Short Stories by Archie

Volume 2

by
Archie Matthews

This book is a work of fiction. The characters, incidents, and dialog are drawn from the author's imagination and not to be construed as real. Any resemblance to actual events or persons, living or dead, is entirely coincidental. (The lawyers made me say that so as to protect the innocent......Me.)

WARNING
English teachers, Punctuation Editors and anyone else with a propensity of critiquing paragraph and or sentence structure, please continue with extreme caution!! Literary sensitive countries should also take heed and be aware that I will not be held liable for inflicting damage to your delicate sensibilities due to my atrocious writing abilities. These stories are intended to only be used for humor and not to be used to teach others "How Not To Write Books"

Books may be purchased for educational, business, or sales promotional use. For information please contact author by email at: archiemmatthews@gmail.com

To order a copy of this book, please contact; LuLu.com or look for "Short Stories by Archie" Volumes One and Two on the web. ISBN 978-1-312-88036-8

DEDICATION

This Book is dedicated to my loving parents Archie H. Matthews, dear old dad, "Thanks for your boot print in my backside and raising me to be a man." and Frieda F. Matthews, sweet, kind mom, "Thanks for all the years of salve applied to dear old dad's boot print".

"Thank you both for sending me on those summer vacations and allowing me to adventure."

And once again, all illustrations by my beloved and extremely talented wife Suzanne Matthews, an accomplished painter and illustrator in her own right, "Thank you for all your help!"

CONTENTS

Short Stories by Archie
Volume 2

The Black Ghouls of River Road

I'll never forget setting in my grandma's café late one evening waiting for my mother to get off work, when the peaceful little community was suddenly thrown into turmoil as old Walt Billows came bursting into the café. The door suddenly flew open and the white haired little old man dashed inside and screamed, "The Black Ghouls got Oliver!" and then grabbing his chest, over the old fellow went, like an ancient tree succumbing to a stiff wind, roots up and limbs down the old fellow hit the floor with a dull "Thud".

Of course being a ten year old kid at the time and eating a hot fudge sundae, there wasn't much that could have drawn my interest, but the mention of "The Black Ghouls" sure captured it and my spoon froze in mid-air. But when the bone chilling announcement set in that they'd "Got Oliver!", I have to admit, I just plum lost my appetite, hot fudge sundae and be-danged. Not to mention the collapse of old Walt upon the café floor.

Now you'd have to know who Oliver Knot was, to know how hard that tidbit of information hit me, for Oliver Knot was just about the biggest mountain of a man you ever did see. The way I figured it, if the Black Ghouls could devour an enormous muscled brute like Oliver Knot, us kids were but finger food and didn't have a chance. Only the dawning realization that you're the potential snack of a Ghoul can quench a kid's appetite for ice cream, let alone a hot fudge sundae.

The blood curdling scream of my aunt Lizzy, not to mention the dropped glass coffee pot, didn't help matters much, when Elmer Fitz hurriedly tried to stand up and ended up falling over backwards, chair and all. But it was dragging the table over with him, when the genuine pandemonium broke out in the little café.

There I sat with my eating elbow froze in place, my hair practically standing straight on end, or would have been if my hat hadn't been holding it down, and bedlam was running amok in the otherwise quiet eatery owned by my grandmother.

Mom came around the corner as if her tail were on fire, to see what all the fuss was about, only to run into the back of her younger sister aunt Lizzy with the still hot grill spatula clutched in her right hand, thus the dropped glass coffee pot and the blood curdling scream. (Funny how a hot spatula to the backside tends to bring about that kind of result.)

And then with a loud gasp of astonishment, mom let out a wail at seeing old Walt Billows laying sprawled out on the café floor and Elmer's feet poking out beneath the over turned table. Yup, bedlam and loud bedlam at that, for just as Lizzy's scream and mom's wail were dissipating, along came grandma from the back kitchen shouting, "What in the world is going on in here?"

All it took was one look at the spilt coffee and broken coffee pot, what appeared like two dead bodies sprawled on her café floor, and poor old grandma all but give up the ghost. With a loud,

The Black Ghouls of River Road

"OH MY GOODNESS!" over she went.......and then suddenly there were three bodies stretched out on the café floor.

I won't bore you with the details of mom and Aunt Liz getting grandma woke up from her faint and back on her feet, not to mention untangling Elmer from the over turned table. I will say, it took them a bit longer to get old Walt to come back around out of the where ever his subconscious went as his body lay practically lifeless. When they did finally get him to stir around, he once again began shouting "The Black Ghouls got Oliver....they swooped down on us and carried him off to purgatory!"

Grandma right quick called my dad and Uncle Bob, and before we knew it, they were both charging through the café entrance to see what all the commotion was about. Uncle Bob and dad listened intently as old Walt began to explain what had happened to him and Oliver.

Walt began by explaining he and his good friend Oliver Knot had been down at the far end of River Road, which as its name warrants, runs along the Snake River to the town of GrandView Idaho. River Road borders the river on one side and on the other is the old Slaughter House where many a critter has been put down and made into table fare. But the old Slaughter House has been empty for many years now, and although many people have whispered it was haunted, Walt eluded that neither him, nor Oliver were afraid of any kinds of haunts.

Of course me being a kid at the time and thoroughly convinced in all kinds of terrors in the darkness, to include Vampires, Werewolves, Mummies, Demons and all other kinds of Hoo-Doo's and Haunts.....especially the Black Ghouls known to haunt River Road. Although I'd never actually seen any of these terrors, as a smaller child, I'd been deathly afraid of the dark, but since I'd grown up, I was now only moderately terrified.

Everyone had heard of the notorious Black Ghouls that had begun to haunt River Road just a couple months back. Many a traveling stranger had remarked about seeing the black Ghoulish

Archie Matthews

shapes flying from the old abandoned Slaughter House across the road. Many a town folk had also witnessed the black shapes disappearing into the dark foreboding water of the perilous Snake River.

Up until now, all the sightings had been just that, sightings, and until now, no one had actually been "Snatched" and apparently "Taken" by the Ghouls. But sure enough here sat old Walt, assuring everyone with an attentive ear sitting around in the café, that his enormous companion, none other than the hulking Oliver Knot had been swooped down upon and carried off.

"We were down fishing by the new bridge at the far end of the road, right up until it got dark for the bite was good and we was catch'n a passel of fish", began old Walt with wide eyes and a still shaking voice.

"Then we reeled in and commenced to meander up the road headed back to town… as we got across from the old Slaughter House, the wind came up out 'a no where and out came several of them vile Black Ghouls" the little old man explained with a look of horror staring off into space.

"They just swooped down on us, all wavering and flapping and then before we knew what happened, one just engulfed Oliver and over the bank they went!" wailed poor old Walt with a wild scared look on his face as his eyes swiveled around from person to person.

"What do you mean….one just gobbled up Oliver?" asked dad a little unbelieving. "What I mean to say, Walt, is Oliver is a mighty big fellow for anything to just up and swallow."

"I'm here to tell you Arch, that Black Ghoul just wrapped itself around big ole'Oliver…..wrapped around him head to boot top, all I could see was his big old boots stick'n out as he was carried head over heels into the river!" wailed Walt.

The Black Ghouls of River Road

"Well what did Oliver do? Did he kick up a fight….or did he just go without a sound?" whispered Uncle Bob, more than a little wide eyed himself.

"Oh, I seen Oliver struggle' n, and of course he was a howling and growling and given that Black Ghoul what for, but it weren't no use! I could see his arms and legs kick'n and a bulge'n that Black Ghoul this'a way and that, but it weren't no use, the Black Ghoul just held him and into the river it took him!" again wailed the little old man loudly.

"But that ain't all, I seen more than one, and one nearly got me! But it missed and only brushed against me as I run my tail out'ta there and made for here!" Walt explained, taking his handkerchief out and mopping his sweat covered brow.

"So Oliver went into the river with the Black Ghoul wrapped around him….his arms and legs kick'n and then what?" urged dad.

"What do you mean, then what? Er you an idgit or something? The Black Ghouls took him down into the black depths of the river! Who knows what for? Maybe they suck your bones of the marrow…….how should I know….then what?!" wailed poor distraught old Walt.

"They've et my buddy and bosom pal Oliver! What are we going to do about it?" Old Walt shouted as he quickly reached out and grabbed dad's shirt front and give him a shake.

I remember dad looking at Uncle Bob and Bob just staring back, all the while the women were cleaning up the spilt coffee and glass, then setting Elmer and his tipped over table up right.

Then another blood curdling scream erupted and once again the café was turned upside down in turmoil.

The scream came from dear sweet mother, who unbeknownst to everyone, including dear old dad, could scream at the perfect

Archie Matthews

pitch and decibel level to break glass. For no sooner did she scream then grandma gave such a start, she wheeled around and accidently broke a whole stack of water glasses on the back counter. As if that wasn't bad enough, Aunt Liz wheeled around and looking down mom's arm like a hunter down a rifle barrel, she too gave a loud scream, but her head was turned in the precise direction as Uncle Bob's ear and only an arms-length away.

If you've ever seen a deer dropped with one well aimed shot, then you'll know just how having his ear drum practically shattered by his wife's scream, dropped Uncle Bob in his tracks.

And for the fourth time that very evening, yet another human body hit the café floor, but this time, no more than a second passed and Uncle Bob was instantly back on his feet. To the day of his death my poor Uncle swore he slipped on some overlooked spilt coffee, but I was there and that floor was as dry as my Uncle Bob's sense of humor. The man was either knocked over by his wife's scream directly striking his eardrum, or he fainted for a second, but coffee didn't have a thing to do with it, other than it happened to be in the same building.

Just then, as dad came back down from the ceiling, Bob once again regained his feet, grandma's attention reverted from the enormous pile of newly broken glass and everyone's attention was immediately drawn to where mom was pointing.

Although I still remained in my chair, I was upon the edge of my seat, what with all the blood curdling screaming and shattered glass, my nerves were all but wound up like a tight rubber band stretched to its breaking point. That's when the café suddenly got so quiet, I am sure to this very day, I heard gray hairs "Popping" out of several of the people now looking out the window, including myself.

To my abject horror, I saw what mom had announced by her glass shattering scream and was still pointing to, for there slowly

14
The Black Ghouls of River Road

plodding up the street outside, was a snow white haired zombie, slowly trudging by the front of the café.

And the last thing I remember was the snowcapped zombie, slowly turned its head and with glassy stare, it looked me right in the eye. The reason I say it was the last thing I remember, was about then, something happened to my rubber band and it snapped without nary a warning, and for the fifth time that night, another body hit the floor…..me.

Evidently, unlike Uncle Bob, my recovery reflex wasn't as experienced and therefore I took much longer to regain my senses, let alone my feet. I remember frolicking across green meadows on a sunny warm day, the birds were calling and calling, and then I realized they were calling my name.

"Archie…..Archie…..son, wake up…" called the little birds, and then gradually the peaceful meadow evaporated and I was suddenly thrust back into the café of horror.

I quickly sat up to see my loving mother knelt by my side and was just about to clamber to my feet, when I was instantly struck with the sight of the white haired zombie sitting only several feet away on a café chair. I gave such a start, the café began to spin and I'd have went back to the peaceful little meadow, if my mother hadn't quickly grabbed me to keep me from going down on the hard café floor. The grab from dear mother instantly brought me to my senses and although the warm sunny meadow beckoned, I resisted the temptation and stayed in the little café of horror.

There not ten feet away sat the white haired zombie that I now recognized as Oliver Knot. Yet, not quite the same Oliver Knot we all knew, for now he sat with the stupefied look of a true zombie, glassy eyes and all. Dad, Uncle Bob and old Walt all three doing their best to get some kind of cognizant response from the quiet idiot that just sat there and drooled, as well as dripped, for he was soaking wet.

Archie Matthews

"My goodness," grandma whispered, "His hair has gone snow white.....I never seen the likes!"

"That's what being born off into the night in the clutches of a Black Ghoul will do to you!" shouted Walt.

"Oliver my friend, what have they done to you", Walt again wailed, but this time he gave the enormous fellow a resounding slap across the face.

Evidently zombies, especially enormous freshly turned zombies, don't like to be slapped, for the large man suddenly jumped to his feet and gave a loud roar and began waving his arms as if battling sanity itself. Walt, dad and Uncle Bob all grabbed Oliver and kept him from over turning tables and hurting himself, all the while Walt kept wailing, "Oh Oliver, Oliver.....what have they done to you?"

This was about the time I decided to put in my two cents worth and without even stopping to think, I quickly shouted, "They've ate his brain and turned him into a zombie!"

Instantly all heads swiveled around, but I'll spare you the intimate details of disgust written clearly upon the adults face at my clinical diagnosis, albeit somewhat non-professional.

Mom patted me on the head and pushed me back into a chair, "You just sit there and don't fuss, Oliver's just had an unfortunate accident and is somewhat addled."

Addled? Boy howdy, adults were dumber than rocks if they couldn't tell right off that Oliver had evidently had his very soul sucked out and was nothing but a shambling zombie, I quickly thought.

I'd seen enough television to know a zombie when I saw one, if this pack of blithering adults didn't. I also knew at any moment, the enormous zombie once known as Oliver Knot, was going to start snapping and biting at everyone and before anyone knew what was happening, we were all going to turn into zombies. Therefore I began to take action, in my own subtle way.

I first began to slowly push my chair back with my feet until the chair was against the wall, then I immediately armed myself with a butter knife in one hand and a salt shaker in the other. The way I figured it, if Oliver the zombie decided to try and bite me and turn me into the walking dead, he was going to get both a butter knife and a salt shaker aside the head. And that's when the arm flailing brute shook off Walt, dad and Uncle Bob and stumbled my way all glassy eyed, if not foaming at the mouth, at least dripping river water.

I'll say this for mom, whether by instinct or thought out self-preservation, she quickly dodged aside and instantly gave me a clear line of fire, which I immediately took advantage of and let fly the glass salt shaker. Now I'm not bragging when I say "I was one heck of a rock chucker back in my day", and although I'd never thrown a heavy commercial grade glass salt shaker before, my aim was dead on.

Walt, dad and Uncle Bob were directly behind Oliver as he'd waved his arms and brushed them aside, and a good thing, for as that salt shaker struck home, right between the hulks glassy eyes, the cap came off and salt flew in every direction. I remember the little silver cap ricocheted off Oliver's forehead and into the glass window with a loud "Ping", and the glass shaker just fell to the floor. But the effect upon the giant white haired zombie was remarkable, for suddenly his brow furrowed and his eyes seemed to clear and his mouth dropped open.

"Whaaaa? What's happening? Why for am I here?" stammered the suddenly aware human, having just now snapped back from zombie hood.

"You was a zombie and you were going to eat our brains, Oliver! So I had to give you a salt shaker betwixt the eyeballs to bring you back!" I quickly explained, hoping beyond hope that the

Archie Matthews

transformation was complete and I wasn't wasting words on a half human, half zombie.

Everyone was frozen in place, trying to grasp the situation until Walt shouted "Oliver, old friend, your back with the living!" ; and with that, Walt jumped to Oliver's side and wrapping his arms around the enormous fellow, he began to shout, "Hallelujah!...Thank You GOD!!! Praise God my Oliver is back with the living!"

I won't go into detail about the straightening up of the salt covered café or the thanksgiving that was shouted for nearly twenty minutes by Walt to the almighty. I will say after nearly half an hour and a whole lot of cleaning salt from table tops, chairs, window sills and not to mention the floor, Oliver sipped a hot cup of coffee and began to tell his side of his harrowing evening.

"We were walking along, me and Walt, when something grabbed me. It just engulfed me and fight as I might, I just couldn't get free. It wrapped around me with its cold clammy wings and I just couldn't get it off me. Then before I knew it, we were in the river, oh my how cold that water was...." Oliver explained and gave a shiver. "I couldn't breathe and all wrapped up like I was, the Black Ghoul just wrapped even tighter and tighter and then I felt the rocky bottom of the river and sure enough, I thought I was a goner." The big fellow, still soaking wet, shook his head and closed his eyes, as if briefly reliving the encounter as he told his tale.

"Then the current pushed me into what felt like that big old tree snag, you know which one Walt...that big old snag that's half in and half out of the water. Well, I felt that Ghoul's grip slipping a bit, so's I give it my last ounce of strength and it just let go, then up I come."

"It just up and let you go?" whispered mom, who like Aunt Liz and grandma, had been hanging upon Oliver's ever word.

"I remember coming to the top of the water and I got to the bank…..then I saw more of the Black Ghouls come flapping, floating and flying up and out the roof of the old slaughter house!" Oliver whispered, "They just kept coming and floated and flapped by me and I just kept thinking if I didn't look and just walked and didn't think or nothing…..they wouldn't take me again. It seemed like I walked forever in the dark. Then I come to standing here, white crystals falling from heaven…..like magic."

"That was the salt from the salt shaker I let you have between the eyes!" I quickly explained. "You was a zombie or on the edge of becoming a zombie and I thought you were coming to eat my brains….but I guess you was just think'n about them Black Ghouls."

"Well, I'm still think'n about them Black Ghouls." Mumbled big Oliver, "I ain't never had ghouls get me before and I doubt I ain't ever gonna forget it, little Arch, I don't recon I'll ever stop think'n about it."

Everyone just stood there watching the enormous man drip river water while sipping his hot coffee, when old Walt once again asked, "An what are we gonna do about it?!" as he looked first at dad and back to Uncle Bob, and then once again gave a pitiful look at poor white haired Oliver.

"Um….well….i just don't rightly know what there is to do?" asked dad as he shrugged his shoulders. I've never seen any of these ghouls, although I've heard a lot of talk. Until now, I just chalked it up to over active imaginations, or at the most a bit too much "Pulling of the cork", but I've never known anyone that was actually attacked."

"That goes double for me…" nodded Uncle Bob, "I ain't ever seen a fella's hair turn white like that either. Bob remarked motioning towards Oliver with a sideways jerk of his head.

Archie Matthews

"You ever saw anything like that Arch?" Uncle Bob asked in a low toned whisper.

I have to hand it to dad, if looks could kill, he'd have at the very least smacked poor Uncle Bob back into yesterday, what with his "Are you kidding me?", not to mention one eye brow up and the other down, dirty look.

"You best get a good gander at that new hair style gentlemen…" growled old Walt, "Cuz, that there's gonna be the new trend in town, if' n we don't do something about them dern Ghouls!"

"And just what the heck do you have in mind Walt?" dad asked giving old man an exasperated look.

"Yeah, Walt?" parroted Uncle Bob, "Just what the heck?"

Well that shut old Walt Billows right up and all he could do was furrow his eyebrows, shake his head and shrug his shoulders.

"I know….I know!" I exclaimed, waving my arm aloft waiting for an adult to pick me to explain my idea.

One hard long look from dad and I knew I was selected and therefore I blurted out, "We go upriver and get Nova Butiza, the gypsy lady!"

Talk about kick'n the bee's nest again and stirring up the hornets all in one fell swoop! The snort of disgust from the women, Mom, Grandma and Aunt Liz, not to mention dad's disgusted look. Uncle Bob did that little face squint and his head hunkered down between his shoulders, for he knew what was coming next.

"She can help us, can't she Uncle Bob?" I said, anxiously nodding my head. "Can't she Uncle Bob, Nova the gypsy lady can cast a spell and send them Ghouls right back to where they come from."

The Black Ghouls of River Road

And as if a pride of lions had just eyeballed a lone wilder beast, all by himself and just ripe for the pick' n, all eyes swiveled from me to poor wilder be….um, I mean Uncle Bob.

"Yeah, Uncle Bob….What About THAT?" Aunt Liz asked as coldly as I've ever heard a woman inquire. That is right up until I married one myself, and then trust me, I heard a lot cooler questions put to me. But that's another story.

Suddenly everyone had something else to do or somewhere else to be at that precise moment. Dad excused himself and went to use the men's room, while grandma and mom suddenly realized they were needed back in the kitchen and quickly dissapeared without another moment's hesitation. Leaving me and old Walt and poor white haired Oliver to watch the scalding looks Aunt Liz kept shooting at Uncle Bob, all the while hunched up Uncle Bob slowly turned around and gave a weak smile to Aunt Liz.

Meanwhile, both old Walt and Oliver kept giving each other puzzled looks. I noticed right off their puzzled expressions, and how they never once looked Aunt Liz in the eye as she kept her piercing gaze turned upon her husband Uncle Bob. Therefore I felt someone should enlighten them as to just who Nova Butiza was, and so I explained.

"Oh, you don't know Nova Butiza?" I began, instantly capturing both Walt and Oliver's attention.

"Well Uncle Bob knows this gypsy woman named Nova Butiza….she's a "Basque"…you know, from the old country, her daddy run sheep in Spain in the mountains and then come to this county. Well, she's lives up the river and knows all kinds of gypsy ways." I began to explain, seeing I had both Walt and Oliver's attention.

"And Uncle Bob used to date her away back when….he said she was a "Witchy Woman" and casts all kinds of spells…." I kept rattling off what I'd heard Uncle Bob tell my dad and other uncles once in a while when the men got together.

Archie Matthews

"Tell them Uncle Bob….tell them about the time she cast that spell on you and turned you into a "Motel"….eyup, tell them that one." I kept bantering, not really noticing Uncle Bob kept getting smaller and smaller, more and more hunched up under the blazing gaze of Aunt Liz.

"Yeah, Uncle Bob", growled Aunt Liz, "Tell us about that "Witchy woman Nova Butiza, and why don't you just go ahead and explain how that "gypsy" woman turned you into a Motel, or should I ask little Archie to explain that, since you've evidently explained it to him."

And at this last juncture, I began nodding my head vigorously, for although I'd heard Uncle Bob tell the guys Nova had "Turned him into a Motel" and more than once to hear him tell it, I never did actually understand how she'd changed him from a human being into a building, let alone back into a human being again.

I was really interested in details, for my mind just couldn't comprehend why on earth a "Witchy woman" like Nova, would turn her boyfriend into such a thing. I suspected my dad knew, but every time I'd asked him about it, he'd just avoid the question or change the subject.

And yet, as curious as I was, I didn't even want to recall the one time I asked my mom about it, for she had "screeched" and ran to poor old dad and they had gone into the bedroom and fought for hours. (Or as mom had explained later, they had things to "discuss", which meant they had fought about something they didn't want me to know about. I was a ten year old boy I knew fighting when I heard it.)

I'll not bore you with the further "verbal flogging" poor Uncle Bob took from Aunt Liz, nor will I go into how quickly both Walt and Oliver disappeared during the "Spanish Inquisition", or that's what I heard Walt mumble to Oliver as they left the café'. A few

The Black Ghouls of River Road

minutes later dad came from the men's room and suggested Uncle Bob take us home, to leave the ladies to close the café'.

Uncle Bob seemed more than happy to drive me and dad home in his old truck. We were all but out the door when suddenly Uncle Bob stopped as if forgetting something, and turning on his heel, went back towards Aunt Liz; his arms out and a pucker on his lips and I thought for sure he was going to give her a "kiss goodbye". But Aunt Liz balled up her fingers into a fist and held it up in front of her face and gave Uncle Bob such a look that he wheeled around in mid-stride and back out the door he came.

I was beside the truck, Uncle Bob was just stepping off the curb and dad was opening up the passenger door, when we heard Aunt Liz through the door, "We'll talk about this in more detail when I get home, BOB!"

Although we only lived about half a mile down the road from the café', it seemed like a long dreary drive home, which was due to the fact that Uncle Bob's truck kept loosing parts and pieces. Therefore he kept stopping to pick them up and put them in the back of the truck bed; which always made any trip seem really long. All the while dad kept snorting and grumbling every time Uncle Bob stopped to pick up another piece.

Uncle Bob was the worst kind of mechanic imaginable, and everyone in the entire county knew it. Poor old Uncle Bob's "Rust Bucket" as everyone nicknamed his pickup, was a perpetual avalanche of truck parts. No matter how hard Uncle Bob worked on it, replacing nuts and bolts and even welding parts back on that were never meant to be welded, they still fell off.

The local garage owner "Blacky Tilt", often called it "an un-natural phenomenon". I'd heard him remark more than once to anyone that was around when Uncle Bob's truck had gone by and lost another part, "Like a show from the Twilight Zone....nee...ner....nee....ner....neeeee....nerrrr" And he'd

Archie Matthews

make that weird spooky sound and then he and whoever he was talking to would laugh and laugh.

Nobody in our family teased poor Uncle Bob about his truck falling apart. Everyone knew it bothered him that he couldn't keep his one and only vehicle together, no matter how the man tried. I'd heard him and dad talk about it more than once, and dad would always give him suggestions as to "lock-tight" and "JB Weld". Finally he'd even bought and given Uncle Bob a store bought book called a "Chilton Manual", which was supposed to help him properly re-assemble his truck. Only afterwards did I hear dad say to mom, "I doubt he even reads it, but I sure wish he'd take time to study the pictures, that truck is an embarrassment, always falling apart like that."

Somewhere along the way, I'd fallen asleep betwixt Uncle Bob and dad in the pickup, despite the clatter of falling parts, the dozen or so stops to pick them up and throw them in the back of the truck.

The next thing I knew, I was waking up in a dark quiet truck, all by myself. Mom and dad had done this to each of us kids at one time or another and we'd been left sleeping in our vehicle parked in front of the house. Now, barely able to keep my eyes open, not to mention make the molasses in my legs work, I opened the pickup door and trudged into the house. I was a bit perplexed at all the debris I was walking over and around while crossing the pitch black living room, and had just turned down the hall towards my bedroom, when I suddenly realized I was in the wrong house.

I'm sure everyone's done that at one point or another in their life, when suddenly half asleep realized they were not where they thought they were just a moment before.

Needless to say, as I realized I wasn't home and suddenly surrounded by strange and unfamiliar darkness, a cold chill ran down my spine. My head snapped up and the molasses in my

The Black Ghouls of River Road

tired and half asleep limbs, suddenly turned into heated steam, ready for action. And with my head up, wide awake, eyes as big as dinner plates, every hair on my body standing at full attention, my body froze in fear while my mind did the fifty yard dash in record time.

The dim moonlight coming through the small windows far up along the far wall, was the only source of light and that gave me just enough to see all kinds of spooky dark shapes and piles strewn around me. Although I had just walked in, what I thought was my house, I didn't have a clue where the door was or for that matter, where I was. Immediately not recognizing anyplace I'd ever been, I knew I was in serious trouble and seeing the outline of a door close at hand, I opened it and being a bit better lit inside, I stepped in and let the door close behind me.

Talk about being instantly transported into a horror movie, as the door behind me closed and I realized I'd just walked through a self-closing door, hearing the latch catch, I wheeled around realizing there was no latch to work on this side. Instantly I recognized my helpless back was facing a vulnerable wide open dark filled space. Immediately I did what any terrified kid would do and wheeled around to face the open dim lit space with my back to the wall.

I don't know if you've ever seen a horror movie involving an animal slaughter facility, or as I suddenly found myself, actually been in a horror movie as an unwilling participant looking around at all kinds of slaughter facility horror props. The only thing worse, being suddenly coming to the realization, your "NOT" in a movie and the hanging meat hooks, large black table tops, complete with strewn old rusty knives and meat cleavers, not to mention the old dusty occasional bone pile, are all "REAL" and not movie props!

Since I was "WAY" past hair raising scared, I felt my body ramping up to the next phase in physical terror. Goose bumps the size of real geese began to raise up on every patch of my skin, not to mention my knees and other parts of my appendages

Archie Matthews

began to quiver and shake. That's when I saw the distant side door with its window, and welcoming patch of moonlight flooding through, and I bolted for it.

Around, over and even through several piles of tables, bone piles and other junk, I traversed until the final obstacle between me and the doorway impeded my progress. What was on the large wooden pallet, in the heavy paper sacks, was beyond my comprehension, as I clawed my way through them, the dust raising up so thick that I almost couldn't breathe. But fear is a catalyst fuel that can propel even the most exhausted kid to perform vast feats of strength, and thus I reached the other side of the dusty barricade and beat on the door until the latch tripped and suddenly I found myself outside.

If I hadn't been so terrified, I might have gave a shout for joy, yet my vocal cords were still far too busy moaning my terror at realizing I was at the one place on earth wild horses couldn't drag me, yet here I had been deposited by Uncle Bob's old rust bucket. I tried to stifle the moaning of fear that just kept emanating out of my own mouth, but I could no more stop the loud groans, than I could stop my legs from shaking, nor my hair from standing straight up atop my head.

And that's when I saw the floating light of doom coming from several yards further behind the building amongst the back corrals that had once held the doomed livestock to be slaughtered. The small little wobbling light began to bounce all over, casting its errant beam in my direction as it quickly and sporadically approached, seemingly with its own high pitched whine.

This approaching bouncing light, instantly inspired my wobbling, shaking legs to do otherwise than just quiver, and with feet churning up a wall of fresh earth that would have made a rototiller proud, my buttocks shifted into high gear and my thighs "Popped" the clutch and I was racing for the front of the building and Uncle Bob's truck of refuge.

The Black Ghouls of River Road

Trust me when I say it takes "WAY" longer to tell the tale of getting around the building, jumping inside Uncle Bob's truck, grabbing the door lever and bracing my feet against the inside door jamb, I locked the door. Or at least held that door shut with every fiber of my being for search as my eyes did, I couldn't see any locking device on that old pickup door.

And not a moment too soon, for I had no more than gotten inside and shut the door, when the wavering light with its high pitched whine, crashed into the outside with a loud "THUNK" . Looking up in horror, I saw a wad of indistinct flesh sliding down the glass with not only a terrible sound, but what appeared to be a huge white eyeball. The sliding flesh seemed to take forever before it disappeared below and out of sight through the truck door window. And then the wavering light once again appeared and was thrust up towards a human face that suddenly appeared outside the window.

"Let me in!" screamed the monster, with the brightly lit face that slowly took on the likeness of Uncle Bob.

Once again, in the high wavering voice, the flashlight not quite so close to his face, Uncle Bob screamed, "Little Archie…..let me in!" The truck began rocking to and fro as he hastily worked not only the door latch, but he kept putting his shoulder against the door as to push it inward, the whole time shouting, "IN, let me IN…!"

And then my worst fear was realized as facing my "Zombie'fied" Uncle Bob, ranting and raving for me to let him in so he could devour my brains, I felt the door inexorably pried open and the dome light came on. Suddenly with a wide eyed look of terror on Uncle Zombie's face, I screamed letting the door latch go, away he flew backwards, once again to disappear into the darkness. And with a valiant heave, I once again pulled the door shut and held on for dear life, until I suddenly felt the driver's side door thrown open and a large iron like hand grasped my shoulder from behind.

Archie Matthews

There comes a time in every meek mouse's life that he is suddenly over taken by a predator of enormous size and strength and the only means left for the timid little fellow to do, is snap his shackles of self-restraint and turn into a fighting tiger.

As that large iron hand suddenly clamped down on my shoulder from behind, trust me when I say, my self-restraint mouse shackles were suddenly snapped. My transformation into a clawing, raging, biting Bengal Tiger was complete as I put up a horrendous fight in the tight confines of that truck cab.

Long story short, after a bloody battle of several seconds, I was pulled across the seat and held at arm's length as dad shouted repeatedly for me to "Calm down......son, calm down.....it's only me and Bob."

After what seemed like an eternity of churning both arms and legs like boat propellers, my adrenaline tank suddenly hit bone dry bottom and I fell utterly limp with exhaustion, not to mention relief as I finally realized it WAS dad and Uncle Bob and neither seemed to want to eat my brains.

Everyone baled into the pickup cab once again, Uncle Bob running around to take his place in the driver's side, while dad quickly went around the back of the truck and jumped in the passenger's side.

"Let's get the HELL out' a here!" growled dad as Uncle Bob seemed to be frantically fiddling with the truck ignition.

And once again I heard as terrifying sound as I've ever heard, when Uncle Bob's head swiveled around with a sick look on his face and said, "She won't start Arch.....she's dead." I'll never forget the cold shiver that mournful "She's Dead" sent up my spine, not to mention the murderous look dad suddenly shot over my head at Uncle Bob.

The Black Ghouls of River Road

"What do you mean she's dead and won't start?" dad once again growled.

"I don't know why, but she won't start, and I just put a new starter on her the other day….but see there…" and Uncle Bob turned the key in the ignition and sure enough, the old truck didn't start.

"Maybe the new starter just fell off….maybe we can pick it up and put it back on?" I said, as hopefully as possible, yet it came out utterly mournful sounding, with my voice almost breaking into a whine.

I won't bore you with the litany of four letter words that ricocheted around the cab of the truck as dad let go with his disappointing barrage of mechanical suggestions. Nor will I go into the hasty search for a flashlight or other light producing contrivance, "heck", I'd have even been happy with a book of matches…..and I told Uncle Bob as much, but to no avail.

Needless to say, it was quickly decided that we were going to have to walk home, which once again raised I and Uncle Bob's neck hair, but only angered dear old dad, for he hadn't any sense when it came to fearing the dark. Nope, not my dad….his favorite saying to me as a kid was, "There is nothing to fear, but fear itself." And in all the years I've known my father, I've never once seen him exhibit any fear, night or day; while I, his son, exhibited plenty of it for both of us, not to mention another fellow or two.

And out of the pickup and down towards River Road we began to walk, and we were almost there, when out of the blue, or should I say "Black", come up the wind. The night had been mostly still, with very little wind, yet that stretch of road along the river was prone for wind gusts, and just now it began to gust.

Who's to say what caused the moaning and groaning of the wind, I can tell you right now, it was the creepy wind and it's moaning and groaning that caused both I and Uncle Bob to moan and groan as we both tried to keep up with the fast pace

Archie Matthews

dad was setting. Dad on the other hand, wasn't moaning or groaning, he was too busy grumbling and growling about all kinds of grouchy topics, most of which concerned Uncle Bob and his "Rust Bucket" as well as old Walt and Oliver and a certain slaughter house….not to mention a hissed oath about "Black Ghouls".

Both I and Uncle Bob were doing our best to keep our feet going to the vigorous pace dad had set and maintained. And then as the wind began to flat blow, and dad was several yards ahead of us, Uncle Bob gave a loud gasp and froze in place, pointing up into the air with a look of horror. And sure enough, although I wanted to, I couldn't help it and looked up where he was pointing. And there coming off the top of the old Slaughter House was a whole army of Black Ghouls, floating off one behind the other in rapid succession headed right for us.

I'll never forget the sight of Uncle Bob standing frozen in place, the look of horror upon his face as an army of wavering black flapping ghouls flew from the lofty height of the Slaughter House roof, headed right at us at a slight downward angle. But unlike Uncle Bob, there wasn't anything frozen about me, my adrenaline tank seemed to be immediately topped off again and with the sight of the legion of fast approaching Black Ghouls, my afterburners suddenly lit and with a loud scream, I broke into a run towards dad.

Only for a brief moment did Uncle Bob remain anchored to his spot, but evidently seeing me take off, he snapped his own anchor chain and became mobile once again, and he passed me as if I had been standing still. With a churning of legs and with his warning siren at full volume, he even sailed by dad.

Dad gave a bit of a start as Uncle Bob, like some kind of Olympic sprinter, whizzed by. Dad briefly stopped to watch the amazing sight of a grown man running for his life screaming at the top of his lungs in the middle of the night. Then he slowly turned around to give me a smile and a bit of a quizzical look, when suddenly he was enveloped by a Black Ghoul amidst River Road.

I'd like to say I ran to my dear old dads side and helped him heroically battle a legion of Black Ghouls.....I'd like to say that.....but discretion being the better part of valor, and knowing there were way too many for just the two of us.....I ran for help!...or should I say, I continued to run for help, for my pace not only didn't slow down, it sped up as I passed Uncle Bob on my way to town at about "Mach Nine".

I passed Uncle Bob and screamed, "They got dad....they got him....they got DAD!" and I'm somewhat ashamed to say, after that, I didn't give Uncle Bob the time of day....or night, for I was suddenly the "Paul Revere" of horror and rushed right into town screaming, "The Ghouls are coming....the Black Ghouls are coming....they got my dad!"

Then a miracle happened right on main street GrandView USA, and a large shadow ran from the sidewalk next to the general store and intercepted me. The "miracle" being it was my Uncle Mel and he stopped me without getting run over or having the arm he grabbed me with, torn from its socket as he latched onto me.

"Whoa there, little Arch....whoa up there, just what's all the screaming about?" Uncle Mel asked quiet and calmly. (I say quiet and calmly, for that was his attitude right up until Uncle Bob went by like a rifle shot, screaming his head off as he passed. For after seeing his cousin Liz's husband, running and screaming up the street from the same direction I'd just come from, Mel's attitude instantly changed.

"Archie, what's going on....who's got your dad!" shouted Uncle Mel angrily, giving me a little shake. "Who's got your dad?"

"The Black Ghouls got dad down on River Road! They got him Uncle Mel, help him... please help him... their all over him down

31
Archie Matthews

there!" I screamed, realizing good old Uncle Mel was a lot like dad, I'd never seen him scared of nothing.

About then, a pickup came roaring up the road and screeched to a halt only a few feet from us, and I instantly recognized Grandpa as he shouted through the opened passenger window, "Mel, something's happened to Archie!"

Uncle Mel, still holding me by one arm, quickly opened the pickup door and pushing me inside, he jumped in and slammed the door. "He's down the road, go Deemer, go!"

And Grandpa Deemer, mom's dad, hit the gas and down River Road we once again sailed, while Mel reached over my head into the back window and the gun rack that hung there. Uncle Mel took down grandpa's old Remington pump shotgun and jacked a round into the chamber, then quickly put it barrel down between my legs and grabbing the 30.30 carbine, he levered a round into it's chamber and put it between his own legs.

In another instant, we saw them crossing the road, almost a solid wall of large black flapping Ghouls, sailing upon the wind from atop the distant Slaughter House roof, swooping down in droves to disappear into the river.

"Oh, my lord....." gasped Grandpa as he hit the brakes and we skidded to a stop.

"Heavens....heavens to mergatroid" wailed Uncle Mel, as we saw dad half stumble and half fight his way up from the river bank, a black Ghoul wrapped around his mid-section all the while he was fighting and shouting unintelligibly.

As if caught up in the "Drive in from Hell", I sat there watching out the front window of my granddad Deemer's truck, as both grandpa and Uncle Mel charged forward with guns blazing. And that's just what guns look like firing into the darkness of night, "About six foot blazing flames" as both grandpa's shotgun and

Uncle Mel's deer rifle fired round after round into the army of Black flapping Ghouls crossing the road attacking dad.

Dad, arms flailing, pulling remnants of vanquished and evidently pulverized Black Ghouls from his legs, began coming towards the truck waving his arms and shouting, when once again an enveloping Black Ghoul took him down the river bank.

My heart was right up in my throat watching my poor dad go down in a struggling heap over the road side and towards the river, his outline momentarily visible within the encased Black Ghoul. Granddad and Uncle Mel firing into the onslaught of Ghouls with nary a sign of hesitation by either side, for the Ghouls kept coming and so did grandpa and Uncle Mel. And then suddenly grandpa went down, a Black Ghoul swooping down and enveloping first his head, flapping far behind and all but dragging him off the road, when another hit him low in the legs and over he went.

The horror of watching first my dad and now my granddad drug down to their deaths, I shouted out the truck door at Uncle Mel, who was spraddle legged, trying to work the jammed lever action on his rifle.

"Uncle Mel……they got grandpa!" I screamed out the wide open driver's door.

Just then, poor old Uncle Mel, turned his head towards me, and then with a wide eyed look of surprise, his head swiveled up wind and he was suddenly sucked inside first one and then another and another of the Black Ghouls. I'll say this about Uncle Mel, he was like dad, and he fought like a tiger, as his hands kept tearing and pushing through first one Ghoul and then another, before he was pushed over the edge of the road and down towards the river.

I'd like to say, I jumped out and ran to my families side, but there isn't a soul that would believe it of a ten year old kid, let alone a coward like me. And suddenly I saw a Ghoul veer towards the

Archie Matthews

truck and head right straight for the open driver's side door, thus I did the only thing I could do, and slammed the door. And not a moment too soon, for I had just pulled it closed and hit that little silver lock button, when with a loud bang, that Black evil Ghoul slammed into the side of the pickup and proceeded to beat it's way inside.

I won't bore you with the horror of sweat filled eons that I spent screaming my head off, the Black Ghoul pounding outside the pickup, its black flapping liked to drove me crazy, not to mention hearing all the wicked laughter coming closer and closer, ever closer to the pickup I was in. The laughter was high pitched and hysterical, and then it was joined with another, lower toned laugh and then yet another, and suddenly I realized they were all three coming closer and closer.

As I sat scrunched down half on the floor board and half on the truck seat, the Black Ghoul beating and pounding upon the driver's side, across the top of the cab and front window, obscuring the further bloody demise of my dad, granddad and Uncle Mel, I realized the passenger door was open and the laughing Ghouls were right on top of me. With a lurch, I bolted for the passenger door and grabbing the door handle, I quickly pulled the door shut and began rolling up the window cranking the knob as if my very life depended upon it.

I had all but six inches or so to go, when in thrust a stark white human arm, and grabbing the door knob, tried to open the passenger's side door. I say "Tried", for that's as far as that arm got before I set upon it "tooth and nail", and brother....back in those days, I could bite and scratch right up there with the best of them, especially when my life depended on it. And suddenly the evil laughter of that particular Ghoul once again shifted back to howling agony, as my incisors' hit bone. But alas, one small ten year old kid cannot overcome overwhelming odds, no matter how much fight is in him, and the door was heaved open.

The Black Ghouls of River Road

There stood dear old dad, one arm inside bleeding from my latest dental work, still somewhat of a smile on his face, albeit a bit strained; bits and pieces of Black Ghoul hanging from his clothing. And just behind him, I could make out Uncle Mel, and grandpa, both laughing their heads off, yet making sure they were behind the windbreak of the pickup, as Black Ghouls sailed all around them, each of them also wore torn and tattered remnants of their antagonists.

I won't bore you with our jovial ride back to town, leaving the army of Black Ghouls far behind, still flocking off the distant Slaughter House Roof, across the space between the old spooky building and over the road to disappear into the swirling water of the Snake River.

I will gladly report, the ride was one filled with three men, laughing and slapping their knees, not only all the way home, but for many years to come, for this tale is a favorite, especially about Halloween time in my family.

And the mystery of the Black Ghouls was soon known to everyone, everyone that is except the little old ditch rider away down river in the next county. For that poor old fellow never did put two and two together, nor did he ever know where all those large four by eight pieces of Black Plastic came from that kept clogging up his stretch of irrigation head gates. If only the old fellow had just come up river and inquired, he'd have heard about the several large bales of black plastic that had come undone atop the old Slaughter House roof, where the company kept them for covering the large butcher tables inside like so many table cloths. It seems over the years the bundle wrappings had worn, and the wind had done the rest.

It's amazing what black plastic looks like flapping off a roof and across a road in the dark of night, let alone falling into a swirling river and mysteriously disappearing. One might even say somewhat like "The Black Ghouls of River Road."

Archie Matthews

The Black Ghouls of River Road

When Pigs Fly

Life on our small farm took a drastic change when my four year old little brother Matthew, ran into the house screaming, "Pigs are flying….pigs are flying!"

In our home, many times one of us four boys would make a request that was met with one parent or another saying, "Yup, you'll get that, when pigs fly". Like the time my brother Roy asked for a 22.caliber rifle just shortly after accidently shooting out dads back car window with his BB gun. As if the laser hot look dad gave him wasn't enough, dad went one step farther and gave a condescending nod and said, "Oh, yeah, I'll get you a higher caliber rifle so you can not only shoot out a car window, but kill a passenger or two while you're at it! Just hold your breath and it will be the same day pigs start to fly!"

There was also the day we were sitting at the dinner table and my four year old little brother Matthew asked, "Dad, when are we going to be rich?"

Talk about a question that froze every bending elbow midway between dinner plate and mouth, including mom and dads. Mom just smiled and asked little Matthew, "Why do you want to be rich?"

"Well, when I asked Roy why we had to do chores, he said, because we was poor, and only rich people didn't have to do chores. So I wanna be rich and not have to do chores." Turning his head back towards dad, little Matthew once again directed himself towards the head of the table and again asked, "Huh, dad? When are we gonna be rich so I don't have to do chores?"

Dad smiled between the dinner roll in his left hand and the fork he held in his right hand and replied, "Well Matthew, just as soon as pigs start flying!"

Needless to say, we kids were anxious for the day that pigs would start flying, what with so many things hinging upon that very miracle. So when dad began working on a pig pen, he had no problem getting all us boys to pitch in and help construct our "deliver's abode". For as the little kids saw it, if we had pigs, it was only a matter of time before one of them could be taught to fly and all our hopes and dreams would come true. Of course, I and my younger brother Ike were older and knew better, but still pitched in constructing the pig pen, just to save dad the trouble of forcing us.

The pig pen was a wire fence nailed to the back wall of the barn and an opening cut into the barn's back wall to allow the pigs to come into a stall constructed inside. We all pitched in putting in the posts and stretching the hog wire nice and tight and then we quickly nailed a big wooden feed trough together to hold their grain and table scraps. An old bathtub was half sunk into the ground and pronounced a "Water Trough" and without so much as a ground breaking ceremony or even a ribbon cutting, the pig pen was pronounced "Finished". But then little Matthew quickly pointed out, "Dad, this pig pen ain't done…there ain't no top dad! When them pigs start flying, they will get out and there will be trouble then dad. We need to put a top on the pen or our pigs will fly away!"

Of course everyone got a big laugh out of that one, except little Matthew and the slightly older, but just as puzzled "Roy", for both had high hopes for flying pigs and the miracles that had been promised, "When Pigs Fly!"

When Pigs Fly

And then the big day came for us to go across the road to the livestock auction house. Yes, I said across the road, for we lived just across the road from the "Sale Barn" as it was called. The livestock sale yard was comprised of approximately fifteen acres of miscellaneous holding pens, some close beside the huge buildings and covered by roofs. Most of the pens were a large series of alleys and fenced pens designed to hold cattle, horse and sheep, while the smaller roofed pens were meant to hold, goats, pigs and sometimes herds of turkeys. Yes, I said "Turkeys", for there were several huge herds of turkeys that were herded just like sheep, by a man and a couple of dogs. The turkey herds were used by many of the large local sugar beet and potato farmers in our area to control bugs. The turkeys didn't bother either the beet or potato plants and were therefore herded through the large green topped plants and allowed to feast on any and all living things hidden amongst the plants. Believe it or not, turkeys will not only eat any and every kind of bug, but also, mice and small snakes. Of course the larger snakes just seeing a herd of turkeys coming, slithered off to the far reaches of the county in hopes of avoiding either being pecked to death or trampled.....but enough about the "Turkey Herds of Idaho", and back to the story at hand.

Mom and dad quickly announced they were going to the auction to "Check out pigs"!

Being thirteen and an official teenager, I quickly asked if I could go along. My eleven year old younger brother Ike didn't much care to go and was quickly put in charge to watch the other two younger boys, Roy and Matthew; Roy being eight and Matthew being the youngest at age four.

And as we walked out of the driveway to cross the road, little Matthew called out, "Pick us out a smart pig dad, he's gotta be a smart pig to learn how to fly!"

Crossing the road and wending our way through the parking lot full of stock trucks and pickups alike, we

39

Archie Matthews

made our way inside and up the tiered wooden bleacher seats and sat down. As with any auction, the things that you're interested in are always offered for sale dead last and "fickle fate" always makes you sit through a long boring litany of things unwanted.

And such was most of our day spent, first the Bulls were offered and then the cows, heifers and so on and so forth until mom finally decided she needed to use the restroom and quickly disappeared into the surrounding crowd.

Soon the young grass calves were offered up for auction and everything went smooth as glass until as scruffy a range calf as I've ever seen was run into the ring. That particular calf was wilder than a "March hare", or so the saying goes, for it charged around the ring doing its best to find a way back to the open spaces where it had been born and apparently raised until now. Such was the meaning of the term "range calf", for it was obvious that this wild calf hadn't been raised on a farm close to humans. Or should I say, "It was obvious to all but one", for after several minutes of all but begging for an extremely low opening bid, someone took the bait and bid.

Everyone was laughing at the ring man as he ducked and dodged behind the protective barriers at each end inside the cables of the big sale ring, avoiding being run over or kicked by the four hundred pound wild bovine. And then the auctioneer pounded his gavel and shouted sold at a minimum bid from "some crazy woman", or so the guys in front of us chuckled.

After several gentler "grass calves" were auctioned and sold, every one of those fetching three and four times what that wild range calf had cost; finally the pigs were up and several came and went with dad bidding conservatively and always stopping short and letting the other bidder win. And then the last four pigs were announced and run into the ring and I could tell right off they were a lot smaller and younger than the others that had run sixty to eighty pounds each. These last four

When Pigs Fly

were in the twenty pound range and being small like they were, the bidding started out at five dollars each and dad opened the bid by nodding his head.

Since most of the crowd had been cattle buyers, the elbow to elbow crowd had thinned somewhat as did the shoulder to shoulder seated crowd, but since a lot of people were getting up from the bleacher seating, there were a lot of people making for the lower tiered exits, which made it hard to see the sale ring. I mention this fact to allow for the little mishap that happened when dad and another bidder began their furious bidding war.

Back and forth the heated bidding went with five quickly becoming seven fifty and then ten and then twelve fifty and so on and so forth until suddenly people began to slow down and stop on their way to the exit and take notice. And then there began a whole lot of whispering and laughing and suddenly the auctioneer took notice and stopped, then as his assistant whispered in his ear, he too began to laugh along with most of the crowd.

"Well now," the auctioneer said with a huge smile, "It's been brought to my attention that we have two people here that desperately want these pigs. It's also been brought to my attention that this lady that's bidding so furiously and the fellow that also seems to need these fine pigs, just so happen to be married!!"

And the crowd burst out laughing and as if by mutual consent parted between dad, who was sitting by my side and mom, who having returned from the ladies room, was standing down by the exit with a startled look at realizing she had been bidding against dad. To say that both mom and dad were a bit red faced was to say the least. But livestock people are usually a jovial bunch and everyone got a huge laugh about the husband and wife doing their best to outbid one another, including the auctioneer and the pig's owner.

After a few minutes, the laughter died down and the auctioneer offered to begin again at five dollars if the pigs owner agreed, which he quickly did with a good

Archie Matthews

natured jibe, "Oh yeah," the fellow called out with a chuckle, "Heaven forbid I'm the cause for dissention in the Matthew's house between husband and wife!"

Thus, we quickly became the owners of four pigs, even though narrowly avoiding a civil war between mom and dad, not to mention the havoc that was almost thrust upon the household bank account and paying through the nose for four scrawny pigs.

After paying for the pigs and transporting them back across the road, which was quite the ordeal all in itself, for dad carried two squealing pigs by their back legs, head down, each letting the entire county know they were not happy with the traveling accommodations. I and mom each carried our squirming burdens clasped firmly in our arms following dad and his two up ended pig sirens.

Depositing the pigs in their new pen, the squealing quickly turned into satisfied little grunts as they roamed around the pen, sniffing and rooting here and there checking out their new home. Even little Matthew seemed satisfied and with a big smile and a nod, he remarked, "Yup dad, I think we got some smart ones! Yup dad, we'll have a flying pig in no time." And everyone and everything seemed content and peaceful, that is until mom made a little announcement.

"Um, I also bought a calf...." Mom said a bit subdued, looking a little sheepish at dad.

"You bought a calf?" dad asked more than a bit puzzled.

"Yes, I got a really good deal and we've talked about getting a calf for the pasture, and the man I was standing next to assured me it was a really good calf at a really good price. I paid for it and all we have to do is go and lead it across the road." Mom said with a satisfied smile.

"And you paid for it already?" dad asked with a puzzled expression.

When Pigs Fly

"Yes, I had some sewing money in cash and I paid for it with that." Mom assured him, with a smile.

I knew mom was proud of sewing wedding dresses for the distant neighbor girls, who had been twins and their parents had paid mom handsomely. At the age of thirteen, I was still a bit confused as to if they'd married one guy, or two separate guys since they were of the Mormon faith. (I never did actually find out.....come to think of it.)

"Okay," dad said, "I'll go get a rope and we can go and lead your calf across the road."

Dad quickly gathered up a rope from the barn and giving me a look and a nod he said, "You might as well come help me, sometimes even a small calf can be a handful."

"Boy Howdy!", if we'd only known just how hard he'd hit that nail on the head, it would have saved a whole lot of trouble and hide. Both of which I'd gladly paid a month's wages to keep. When I was thirteen minimum wage wasn't much money, but hard earned, yet so was hide back in those days, as you will soon find out.

So back across the road I and dad went into the auction office and after waiting in line a bit, we were told to go out the back door and give the slip to the stockyard man and he'd get our "Calf". The smile and chuckle that followed the announcement of "Calf" should have been our first warning, but both I and dear old dad missed it clean and it went way over our heads that the joke was on us.

After several minutes of waiting a fellow came down the walkway and took the slip from dad and reading it, he smiled and asked, "What kind of an outfit are you driving, pickup with racks or truck and trailer?"

Archie Matthews

Dad lifted the rope and said, "We live across the road and we'll lead it home if it's broke to lead, if not, I brought my son and we'll drag it across if we have to."

The smile and twinkle in the fellow's eyes should have been our second warning that somehow something was up. The fellow called out to another guy up on top of the catwalk that ran several feet above the many corrals and pens down the long expansive stockyard.

"Send me the tornado, Walt!", and hearing that, I saw dad's brow furrow.

"I've got a feeling something's up. Now I'm beginning to wonder what your mother's got us into with this calf?" dad said with a strange look directed at me.

I just shrugged my shoulders, and then hearing the two guy's laughing, we heard the fellow shout, "Yup, you fellows just wait right there with your rope and we'll trot your calf out to you!" And then as if laughter were some kind of infectious disease, we heard more distant laughter and after a couple more minutes we were quickly let on to the joke.

In a fast approaching cloud of dust, stampeding hooves and wild bucks and bounds, down the narrow alley came that wild range grass calf that weighted a good four or five hundred pounds, which was about twice the size of even the biggest calf, either dad or myself had imagined.

"There you go fellers!" roared the young fellow with laughter, "Get your rope ready and just lead away!"

Dad's face turned more than a bit red, and he hesitated, and that should have been my warning that danger was upon us, for dad wasn't a man that hesitated. With several people chuckling if not down and out right laughing at us, dad quickly lassoed the large wild calf as it had stopped in front of us suddenly sprattle legged and head down, not knowing what to do or where to go.

The next thing I know, dad flipped the end of the rope to me and said, "Whatever you do, hold on and don't let go!"

I had just grabbed the rope and gave it a twist around my wrist, when some helpful rascal threw open the alley gate and with a jerk, we were headed outside and home.

I have to admit, we were suddenly outside, but the huge calf immediately transmitted to both I and dad that he had other ideas than being lead, drug or going quietly across the road to his new home. Immediately upon stepping out from under the catwalk and through the open gate into the broad expanse outside the confines of the stock pens, the range calf decided to bolt for parts unknown....or should I say, parts only known to him.

If you've ever tied a rope around the back bumper of a truck that suddenly takes a notion to head for the high country, you'll know what I'm talking about, when I say, I was quickly jerked off my feet and away we went.

Now when I say "We", I don't want you to be confused and think I meant I and dad, oh no my friend. Remember when I told you dad didn't hesitate. Nor did he in this instance, for upon seeing the calf take off like a sixty seven Chevy, dear old dad decided to do just exactly what he told me not to. "No matter what happens, don't let go" had been his very words, but evidently in his own mind, that only pertained to me, for dad "Let go".

To this day dad claims the rope slipped out of his hands, but need I remind everyone, I was there. There is a distinctive difference in a rope running through a fellows hand and slipping out, and the quick instinctive reaction of throwing one's hands wide open in order to save ones self. A very distinctive difference, the difference is especially noticeable to the fellow left holding on to the rope and nearly drug to death.

45
Archie Matthews

I'd like to say, the reason I didn't throw open my hands and think of myself was because as the first born son, I was ever loyal, staunch and true to the teachings of my father…..I'd like to say that. But the real reason was, I'd taken that little loop around my arm with the rope, and with that quick ignorant act, had become inexorably fastened as if by steel chain and manacles to the now galloping calf.

Before I knew what was happening, I was being drug across the heavily graveled parking lot, I say heavily graveled, because as my pants pockets quickly scooped up gravel, it got enormously heavy, as did my cowboy boots. I hadn't noticed just how heavy my pockets were with gravel, not to mention my boots, until the calf decided to jump into the canal that ran alongside the parking lot. Oh….but I happened to get ahead of myself and forgot to mention the really tightly strung four strand barbwire fence separating the parking lot and the canal. But of course, we were through it so fast, I hardly had any time at all to notice how much clothing, let alone hide I'd left behind on those barbs, before we hit the deep cold canal water.

Now I've always wondered what water skiing was like, for I was raised in Southern Idaho and since its arid country, I never had an opportunity to give it a try, that is, until that precise moment the calf drug me at top speed through the water. I've seen surfers crash and become overwhelmed by massive waves on television, and perhaps that better describes my experience in being drug across the canal, for there never really was any time spent atop the water and a whole lot of time thrashing around under water.

Then suddenly out the other side of the canal the kind calf drug me, just in the nick of time for me to catch my breath and give out a scream as once again I was drug through another four strands of brutal barb wire. Once again, there was a loud screech of stretched fencing wire and groaning wooden posts as I went through another fence. To this day, I don't know which of us

"Screeched" louder, me or the fencing, but I'll bet you can guess where the loudest groaning came from.

Somehow, and I can only surmise at this point in time, my left boot decided to abandon the rodeo and was thus left behind. I suppose I should be grateful that it was the only thing that left my body at that particular point in my adventure, but it's hard to count one's blessings as you are being drug to death by an insane calf bent upon alternately shredding and then drowning you.

It was several yards after the last barbwire fence crossing that the little calf decided it favored the original side of the canal and without breaking stride, back through the fence he went, I of course tried my best to follow, what with my arm being tied to him. The reason I say "I tried my best", was if you've ever been forcefully pulled through a fence and gotten hung up on the wire, one tends to try his best to go with the flow. Hence, I tried my best to get free of the entangled wire and relieve the sixty thousand pounds per square inch that was doing its best in ripping my rope wrapped arm from its socket; all while the barb wire did its best to rip the remaining tattered wet clothing from my bleeding body.

I'd like to say, "It's funny the things that run through ones head at such times." But trust me, I just couldn't find the humor, then or even now. I did think of dear sweet mother, and for a fleeting moment I recalled her smile at thinking she got such a good deal on this calf. Then I thought about how disappointed she was going to be at the cost of my funeral that is, if there were anything left of me to bury. That's when I became a scuba diver once again and I'm sad to admit, I didn't give dear sweet mother another thought.

I'll never forget being drug across the bottom of the muddy canal and seeing a huge crawdad lift his claws menacingly, as if to warn me not to try anything funny. Little did that plucky crustacean have to fear from me, for at this point, I had no humor left in me, let alone perpetrate upon a crawfish.

Archie Matthews

Then once again, up the side of the canal went the little calf, immediately followed by me, the human plow. Realizing I could once again inhale air and not just muddy canal water, I sucked in an immense lung full and was just revving up my scream mechanism for the up and coming barbwire fence crossing. Suddenly the world stopped grinding away at my underside and I stopped just a few feet short of another barbwire peeling.

I often recall my harrowing experience of being peeled and then doused and then peeled and then doused, now that I am married and am often appointed to peel vegetables at the sink for a roast or other culinary delight. My wife often has had to take the metal peeler from my quivering hands as I stand frozen and mesmerized at the sink while holding the half peeled carrot or other vegetable under the running water. Then leading me to my recliner, she gets me set down and lets my post-traumatic stress syndrome work itself out as I mumble "wire, water, wire, water.....bad calf....bad calf."...sometimes for hours.

Needless to say, the calf incident left a lasting impression upon me; to this day I still have impressions of the barb wire fence on multiple parts of my anatomy as well as my mind. But even while dating, my beloved wife had been warned by many a relative about my having one or two screws loosed by an adventure or two while growing up....but back to the story at hand.

Suddenly stopping as we did, I realized several people had captured the calf as it had been slowed down going through the barbwire fence. Which was puzzling, for believe me, through the whole harrowing experience, I never noticed any diminished speed. The wild calf seemed to maintain it's faster than the speed of sound gallop through canal crossings as well as charging through barb wire fences.

I do have to admit, what with coming to a stop, sound immediately caught up and never was a more mournful

48
When Pigs Fly

"Mooing" heard as the calf was roped and brought to an abrupt halt. Of course, as dad now points out, it wasn't long after he got me untied that I stopped "Mooing" so mournfully.

Then with the help of a couple very kind sale yard cowboys, smart lad's both, for they rode horses and didn't try to drag a nine hundred pound gorilla cow bare handed! Thus after settling their ropes upon the bovine tractor, the wild calf was drug to his new home across the street, but without me, his human plow.

Upon seeing dad coming through the door half carrying and half dragging the remnants of a three time barbwire shredded human being, not to mention twice drowned, or as close to being drowned as I ever want to come, dear mother gave a shout and came to my aid. The aid being, to direct my dad to drag what remained of my wet bleeding carcass back out to the porch. It wasn't too long a wait, until she came with a housecoat and some bandages so she could "Staunch the bleeding" before I was allowed upon her carpet. You know how women are when their floors have just been cleaned, not to mention their freshly vacuumed carpet!

After a couple weeks of mending, both physically and mentally, I was right as rain and able to walk upright again as well as look mom in the eye without sneering and muttering, "You and your #$@%^*** cheap calf! Not to mention how long it took for me to forgive dear old dad and his cowardly act of letting go of his section of rope.

(Authors note; The psychologist still thinks the post-traumatic stress will go away someday, while the local pastor at our church still works with me on the "forgive part".....but even now, I am shooting my beloved father an evil look, and it's been just over thirty-five years past.....and still I harbor vengeful thoughts towards the entire bovine species, and every time I look at a cow, I imagine it under knife and fork, slathered in steak sauce...."ah, revenge is sweet...or at least salt and peppery.)

Archie Matthews

The long story short, the cow got bigger and we eventually ate it and never a sweeter meat did I ever partake in, for every time we had beef, I giggled like a mad man and wouldn't have stopped if dad hadn't drug me from the table and locked me in my bedroom until my sanity returned.

But enough about the calf, other than to say dad never did forget about all those Auction fellows laughing at us that day while we wrangled the calf, and dad wasn't one to forget being the brunt of a joke. Little did any of us know at that time, dad and I were going to get even with those Livestock Auction people and have our own laugh at their expense, and when I say "Expense", I mean it cost them a lot of money, and we're still laughing!

But enough of that now, back to the pigs, which believe it or not, this story is all about.

And so the four little pigs were fed and kept in the luxurious accommodations of a pig pen completely outfitted with suitable water and feeding trough, as well as fresh straw lined sleeping quarters just a step away inside the barn. And life with four little pigs seemed to be good and right and everyone was happy, that is except for one little pig that seemed to long for more.

The first sign that we had a disgruntled pig on our hands, was when I went out to irrigate the back field one evening and realized there was no water in our two foot wide irrigation ditch, let alone the smaller ditches it fed. Upon tracing the ditch back towards the canal, I quickly discovered a flooded field and the side of the ditch which was slightly elevated with a berm on our side, was breached with several large holes.

After trudging through the flooded field up to the canal and shutting the water off at the head gate, I quickly assessed the situation and was immediately rewarded by finding a pig rooting around boring holes in the side of the ditch. After several minutes of trying to herd the little "backhoe" back towards its pen, and finding that pigs don't herd worth a darn, I went to the house and sought help.

Rounding up my brothers, mom and dad, we spent the next couple of hours herding and cussing the fast dodging little spawn of the devil. I must admit, I began to build up a deep seated internal resentment for pigs in general. (not quite as much as cows, but close.) Only after everyone was covered in a thick layer of sweat, mud and freshly churned up pasture grass, did the pig crash into mom, at which time she grabbed him by the back leg and hung on for dear life.

There has been much contention as to "Who's life she was hanging onto, hers or the pigs", for she was howling her head off stretched out as if on the torturer's rack, the pig squealing for all it was worth, both screaming as if their lives depended on it.

I won't go into the boring detail of fixing the irrigation ditch or the arduous journey carrying a mud covered traumatized, free ranging pig back to its captivity, let's just say it wasn't easy and leave it at that.

Back into its pen it went and once inside everyone began to give the fence a once over and try and find out how it had gotten out. The biggest mystery remained, and by "remained", I mean to say the other three little pigs remained secure in the pen. After several minutes of close scrutiny, no breach in the fence was found, nor within the barn, as the gate inside was found still closed and latched. Everyone scratched their head and looked at everyone else and since Matthew had been left behind on the back porch to watch the pig round up from afar, he was the only one laughing now at seeing everyone covered in mud. Thus suspicion was immediately cast his way as to the most likely culprit to have let the pig out.

Dad was the first to cast muddy looks little Matthew's way by saying, "Matthew, did you let that pig out of the pen?"

Archie Matthews

Of course what with dad being covered in mud, you'd think his anger might be a bit masked, but I assure you, even a four year old could see dad was hot under the collar. Therefore, little Matthew never hesitated or batted an eye and quickly assured everyone "NO, I didn't let the pig out!" Of course if I'd been Matthew, I wouldn't have admitted to it either, for not only was dad hot under the collar, but there stood mom covered in mud, clutching and unclutching her hands, and I don't think it was to regain her circulation from clutching the pig.

And thus began the month long mystery of "Houdini", the miraculous escaping pig. For just a few days later that very same pig escaped once again. And once again after a huge pig round up, complete with running, screaming and angry words, the pig was again penned up. And just as before, the pig pen was given careful scrutiny as to its pig holding abilities, but yet again it was one pig loose and three pigs held within. Need I say the mystery deepened, but this time the adults began to cast suspicious eyes upon the four younger members of the family.

The gate inside the barn was scrutinized, but this time a piece of wire was expertly twisted around the latch, in just such a fashion that any tampering would instantly be detected. Then with a smug satisfied look shot in the direction of us kids, dad gave a knowing nod as if the trap to catch a "Gate Opening Kid" was set.

Once more the very next day, there was "Houdini" the escape pig, prancing around the pasture drilling for water in the side of the ditch, doing his best to turn our pasture into a submerged rice patty. The wild calf stood hoof deep in the water, a disgusted look on his face as he'd have to go scuba diving for his sweet grass, inches under water. And after another muddy roundup and hours of chasing the squealing "Houdini", he was captured and carried back to captivity. Upon dropping the little rascal back in his pen, dad immediately scrutinized his intricately wrapped wire around the gate latch and with faint grumblings and evil glances us kids direction, he concluded the pig evidently didn't come through the gate.

Two more times the very same pig was found outside the pen and two more times there was bedlam amidst the Matthews clan, the likes the neighbors had never witnessed before, nor after that wild summer, I am confident to claim. And after the latest rash of escapes by the "Houdini Pig", the accusations from both mom and dad began to fly wide and right out into the open.

With us four boys lined up before the barn wall as neatly as any suspects had ever been lined up before a firing squad, and with his finger pointed at each and every one of us boy's nose in turn, dear old dad began to seek to get to the bottom of the mystery of the escaping pig.

"Someone is letting that pig out...."Dad began, "There isn't a hole in the fence. There isn't a hole under the fence, and since pigs don't fly there is no way over the fence. Therefore the only other alternative is the gate."

Dad marched up and down the line of suspects and gave each of us a stern questioning look, but was received with nothing other than innocent looks.

"Someone is trying to pull a fast one. Whether a joke or trying my patience, I don't know, nor do I care. I will say this.....If I catch someone letting that pig out, the joke will be on them, in the form of my belt on their backside. Does everyone get my meaning!?" roared dear old dad, not only at the end of his patience, but evidently several paces past.

Then a couple days went by and sure enough, the pig was out once again. And once more with everyone's help the little culprit was caught but this time, dear old dad had an idea.

"We're going to lock the rascal in the horse trailer!" dad exclaimed as he carried the squealing pig to the tall steel sided horse trailer. And as I quickly opened the

53
Archie Matthews

trailer door, dad thrust the pig inside and we closed the door. Now if you've ever seen a steel sided horse trailer, you'd know it's a good five feet of slick steel at the lowest point which would be the back door. And after shutting the horse trailer door, dad stepped inside the barn and quickly returned with a padlock in his hand and with a grunt of satisfaction, he slipped it through the door hasp and snapped it shut.

"Now, let's see that pig get out!" dad huffed, "The only way is if pigs start flying and over the door he goes!"

Little did we know, dear old dad had the ability to prophesy, nor did we have long to wait, for the very next day, there stood the pig proud as you please rooting around the barn.

I've never seen such a murderous look on my father's face as I did that Sunday morning as we stepped outside and there stood the pig. All I can say is the pig was lucky dad wasn't wearing a gun belt, or he'd have slapped leather and we'd have eaten pork that very day for lunch. Be that as it may, there for a few seconds, I wasn't too sure dad wasn't going to run for the house and get a gun and shoot that pig dead, for like I said, dad had a murderous look on his face.

After we ran the little pink Houdini down and locked him yet again inside the horse trailer, dad conducted a long careful inspection of the horse trailer, both inside and out; then with a scratch of his head and mumbled words that no kid should ever hear, off dad stalked to do his chores.

Since it was Sunday it was a day of relaxation and after everyone did their individual chores, each kid meandered off in a different direction and did whatever it is kids do. Meanwhile dad retired inside to sit in his chair and relax in front of the television that he seldom took time to watch. The morning wended away and that Sunday was serene and quiet. That is right up until little Matthew came screaming into the house.

When Pigs Fly

"Pigs are flying, Pigs are flying!" he continually screamed as he ran in the back door, through the living room, around the dining room and kitchen and back out the door he had just come in.

"What in the world?" mom shouted as she came charging down the hall from her bedroom where she had been doing whatever it is mother's do in their bedrooms.

Dad quickly sat up and leapt from his chair, not even bothering to take notice of the television remote as it shot across the room from his lap. "What the heck was that kid yelling about pigs flying?" And out the back door dad went quickly followed by mom and I.

As we ran out the back door we could see little Matthew standing pointing at "Houdini" the pig smugly standing in the middle of the barnyard, ready to receive applause at his miraculous and amazing escape from a locked horse trailer.

"Pigs can fly....pigs can fly" little Matthew kept howling as he ran around the pig pointing his finger. "That pig can fly!"

"Matthew, what did you see?" dad asked as he ran too little Matthew and snatched him by the back of his little Oshkosh overalls. "How did that pig get out of the horse trailer?"

"That pig flied out....That pig flied out dad! That pig can fly!" little Matthew claimed with wide eyes, still jumping up and down with excitement with dad doing his best to hold him still.

"What do you mean that pig flew out?" dad asked again, "Tell me what you saw, just where were you and what did you see?"

"I standed by the barn and played with my truck," little Matthew said as he pointed to the fresh dug hole between the horse trailer and the barn, there sat a large

Archie Matthews

yellow Tonka truck next to a freshly dug hole. "I standed there dad and digged my hole and out flied the pig!"

Dad gave Matthew a puzzled look and then releasing his grasp on Matthew's overalls, he said, "Show me where you were". And following little Matthew over to the dirt pile, sure enough, there were little Matthew's foot prints, and straight out from the horse trailer door were the pigs foot prints plain as day.

Dad had been raised in the woods of central Idaho in a little town called Ola. He had hunted and trapped and fished and traipsed all over the hills, and in doing so, had learned to track small as well as large game. Seeing the tracks suddenly appear just outside the door of the horse trailer, dad's face turned from puzzled to down and outright astonishment.

"Pigs fly dad, they do." Little Matthew assured us. "That pig flied out."

And thus did the mystery of the escaping pig deepen even more so. Of course there was another pig chase and soon the pig was once again in its original pig pen with its siblings. Dad's theory was, "We might as well put him back in the pen, where he's got food and water handier than feeding and watering him in that horse trailer. Besides, if the horse trailer won't hold him, I don't know what will."

And then with a sly smile, dad seemed to get a stroke of genius and said, "I know where we can lock him, and he won't get out! We'll lock him inside the barn!"

That relaxing Sunday afternoon quickly took an immediate turn into another work day on the farm as we fastened a board over the door from the pig pen to close off the barn opening allowing the pigs access from the fence enclosure to the barn. After the board was fastened, dad gave a satisfied grunt and smiled.

When Pigs Fly

"There you little pest, I'd like to see you get out of this barn....you do that and I'll sell you as "Houdini The Amazing Escaping Pig" and won't have to work for a living anymore!"

"Yeah dad," affirmed little Matthew, "And flying pigs are worth a lot of money, huh dad, then we'd be rich and no more chores!"

"Well...." Dad began. "I'm not sure what's going on, but I'm pretty sure pigs don't fly. If he does fly, we're rich and no more chores." Dad laughed with a wink at Matthew.

Now I have to admit, I was in agreement with dad in looking over the barn situation, I couldn't see anyway that pig could get out now. The barn was the typical two story affair, with a ground floor and a loft some ten feet above where we stored hay for the winter. The ground floor had a concrete slab and there was no digging out, and what with the barn itself being solid post and beam frame with age hardened pine siding, that pig would have to either dig through concrete or bust through the tough wooden siding. And with that, we left the pig in the inside pen and walking through the barn door, dad not only fastened the lever latch on the door, but since the wooden door opened outward, he also turned the upper wooden latch that spun on a nail that would be out of reach from anyone but himself, mom or I.

"That pig gets out now, I'll eat my hat!" announced dad with a firm nod.

But the look mom gave him told me she was contemplating just how she might cook up that hat to make it palatable, for I could tell she was beginning to have her doubts about keeping that pig locked anywhere.

And a couple more days slipped by and since it was summer there was no school and us kids would do our chores and then the rest of the day was our own to do

57
Archie Matthews

whatever it is kids did. So little Matthew and Roy were out playing with their trucks by the barn most of the day, and I and my brother Ike were out setting irrigation that afternoon when dad come home from work. I saw him pull up in his pickup and park then stepping out he walked over to the barn, opened the door and went inside. A few minutes later out he came with a satisfied look.

I and Ike finished irrigating and soon joined dad on the back porch and were visiting about our day fixing irrigation ditches and dad's day working at the big feedlot where he was the foreman, when here came Matthew and Roy.

"Hey dad, we heard funny noises in the barn." Roy claimed, looking a bit scared back over his shoulder at the barn.

"Yeah, dad…." Little Matthew began nodding in agreement, "Funny noises in the barn, dad."

"What kind of noises?" dad asked with a bit of a smile.

"Like huffing and puffing noises and then grunting, like the big bad wolf when he got after them three little pigs….." explained eight year old Roy, with another wary look back towards the barn.

"Yeah, dad, huffing and puffing like a wolf in the barn eating our flying pig! You better come quick dad, we need that pig to be rich dad….I hate chores and being poor!" wailed little Matthew as he began to shoot suspicious looks towards the barn.

And with that, we were all on our feet and headed towards the barn, dad in the lead and I and Ike close behind, but not too close, after all, someone did mention the possibility of a wolf inside eating the pig. Mom must have seen us through the kitchen window, for here she came too. Just as we approached the barn, sure enough you could hear loud snorting and wheezing inside the barn.

When Pigs Fly

"Dad!" wailed little Matthew, "Better get your gun dad! Don't let the wolf eat our flying pig dad....don't let it get you dad!"

I have to hand it to dad, he wasn't anyone's fool and hearing something strange coming from the barn, made a quick little detour over to the inside of the little tack room attached to the barn. Reaching inside and up over the door, his arm came back out with an old single shot shotgun he kept hidden there. Snapping the breach open, he checked to make sure it was loaded and with the quick flip of his wrist snapped it shut and gave everyone a serious look.

"Stay back, I'll take a look....." he warned as he stepped up to the door.

I'd like to say, I clamored for a chance to assist dear old dad in fighting whatever was making those strange sounds, and was apparently just finishing up eating the pig, for suddenly the sounds ceased and the inside of the barn was quiet. But I didn't, I was happy to stay back and let dad and his shoot' n iron face the unknown pig assailant.

Dad eased both the upper latch and the lower latch open and then throwing the door open, in he went. A few minutes ticked by with me and everyone else holding their breath when we heard a loud exclamation from dad inside the barn. After a few more minutes and not hearing any gun shot, mom called out, "Archie, what is it? Archie are you okay in there?"

Then dad appeared in the door with the strangest look on his face and said, "There isn't anything in here......no nothing.....no pig, no wolf, no anything?"

Of course that sent a flood of bodies into the barn as dad turned around and led us back inside, and sure enough, there was nothing. The pig pen was empty as was the rest of the barn, oh sure, there were a few odds and ends here and there. A stack of boards against the

Archie Matthews

far side, a few bags of pig feed and a bag of oats, several buckets here and there and some other stuff, but no pig and certainly no wolf, with or without a pile of pig bones.

Everyone was just as astonished as dad had been, and then dad's brow began to crease and his head slowly swiveled around to Matthew and Roy.

"If you boys are playing a prank on me, I'll tan your hides!" growled dad with a stern look. "I've had just about enough of this whole mysterious escaping pig!"

Both Matthew and Roy gave startled looks and it became obvious that they knew just about as much as the rest of us as to what had happened to the disappearing pig. And then little Matthew's mouth dropped open and his eyes opened big and wide and he began jumping up and down.

"Dad, dad.....I know, I know...." Shouted little Matthew raising his hand as if to ask permission to speak.

"What do you know?" asked mom quickly.

"I know what happened to the flying pig!" shouted little Matthew.

"What?" asked dad.

"He's not only a flying pig, but he's an invisible flying pig!" explained little Matthew with a serious look. "Yup, that's it dad, he's an invisible flying pig, dad! He's probably flying around in here right now and we can't see him!"

After several minutes of snorting and laughing, that is, everyone but Matthew, the barn once again became quiet, and dad was about to say something when we heard a loud bang on the roof of the barn, and as I've stated before, Dad didn't hesitate.

When Pigs Fly

Dad darted for the barn door and everyone piled out behind him as we heard a scraping sound along the tin roof. Everyone was looking up expectantly, while backing up to try and see what was on the roof, when with a loud squeal, over the edge of the roof came the missing pig.

All I can say is if little Matthew had been two feet more to his left, he'd have been squished flat, as a thirty pound pig came crashing down to earth. I'll say this about pigs, although they are not well suited for flying, they sure as heck can crash land, for the little pig hit the ground with its legs neatly tucked underneath and as it slammed to earth, out popped its landing gear and as if by magic, it stood up un-hurt.

Everyone but Matthew was so utterly surprised by the crash landing that we all stood there with our mouths open, not uttering a sound, but not so for little Matthew, for he took off at a dead run for the house screaming to the top of his lungs.

"Run for your lives…flying pigs are crashing! Flying pigs are crashing! Runnnnnnnnnnn……!" And away he went towards the house as fast as his short little legs could carry him, without even a backwards glance, across the lawn, up the back porch and into the house, "Banging" the back screen door and door as he barricaded himself inside.

After a few more seconds of shocked surprise at seeing a pig fall from the sky, dad began laughing and laughing. Then reaching over and grabbing the pig, he carried it inside and placed it back in the wire pen within the barn. Then coming back outside he quickly shut the door and walked over to a handy knothole in the wall and began stealthily watching the pig. At this realization, the rest of us all fanned out and everyone sought a viewing point as well. And sure enough, after several minutes of careful quiet observation, we were not disappointed by our vigil and saw the little "Houdini pig" begin his escape attempt.

Archie Matthews

The little pig circled the small pen a few times and then walking over to the wire fencing, jumped its front feet up and hooking them into the wire, climbed up the wire as deftly as any skilled rock climber did the vertical side of a mountain. Reaching the top, the pig simply fell over the other side and then getting to its feet, it sniffed around a few minutes and then walking over to the wooden ladder that led to the loft above, the little climber once again kicked its front feet up and hooked them over the wooden ladder rungs and began to climb up towards the loft, hoof over hoof.

Dad, seeing his chance, immediately ran for the barn door and throwing it open ran inside to snatch the pig as it was now just about five foot up the ladder. Grabbing the pig, dad was immediately rewarded with the loud squeal of a frustrated pig, for now the "Jig" was up and not the "Pig". With a grunt of satisfaction, dad carried the squealing rascal outside and over to the horse trailer, lifting him over the rear door, dad dropped him the last couple of feet inside.

"Now everyone stand back! I want to see how he does this little trick!" dad exclaimed as he stepped way back and quietly watched.

You could've heard a pin drop as everyone held their breaths waiting expectantly to see how the little porker made it up the five foot slick steel rear door, nor did it take long. Sure enough, we suddenly heard the thunder of little pig feet running and a dull "Thud" as two little pig feet suddenly appeared over the top of the horse trailer door. Then working his little feet and then his pork hocks over the metal door, slowly the little acrobat chinned himself up until his head and shoulders where above the edge of the trailer door. And with another kick of his front feet, the little escape artist pushed his legs out until the door edge was now clear under his armpits and then with another big heave, over the edge he went, head over heels to land on the outside.

And thus was the mystery of the "Flying Pig" solved, but this wasn't the end of the little "Houdini Pig", by any means. For as I said earlier in the story, dad didn't like to get laughed at, and little did we know at that very moment dad had formulated a devious plan for some "payback" to get those livestock people that had laughed at us during the wild calf rodeo.

The day before the next livestock auction, saw us take the little pig back across the street. The Livestock Barn would take animals in for the auction all week, but dad waited until the very day before. There were only a handful of Livestock Auction workers there with the occasional livestock owner dropping animals off. Therefore there weren't a lot of people around, and that's just what dad was counting on.

Dad went into the office and did the paper work, which although the paper work was simple, wasn't easy for dad, for all the clerks as well as the pen wrangler all joked and chuckled over our last "debacle" involving the "Wild Calf". But come to find out, dad was about to get his much deserved "Pay Backs" and therefore he just smiled knowingly, and took the jibs in stride.

After dropping off the pig, dad came out of the livestock office and giving me a wide grin, he said, "Let's go home.....if things happen the way I think they will, those boys won't be laughing for long and we need to be ready at home."

What that meant I didn't have a clue, but I followed dad back to the house and we sat on the front porch, I sipping a cola, while dad enjoyed a nice cool beer. And then about twenty minutes went by when dad began chuckling and bumping my knee with his and getting my attention, he motioned over towards the front of our driveway by the barn and here came "Houdini" the freshly escaped pig.

I'm not going to bore you with long drawn out details about how many times my dad took that pig to the sale, filed paperwork, left the pig in the care of the livestock

63

Archie Matthews

yard to sell. I will tell you each and every time at the end of the sale the very next day, dad would go into the office and there would be a scurry of the office personnel to try and figure out what happened to dads pig.

It seems they never had a record of it selling and there was always a long drawn out conversation between the clerks and the pen wranglers in the back. Dad always had a receipt for the missing pig and thus, with a huge smile and a chuckle dad would collect whatever the going price was for the missing pig.

Honestly......I don't have a clue how many times he took the pig to the sale, only to have it escape and come home. I do know finally after several months, one day here came the pig, but this time, there were several pen men and a couple clerks from the livestock auction in hot pursuit. And there we were as usual, but this time, it was I and dad laughing and those other people being led around by nothing other than a flying pig.

This tale doesn't really end here either. I'd like to say it was a big happy ending with the laughter on the front porch, but two lives were dramatically affected by that summer and the myth of the Flying Pig.

One life forever changed was "Houdini" the pig, for once the jig was up about Houdini's climbing abilities; he was put in an escape proof pen and finally sold. We were later told by the fellow that had ended up buying him, he met a terrible end, for the new owner didn't know about his new pig's acrobatic skills and the pig climbed over his fence and fell head first into a rain barrel and drowned. Which in my opinion served the little rascal right, but that's just my opinion, despite it being somewhat jaded by all the times I'd spent covered in mud and sweat from having to chase him down.

But the other life dramatically affected that summer by the Flying Pig was little Matthew. No matter how hard anyone in the family tried, we could never get him to understand the pig didn't really fly. And thus for years

When Pigs Fly

little Matthew assured everyone at school during show and tell, he'd seen a pig fly and no amount of laughter would dissuade him.

In fact to this day, many years later, little Matthew is now Big Matthew, with kids of his own. And when he comes to visit our farm and he thinks no one is around, if you watch him carefully you might catch a glimpse of him out by my pig pen with a twinkle in his eye, encouraging them to fly.

After all, he's always wanted to be "Rich!"

Archie Matthews

When Pigs Fly

The Legend of Stink Foot

Now everyone's heard of the Legend of Big Foot, although shrouded in deep mystery and heated debate about whether or not Big Foot actually exists. But in my family, we have a Legend of just such a mysterious being, yet we have irrefutable evidence that "Stink Foot" actually exists, and I'm not talking about grainy photo footage, questionable foot prints or unidentified hair samples, for we actually have in our midst, the living breathing Stink Foot.

It all started away back when I was six and dear old dad broke his foot and had to have a cast put on it. Now you must understand my beloved father and leader of our household, was not the most patient man on the face of the earth. In fact, his GOD given allotment of patience could be measured by the partitioned marks within a thimble. Yes, you heard me right.....not a cup, not a half or even a quarter cup, my father's patience equaled about a tenth mark on a woman's sewing thimble. And believe it or not, I think that's a fairly generous assessment, as you will see by this story.

Now dear old dad came home that afternoon with a large white plaster cast on his right leg, encompassing his entire foot and leg up to just below the knee. When he arrived home, or how, I can't tell you, for I was off playing with some friends, and upon arriving home, was surprised to see dad's pickup already in the driveway. Since dad usually worked until 5:00 every evening, seeing his pickup already home at 3:00 was a bit of a shock, for my dad just didn't miss work, unless it was something serious....such as a broken foot.

Poor old dad sat in his favorite chair with his broken foot in his freshly wrapped plaster cast propped up on a stool in the family room. I could tell his foot was really bothering him, for every time one or the other of us kids would race by his foot stool, the old man would growl and flinch and warn of instant death if someone actually ran into his throbbing appendage. Needless to say, it was a touchy afternoon and evening, but before long, it was bedtime and everyone was tucked in for the night.

That is until about midnight, when I awoke to a weird thumping sound out my bedroom window. Getting out of bed, I went to the window facing our back yard and instantly noticed the detached garage light was on. Now although I was scared to death of the dark, our back porch light was on, lighting the walkway to the well-lit interior of the garage. Therefore, being a curious kid of six, I decided to go see who was working in the garage this late at night.

Getting my slippers and housecoat on, I proceeded to go out the back door and across the walkway to the garage several yards from the house. Imagine my surprise at opening the garage door and peering in to see poor old dad gingerly chipping away at his plaster cast with a ball peen hammer.

"Whatcha doing dad?" I shouted, trying to make myself heard above the gentle hammer blows, as I threw open the garage door and stepped quickly inside.

The Legend of Stink Foot

I could instantly tell poor dad's foot was killing him, for he gave such a start that he missed the plaster cast and "Whacked" his big toe. Thus his brief "Howl", not to mention the violently flung hammer; which I knew wasn't intentionally aimed at me, but probably more of a pain reflex resulting in the instant releasing of the hammer in my direction.

After a few minutes of dancing around on his left foot, as it was the only one he was standing upon, his right leg being propped up on the table saw all stretched out, surrounded by chipped away plaster chunks, dad eventually stopped talking in that strange foreign language he spoke in sometimes. Although dad spoke some Basque and Spanish, this wasn't that kind of language, and to my knowledge he only spoke it when he smashed, cut or otherwise damaged one of his body parts. And usually, just like now, he only spoke several growled words and then soon began to speak English once again.

"Get me that hammer and hand it back to me..." grumbled dad with a pained look, "What are you doing up at this hour?"

I smiled at dad and then shuffled over and picked up the hammer that had slipped out of his hand and said, "Well, dad, I heard some funny tapping sounds and thought it might be a woodpecker in the garage".

Gathering up the hammer I had just dodged, I have to admit I was a bit hesitant in reloading dad, but handed him back the hammer all the same. Handle first and then as he took it, I stepped away and put some distance between us, just in case he was still harboring some ill feelings about that startle and the toe whack.

Funny thing about dads, often they will attribute their misfortunes upon their children, and since I was the only one handy at the time, I knew I would probably be the one that got blamed if

Archie Matthews

something went wrong. Thus was my caution purely a practical application and nothing personal against dear old dad.

"So whatchadoin dad?....don't you like your new foot cast? It's kind of a dumb color, but we could spray paint it....do ya want me to get the spray paint dad?" I asked, as I stepped up and was looking over the mess of plaster chips surrounding dad's propped up leg.

"I gotta get this dern cast off.....that doctor tried to tell me to wait a day or two for the swelling to go down before he put this @#$#%@## cast put on. But OH NO.....I argued with him and insisted he put it on while I was there.....now my foot's swollen and this @#$%# cast is killing me!"

Dad was funny that way, he'd revert in and out of that foreign language sometimes, that's how I knew his foot hurt. He also did that once in a while after him and mom had one of their "discussions" but he never did it while in the discussion, but only afterwards when mom wasn't around.

After explaining his need to get the cast off, he quickly went back to gingerly chipping away the cast. And I could tell he was having a hard time of it, what with wobbling all over while on that one leg, not to mention taking those itsy bitsy swings. I knew if I had a hammer, I'd have that cast off there quick, then dad could rest his leg.

"I'll get a hammer and help you dad...." I offered as I began looking for a hammer.

"Oh, no you don't....you just come over here and help steady me. I'm almost done around the toes, but my good leg is getting tired and I keep swaying.

"Sure enough dad....anything to help." I said cheerfully, as I hurried to his side, but quickly realized he was dressed like I was, in just his housecoat, with a flimsy sash tied around his

The Legend of Stink Foot

waist, which was incredibly hard to hold on to with any kind of firm grip. And as hard as I tried to get a good hold, dad kept complaining "Your pinching the daylights out of me…that's my hide under that housecoat….you know!"

"Well, it's hard to tell where your housecoat ends and you begin….dad", I tied to explain, but no matter how hard I tried, my grabbing handfuls of housecoat, just resulted in more complaints.

Therefore looking around I saw dads "Work Mate" bench, which was a portable table like workbench, which split down the middle and could be loosened or tightened with a big crank, thus enabling it to become like a giant vise.   Pulling the workbench over to dad's left leg, I opened up the vise as wide as his leg was and pushed it into place surrounding his leg up above the knee and midway up his thigh.   Of course as I was getting the bench moved into place, poor old dad had been carefully concentrating on not thumping his toes again, but suddenly he took great notice of my ingenuity.

"What in the heck are you trying to do to me……." Dad grumbled…….."I asked you to help steady me….."

"This will help dad….see…." and with that I spun the crank snug and sure enough, dad was much more stable with the vise holding on to his mid-thigh, what with its wide legged base distributing his weight more broadly.

"Hey….that does help." Dad said with a tight smile, and once again began carefully chipping away at the plaster, the bottom of his cast wedged up against the raised up table saw blade, amidst a growing pile of plaster chips.

"Want me to raise up that saw blade some more dad?" I asked hastily "That'll help ya dad…." as I grabbed the crank on the saw and gave it a quick spin or two, but instead of raising the blade

Archie Matthews

beyond the four inches it was now sticking up, the blade tilted about half an inch and dug into the bottom of dads cast.

"No…stop turning that crank!" dad grouched, still focused on not hitting his toes.

"Okay dad." I quickly said, as I began to look for the other crank that raised and lowered the blade. But unfortunately, as my hands were searching around the side of the saw, I must have accidently bumped the switch, for the saw kicked on.

It's funny how little accidents like that happen so quickly, but I instantly rectified the situation by quickly depressing the button again. And only a split second of about thirty thousand revolutions of the blade as it ground into the bottom of dads plaster foot cast. Thus quickly stopping in a loud screech and hail of plaster dust; the screech of course coming from dad and the plaster dust from the slightly mangled cast.

I'd have giggled out loud at the astonished look on my father's face, if the steam coming out his ears and the flames inside his eyes hadn't been so scary. But not to worry, that bench vise held him upright, or I'm sure from his looks, he'd have probably fell over. He was momentarily white as a sheet and taking big gulps of air, kind of like a fish does after it's been freshly jerked out of the water and is about to die on dry land.

"Um, sorry about that……" I hastily apologized as the little cloud of plaster saw dust began to dissipate, and I could see dads open mouth begin to take shape to say something. But I won't bore you with the twenty minute rant session dad went into, speaking that angry foreign language and waving around his hammer.

It's important to remember poor old dad's foot must have hurt something awful and thus he wasn't in his right mind. What with his toes all puffed up and purple like, not to mention the

The Legend of Stink Foot

increased sweating since I'd joined him, especially after that little table saw debacle.

Long story short, although he never did say so, I could tell those several thousand revolutions of that saw blade no matter how brief, had loosened up the bottom of the cast significantly, what with all those deep gouges in the plaster. Good thing I'd shut it off fast, another half dozen turns and dad might have one leg shorter than the other.

Whether dad wanted to admit it or not, the thinned down bottom of the cast was all but gone, for after just a few more hammer blows, the whole bottom of that cast come off. And with a surprised if not tense look, he asked me to hand him the big rasp. Then taking it from me he began to file the ragged edges off around the top of his exposed ankle, when I felt the urgent need to run into the house and water my mules.

Now, since we lived in town, and not out in the county at this particular point in our lives, we had no pasture and no livestock......let alone mules. Thus I feel the need to explain my "Urgent need to run water my mules".

Grandmother had always showed deep disdain at saying a fellow needed to go "Pee". Therefore she had always explained her grandson's must "Water their mules"; which simply meant, going off and relieving our bladders, but allowing everyone else the fantasy that we were big time livestock owners and evidently had a mysterious set of mules that needed constant water. I know it's kind of confusing, but wait until I have to explain how "Girls visited the water closet", despite there being no "closet", not to mention the only "water" was that which they brought with them. That'll set your noggin spin'n.....

Thus feeling the urge to water my desperately dry mules, I quickly exited the garage without any fanfare or even a word to dear old dad, who seemed rather intent, what with filing down the jagged edges of his cast.

Archie Matthews

Returning in through the back door, I wended my way down the hallway and quickly and efficiently, "watered my mules….as well as pitched them some hay". (I trust I don't have to explain that added little livestock metaphor….if you get my meaning.)

Afterwards, with a flurry of yawns and struggling to keep my eyes open, I trudged back to bed and having just enough energy reserve left to drop my housecoat and slippers by the bed, I crawled under the covers and was fast asleep.

It wasn't long before I began to have the nicest dream, of being back with my beloved grandparents in the hills of central Idaho. I dreamt it was such a nice warm summer and we were all playing and having such a good time in the grandparent's yard with everyone laughing and the frogs croaking. And then grandpa came to me in my dream with a smile upon his face and opening his mouth to speak, a loud "Croak" came out. Then along came Grandma and she began croaking, and soon everyone was croaking and croaking and I remember thinking that croaking sounded more and more familiar. Until listening ever intently it actually became my dad's voice, croaking for "Help…Croak...Help…Croak….someone HELP!"

And thus a perfectly wonderful dream slowly evaporated as I heard mom come rushing down the hallway, calling out, "Archie...Where are you...Archie?" Then I heard the distinctive sound of the back door opening up and then the shop door banging open and another flurry of dad's foreign language. I couldn't quite tell what exactly was said, but suddenly realizing I'd left dear old dad precariously clamped in his workbench, I could guess, for I'd heard them a time or two before.

After several minutes I heard mom and dad's voices coming closer as they approached the house from the garage, and I quickly peeked out the corner of my bedroom window, to see mom doing her best to help poor old dad hobble to the house in his busted up cast.

The Legend of Stink Foot

"Why on earth did you have your leg clamped in that workbench to begin with?" mom was asking quite exasperated.

"That son of yours imprisoned me in it!" wailed dad as he grunted and groaned all the way from the garage to the back door.

"How on earth did "OUR" son imprison you in your own workbench...and why in heavens name did you try and saw your cast off using the table saw?" mom quickly asked doing her best to keep poor old dad upright and hobbling forward into the house.

"I didn't try to use the table saw to cut my cast off, your...I mean "OUR" son also did that to me! The kids not only a menace to society but he'll be the death of his family....each and every one of us...believe it or not, he just tried to whittle me down! He'll never stop until he kills us all!" dad babbled as he hobbled across the kitchen and down the hallway, with mom's help.

Of course once they were down the hallway and into their bedroom, I could hardly hear the rest of the conversation; that is until I got close to their door and put my ear up against it. Then, oh boy howdy, could I hear the rest of the conversation. Let me just say, poor old dad must have been half out of his mind with pain, for he began a litany of all kinds of woe's and misery that somehow his poor disillusioned mind blamed me for. Long story short, it took mom quite a while to get him calmed down and back into bed. Of course, I can only surmise, for I'd gone back to bed, once his pain filled ramblings had been realized for what they were.

The following morning at the breakfast table, there sat poor old dad with his raggedy looking cast propped on a chair, smudged from the oil and grease and what-not on and around the table saw, not to mention his exposed good leg with its odd looking black and blue stripe around his thigh.

Archie Matthews

"How ya doin this morning dad?" I asked with a smile, trying my best to lighten the poor fellows' gloomy mood as I entered the room.

"Oh, I'm just doing fine and dandy, ever since your mother came and opened up my workbench vise and rescued me last night….." grumbled dad with a dark look. "Where in the heck did you make off to last night?"

"Oh, I had to water my mules' dad…..then I got tired and went back to bed." I quickly explained, shoving a piece of bacon in my pie hole.

"Yeah….back to bed…and left me out in the garage all locked up and helpless".

"Well, dad it was "YOUR" workbench….I figured you knew how to open it by just twisting that little handle….did you forget how?" I asked somewhat puzzled around another slice of bacon, just before it too was shoved inside my half full mouth.

"Never mind…" growled dad with scowl.

"Now don't you worry honey, I'll get the kids off to school and then I'll take you back to the doctors and have the doctor fix that cast." Mom said jovially as she brought more bacon and some eggs to the table for the starving horde.

As you can probably tell, I and mom were jovial people, unlike dad, who often let the little things get him down.

I won't go into the details of the long boring day at school that I was forced to endure, nor the long arduous walk home, since we only lived across the street from the school. But that late afternoon when I got home, dad was there once again, early in the day sitting in his chair with his leg propped up with a new white plaster cast. But this time, there looked to be lots of cotton

The Legend of Stink Foot

cloth or some such fabric all around his exposed toe tips and around the top of his cast.

"How's the leg doing dad?" I inquired coming in and walking right up and beginning to explore dads new leg addition, not to mention gently pinching the fat black and blue toes.

"Fine....fine....don't touch....don't touch!" dad insisted, still quite grouchy, as he waved his arms and gave me a mean look. Which was pretty funny, for dad wasn't mean at all, just what mom called, "A little on edge sometimes...especially around children."

Needless to say for the next couple of weeks, dad was a bit on edge, but soon just sitting around began to wear on him, for dad never was a lazy lay-about of a guy. Therefore he began to hobble around the house on his cast, despite what mother called "Contrary to Doctor's orders" and the fact that as mother continually pointed out, "Your not supposed to be up walking around on that cast, it's not a walking cast!"

That next Saturday, when my bikes front fork broke, and I was wailing my head off, dear old dad assured me he'd just weld it back on and it'd be good as new. Of course what with him walking around on his cast, I took that to mean right away.....right now...even.

Thus began the lengthy trial of patience that pitted son against father as to who was going to wear down first. For as with any six year old, when told his bike is going to be fixed, we think that means, "Right Now...this minute". But apparently when you're a father, with a cast on your broken foot, that kind of promise takes on a whole different meaning, such as "Someday, away far down the road of life....like when you're in college."

And as boys will do, I tried to be patient with my subtle questions and hints to dear old dad as to just when he might get around to welding my only means of transportation. But on the other hand,

77
Archie Matthews

dad was not a patient man, unless it came to taking his own sweet time in fixing his kids bike.

"Dad... I need my bike fixed dad....when you gonna fix it? Huh dad?....when?" I asked only every day of the week, two or three times at breakfast, and then nine or ten times every evening. Although I knew dad was especially grumpy at the evening news time, the man was severely troubled with world events. I tried my best to get between him and the television to get his full attention and make him understand the dire need I had in getting my bike fixed, but he kept squirming and twisting around doing his best to see the news around me.

"I'll get to it, I'll get it fixed.....did you notice this thing on my leg? I broke my foot you know....I'm supposed to stay off it and rest!" dad tried to point out, as if the poor fellow had just noticed he had a cast on his leg, and happened to be reliving the doctors instructions at that very moment.

It didn't take me long at that point in time, to realize the old fellow was probably not only on heavy medication, but a bit out of his mind with pain, and that mom was going to be the only lucid adult available for me to reason with. Thus I sought her out in the kitchen and did my best to get her to understand my bicycle plight. Of course, feeding a horde is not an easy affair....which she continually pointed out to me for the twenty minutes I kept following her around as she chopped, diced, peeled and pureed things and shoved them into the half dozen boiling containers atop the stove.

Finally, I just threw my arms up and decided to go out to the shop and try this welding thing for myself.

Now I'd watched dad many a time, run his welder. Of course I knew how to turn the thing on, and that the holder with the long metal rod was what melted the two pieces together. I also knew you had to watch everything behind that black colored glass, for I had tried watching from a distance once, even though I'd been

The Legend of Stink Foot

told not to. Wow, had my eyes hurt for the rest of the day, and a day or so afterwards. Shortly after that dad preached the "Archie's Welding and How Not to Become Blind" short course, by explaining about his welding hood and how you could only watch the bright welding light through it, or you paid the price with painful eyes. So with this knowledge, I decided I'd just go ahead and fix my bike myself......after all, how hard could it be?

Since mom was so busy cooking and dad was in glued to the "boob tube", as mom called it, which never made any sense to me, but I knew mom got mad when dad didn't do things that she asked, and that's usually when she called it the "Boob Tube". I knew I had a while to weld my bike back together, that is if I could keep little brother Ike out from under foot, and then I realized my younger brother was nowhere to be found, and therefore, not a problem.

Thus making my way out into the garage, I drug my bike and the broken front fork up to dads welding table. I knew that dad sat things that needed welded on that table. I quickly propped my bike up to the best of my ability and lay the fork and front tire as close together as I could get them. Then getting down dad's welding helmet, which was about twenty times too big for me, I switched the welder on and picked up the welding handle that held that long stick of welding rod.

Having everything just where I wanted it and just as I was about to begin my welding career, I heard the back door of the house open and heard my "Pain in the backside brother Ike" call out, "Archie.....where are ya?"

Not wanting the biggest snitch in the county to find me messing with dad's welder, I quickly dropped what I was doing and ran for the garage door and stepping out, I closed the door and left the running welder behind me.

"Here I am......" I quickly answered, with as innocent a smile as was ever displayed to an idiot little brother.

Archie Matthews

And thus dinner happened and as is wont with six year olds my welding project was forgotten, at least until several days later.

Since I was at school, it seems I missed the excitement of the original discovery, for as the story goes, mom happened to be washing dishes when she noticed a black tendril of smoke coming out of the crack around the garage door. Upon her entering the garage, she discovered a couple things. One was dads welder was just humming away, the other was a black bubbling mass smoking atop dads welding table.

Of course, I heard all about the amazing "Garage Welding Incident", as it is still referred to today neither I or my younger brother Ike knew any of the true or false questions, nor the multiple choice, let alone the much harder essay questions, no matter how much dad screamed and shouted pointing an accusing finger here and there.

The really sad thing was, somehow, the aluminum forks, rim and tire, not to mention the tube, was forever missing from my bike, never to be seen again. The good part, or as good a part to this tragedy as could be deemed, was somehow, after the front of my bike turned to its former liquid state, the back half of my bike fell off the table and rolled far enough away that my role in the little fiasco, remained undiscovered.

Dad would say the ultimate tragedy was after mom shut off his welder, the black smoking puddle atop his superheated welding table top, solidified, and as such, was never to be removed, but became as much of the table as any other part. The problem with that, as dad found out later, the table top was never conducive for welding ever again and the entire welding table was rendered useless and eventually hauled off. But of course that was much later….after the Legend of Stink Foot was well established.

The Legend of Stink Foot

And after a week or so of searching for my missing bike forks, I was reduced to scavenging a set of old steel forks from another bike a friend had. And after another full week of reminding dad patiently of his promise, finally he succumbed and that next Saturday, complete with cast still on his leg, he decided to help.

Oh, but I've gotten ahead of myself a bit.....for I failed to mention that same day dear sweet mother was discovering the "Garage Welding Incident", dad had finally gone back in and finally gotten yet another cast put on his foot. It seems even the second cast couldn't with stand dads stomping around and was thus replaced with a thick sturdy walking cast.

It seems since dear old dad and the local "Quack", that was evidently old Doc Helverson's nickname, or at least that's what dad called him, had somewhat harsh words that initial day when he had put the original cast on. And then dads apparent walking on his second cast had finally broken down the second cast and therefore the third cast was needed. This was when the old doctor had instilled a bit of professional payback.

As dad had explained the night he was chipping away the "tight cast" from around his painfully swollen toes, the doctor had tried to get him to understand the need for waiting for the swelling to go down before he could get the proper fit to the cast. But as dad had bemoaned that late evening during his little "chip 'n" session, he had insisted and the doctor had put the cast on despite the severely swelling foot. Thus dad had chipped that cast away in the dead of night; with a little help from his oldest son.....yours truly.

And as you will recall, dear old dad went and came back with yet another white plaster cast replacing that chipped away cast, but what I didn't tell you was, despite the old doctor's insistence, that dad stay off that foot, for that second cast wasn't a walking cast. But as you can probably tell by now in reading this story thus far, dear old dad isn't known for his patience, and thus had been

Archie Matthews

walking around on that "plaster of paris" and had practically busted it to "smithereens".

And therefore dad had once again returned to the "Quack" and had yet another even sturdier cast applied. This time when dad came home, the cast looked odd, but extremely tough, and mother had patiently explained to the young inquiring minds that wanted to know, that dads new cast was made of fiberglass a kind of boat building material; which didn't mean much to us kids, but was about to mean a great deal in the shaping, and forming or the Legend of Stink Foot.

Now that you are brought up to speed, we will once again resume with dear old dad finally breaking down and fulfilling his promise to fix my bike; which after a brief harangue by not only me, but mom, dad acquiesced and stomped out to the garage. I say he stomped, and that's just exactly what he did in the large bulky heavy fiberglass cast. The "Thumpity….thump…thump" of his boat material encased leg booming along the walk between the house and the garage.

Of course I was too young to recognize a grown up having a bit of a traveling fit, for it wasn't until much later in life that I began to recognize when an adult was angry, they tended to walk fast while grumbling, or at least dad did. But be that as it may, I followed along chattering happily, knowing my bike was about to get fixed and I'd be able to once again join my pedal gang into and around town.

I won't bore you with all the technical "mumbo-jumbo" as dad tried to figure out how to put the two totally different bike halves together, but finally dear old dad just decided to weld the front piece to the back piece. After some grinding with his angle grinder, at which time, I noticed a lot of sparks dancing around dads exposed toes. Of course dad had noticed about the same time, as he was the one grumbling and wiggling his exposed little pink porkers fervently doing his best to keep them out of the spark shower.

The Legend of Stink Foot

After several minutes of grinding, dad asked me to go in and get him a sock to put over his toes and the end of his cast; which I quickly set off to do, despite my disgust at having to run errands for the surgeon. I was a tad disgruntled at having to leave my "baby" without its loving owner to over see the operation. This is why, as I exited the back door, on my way to the house, I recognized a quicker solution to the problem.

Every spring after dad was done using the old rotor-tiller to till up mom's garden plot; he would cover the carburetor with an old wool sock. He claimed the sock kept dirt and stuff from getting into the old leaky carburetor. Seeing the old sock just a step off the walkway to the house, I quickly grabbed it and pulled it off the rotor-tiller carburetor and returned inside the garage.

Dad was still a bit cranky at having been what he called "Shanghaied" by a "female siren and her evil progeny", which I didn't understand a word of, but if it meant he was welding my bike, I was all for it. And "Thumping" around the garage, getting his welder turned on and then arranging the bike just so, on the edge of his "ruined" welding table, I decided to do old dad a favor.

Thus I bent down and slid the somewhat damp gas soaked, stinky sock over the end of dads exposed toes and up and over the heel of his massive foot cast. Of course, dad had stopped to lift his foot, allowing me to pull the old rotor-tiller sock on his cast. And believe it or not, the grump even mumbled a hasty "Thank you…" before he once again hurried to complete the weld and get back to his Saturday morning leisure.

But …."Oh the plans of mice and men…." Or so I'd heard adults say when their carefully laid plans suddenly fall asunder and turn into catastrophe…..and what a catastrophe, yet all in the making of the Legend of Stink Foot.

Archie Matthews

"Close that garage door will you.....I can't stand the smell of that dern toilet!" dad groused, as he motioned me towards the open garage door. I immediately went to close the open door wafting the odorous fumes of our neighbor's construction porta-potty.

Old Sam had been undergoing an extensive bathroom remodel the past couple of weeks, and therefore had a large plastic construction toilet placed beside his house, directly up wind it seemed from our garage. Both mom and dad complained about it, but only to each other, despite my suggestion that they go tell the neighbor it stunk. Both had assured me, we were just going to have to put up with it as a sign of being good neighbors until old Sam had his new bathroom in place. Therefore we had put up with the stench week after week. The smell really wasn't to awful bad from about Monday morning until Wednesday, for a big truck came every Monday and pumped out the foul smelling blue muck and replaced it with fresher smelling blue muck. But as every Saturday and Sunday, the last couple of days of the week and the neighbor's toilet "reeked to high heaven", or so dad claimed.

Shutting the garage door, I turned around to see dad holding up his hand palm towards me. "You need to be on the other side of the door until I'm finished welding, so you don't burn your eyes watching me weld again."

Although I hated to do it, I had already suffered flash burning my eyes once watching dad weld, and didn't want to go through that again, so I nodded and was about to step out when I realized something.

"How will I know when you're done?" I quickly asked dad.

I won't go into detail about his disgusted look, but he replied, "I'll holler at you".

"But maybe I won't know one holler from another.....how about a secret password?" I offered. As a kid constantly watching

84
The Legend of Stink Foot

television, I knew secret passwords were important things to know in order for one fellow to impart to another fellow upon opposite sides of a door, when it was safe to enter.

"Okay, I'll say…Come In…and then you'll come in." the grouchy old welder suggested with a bit of sarcasm. But at the age of six, I assure you, the sarcasm went totally over my head at the time.

I just nodded, since I could tell dear old dad was getting a might apprehensive and wanting to get my bike up and running as fast he could, due to his putting it off as long as he did. I had heard mom light into him that morning about his continually putting me off, and his loud and hasty agreement, "Okay…okay, so I've been a lousy father and shouldn't pamper my broken foot any longer and fix the kids bike….I get it…I get it!" I knew although it'd taken dear old dad a while to come to that conclusion, he was on the job now.

Therefore with no further "ado", I quickly exited the garage door and stepped outside. But as I closed the door, that dern sticky knob wouldn't release the latch again, and what with the stink wind blowing our way from the neighbor's toilet, I couldn't get the door to stay shut. Therefore, in order for it to stay closed, I reached up and flipped over the hasp from the door jamb to the door and turned that nifty little square knob that locked it in place; thus effectively locking the door closed until the password was given.

For a brief instant I was standing there with the door shut, day dreaming about my fixed bike, the humming drone of dads welder the only sound coming from the garage, and the next thing I know…..Screaming Pandemonium!

Did I mention that the garage door had a window in it? Yup, although somewhat smudged and dirty, it was still a window, and before I could get up on my tiptoes to look inside and see what all the screaming and banging in the shop was all about, there

Archie Matthews

was dad sucked up to the window shouting his head off rattling the door for all he was worth.

"OPEN THE DOOR….OPEN THE DOOOOR!" dad kept screaming almost pulling the door completely off the hinges, let alone almost breaking the hasp.

"That's not the secret password dad…." I tried to point out, "Your supposed to say….Come in…..remember?"

But then what with all the begging, pleading and blood curdling threats, I decided to go ahead and violate security measures this once and forgo the password. Dad's panicked look, not to mention high pitched screaming helped me right along with my quick decision. And thus began the struggle to turn that square little hasp knob, what with two thousand pounds of enflamed gorilla doing his best to pull the door off its hinges from the inside. But after what seemed a long while, especially when your own father is screaming death threats through a door window at you, I finally got the hasp turned and the door burst open and dad came "Thumpity, thumping" out, with his wool sock, not to mention his fiberglass cast fully engulfed in flame….well not fully, for only the foot portion and maybe half way up the leg was actually ablaze, the way I figured it, there was still about six inches of cast to go.

No one ever did explain to me if it was the carburetor gas soaked sock, or the fiberglass that made the flame burn that odd color, but what ever it was, it sure sparkled and popped dazzling multi-colored flames. That is, all the way to the nearest water source which happened to be the neighbor's chemical construction toilet. If I'd have been dad, it wouldn't have been my first choice, but of course, I wasn't the one with the brightly burning foot.

I have to say, for a man with a heavy fiberglass cast on his foot, the old man veritably flew across the twenty odd feet between our garage and the neighbor's outdoor toilet. And after throwing wide open the door and seeing dad thrust his flaming foot down the toilet hole, as the door returned and slammed shut due to that door spring, all I could hear was a loud "Hissing" and a very relieved sigh… well at least for that first few seconds, and then the loudest series of cussing and unintelligible growling I've ever heard before or after coming from an outdoor toilet….well, except for that time I stole the hot fudge….. But that's another story.

I won't embarrass "Old Stink Foot" by going into detail about getting stuck in the neighbors toilet with his cast shoved down into that vile blue muck. Nor the even more embarrassing need to be assisted by not only the toilet's renter, but the company that supplied the toilet. I will say, it was quite a crowd gatherer, and people came from blocks around to see that chemical toilet taken apart piece by smelly piece to extricate "some fuming crazy man", or so I'd heard a few descriptions mentioned while I mingled with my friends in the crowd.

And thus the Legend of Stink Foot was etched into not only our household, but the neighborhood as well, for I'm sure I don't have to describe the unimaginable horrid smell as dad and his singed fiberglass leg cast was extricated from the neighbors toilet. To say the smell was horrid, would have been like trying to say a skunk smells like tulips, until you've actually smelt it, you have no idea.

But of course, since it was Saturday, and the following day was Sunday, the "Quack" couldn't be reached until that following Monday. And thus dear old dad was stuck….as were we his family, with as stinky a foot as you can imagine. Of course the old fellow tried his best to once again chip away the befouled foot covering, but fiberglass is tough…."That must be why they make boats out of it." I pointed out, seeing both mom and dad doing their best that evening out in the garage, chipping away….or should I say, trying to chip away, for try as they might, they couldn't even make a dent in the stuff.

Archie Matthews

Needless to say, it was a long weekend, but finally Monday came and dad went to the doctors, yet when he came home, there was no cast. Upon asking mom about it, she quietly explained there had been a little misunderstanding at the doctor's office and dad's foot wasn't actually broken. It seems dear old dad just had a sprained ankle; therefore there was no further need of the cast. It was also pointed out, that dad still had a mighty tender toe or two, for evidently the little chipping hammer episode had left him with two broken toes, hence the black and blue swollen little piggies.

"So dad went through all that for no reason?" I so eloquently put it, but mom quickly shoved her hand over my mouth and told me not to say that where dad could hear me.

Thus was the Legend of Stink Foot born, but believe me when I say, it was NOT a short lived Legend; for years afterwards, anytime dear old dad gets that foot wet, that distinctive odor of gasoline soaked wool and burning fiberglass is once again renewed, not to mention the wafting aroma of toilet chemical, blue muck and all.

And here we are, Mom and dad living with me and my beloved wife Suzy on our Big Montana Cattle Ranch in the middle of Washington State. All one big happy family, mom and dad retired, Suzy working as a Para educator at the local school district, and I with my government job during the day and book writing in the evening….but wait…I can't write anymore, I've got to go…for I can smell dad coming down the hallway….fresh out of the shower…..and thus lives on….the Legend of Stink Foot!

Show and Tell

Back when I was in grade school, there were a few big events every kid longed for, recesses and lunch were both big, but even more exciting than those was "Show and Tell"!

Now for you young people of today, I will explain the long lost archaic art of "Show and Tell". Depending upon your gifts, and when I say "Gifts", I'm not talking about those GOD given talents we all have, but the material ones bestowed upon a child by a relative for your birthday or perhaps Santa for Christmas time. Either way, I'm talking about a spectacular gift you could bring to school, show and brag about to your entire class. But back in those days, "Brag'n" was a bad thing, therefore they called it "Tell'n". Or if you were like me, I got crappy gifts such as socks or handkerchiefs generally, and therefore I was either reduced to "Tell" or make my own "Show" items.

Now "Telling" even as a young lad didn't present to hard a task for me, for as you can imagine, I'm a fairly good "Tale Teller" as an adult, and even more so as a kid. Of course as an adult, there are moral and civil restraints a grownup feels in "spinning a tale" to an audience, but as a child…..well, let me just say, I spun some "Whoppers" back in my day, with no moral or social restraints holding me back. In fact, some of my "Show and Tells" were not only "Show stopping" but almost "Heart stopping", as you will see by this story.

My story begins back in first grade as everyone in the class had just come back from Christmas break and artfully wended away the morning class hours by displaying a virtual cornucopia of magnificent gifts and plunder they'd gotten for Christmas, not to mention the glorious stories of travel to far and distant relative's houses.

Because I had been once again doomed to getting both socks and handkerchiefs and staying home for Christmas, I sat at my desk, with the choice of showing off my newly acquired wool socks, or spinning a "Yarn" as my old Grumps would have called it.

See, that's also the peculiarity of "Show and Tell", for really it should be "Show and/or Tell", for you can have a "Show and a Tell" or you can just have a "Tell", but you just can't get by standing their like an idiot holding up something for "Show" and not tell about it…..but you can, just "Tell", if like me, you just got junk and don't want to display it.

(I know it's complicated, but I didn't make up the rules, nor do I think it was an American invention, but probably originated in Poland somewhere, for the "Have's" to show the "Have-not's", what kind of things they "Had", and thus slowly but surely educating the countryside, due to the lack of television…..or at least that's my theory.)

As you can imagine, faced with the prospect of standing in front of a classroom of my peers and pulling up my pant legs to display my new wool socks poking out the top of my boots, or telling an exciting tale of woe and horror, which would you have done?

Show and Tell

"YUP", precisely......and thus went my story for "Show and Tell".

Of course I patiently waited my turn; all the while my active imagination kicking into overdrive I began to devise the veritable beginning of my "Ultimate" first grade "Super Tells". And thus I was soon ready as it came my turn and our first grade teacher Mrs. Bee called my name and I sauntered towards the front of the class.

I'll just take for granted that everyone understands the logistics of a first grade sauntering, even if it was my first time to the head of the class. I won't risk boring my readers with the smiling and waving at my fans on my way by as I strode valiantly to take center stage at the head of the class.

Taking my spot front row and center, Mrs. Bee of course still setting at her desk and behind me, I faced my audience and opened my first show and tell with a dramatic look of enlarged eyes, upraised arms and an astonished look on my face,....I shouted.....

"An alligator ate my little brother on the way to school this morning!"

Of course there were several sharp intakes of breath and several little frightened squeals from the girls around the room some of which even knew my younger brother Ike, or otherwise known for the next couple of years in grade school as "gator bait".

Upon seeing a lot of jaws dropped, not to mention extremely surprised looks for many of my friends, let alone the acquaintances. I immediately recognized I had captured my audience's attention and thus I waded headlong into my fantastic morning adventure.

"Yup, on our way to school this morning as we were passing by a huge tree, my brother Ike was but a few feet behind me, when all of a sudden I heard a faint rustling of leaves; I felt a rush of air overhead and heard a "Yelp". Turning around, all that was left of

Archie Matthews

dear little brother Ike, was his empty ball cap sitting upon the ground!" I wailed, continuing my dramatic look of horror at having lost the brother that up until now was a pain in my backside, but having become alligator food, I now missed beyond words……almost.

"Then, looking up, I saw the huge beast with it's long snout still dripping with bit's of bone and bloody guts, getting ready to snatch me, I battled him tooth and nail and got away clean." And with that, I threw my arms up triumphantly with a heroic smile. But seeing the disgusted look of several of my brother's friends, girls ever one, I added; "Poor Ike and me with a broken heart, what with my dear little brother ate and in the belly of an alligator somewhere up in a large tree."

And watching the audience closely, I could see the level of disgust by the girls, ease a bit, if not take a gentle nudge into the direction of sweet compassion for my horrible loss….but then I noticed several shocked expressions turning into puzzlement and gradually swinging into disbelief…..

And since it was customary for both the "Show and the Tell" to take questions, even without me asking, there was a flurry of raised hands and several "Wisen-Heimer's" began to formulate their attacks to the veracity of my "Tell".

Now I don't know what idiot designed the "Question" part of the Show and Tell procedure, but I never have liked that stupid part. It always seems to bog down the thrill of the story and can very quickly "deflate" even the most inflated tales of adventure, not to mention gore and horror.

Thus the questions began to be fired at me; first it was just a random "Pot shot", from Doogie Mayer as he asked, "But Arch, you just live across the street from the school and there ain't but a few itty bitty trees between here and there…..where was you at when you walked under that big tree?"

Show and Tell

Suddenly I could see my "Tells" were going to have to involve a bit more research as to terrain and the size of its content, not to mention geographical settings, since I did only live across the street from the local grade school. I could see right off, I needed to put a bit more preparation in my "Tell's", in hopes of avoiding all these embarrassing questions.

And then hails of well-aimed questions were soon being fired at me, if not a virtual machine gun barrage of "Where, How, What...?" Not to mention all the stupid innuendo's about the possibility of alligators inhabiting trees in the lower portion of Idaho, let alone the arid county we inhabited and "did I bump my head on the way to school?"

All I can say for the rowdy mob, was they were lucky Mrs. Bee stepped in when she did, before I had the opportunity to actually begin explaining to these local hillbillies with their low I.Q's, not to mention limited imaginations, the absolute fact involving the alligator in the tree.

But be that as it may, for Mrs. Bee stepped forward and hastily patted me on the head for doing my best in entertaining a bunch of half-wits, and I was sent down the gauntlet aisle towards my distant seat, followed by the stupid looks of my classmates.

Taking my seat, I smiled at dear Mrs. Bee as she shook her head at the apparent stupidity of my audience, not to mention the uneducated simpleton's questioning the voracity of my exciting alligator in the tree tale. And patting her forehead with her white lace fringed handkerchief, she quickly decided my harrowing tale was excitement enough for this inexperienced pack of hay-seeds and we went quickly into the lessons of the day.

I'll spare you the bloody details of answering some pretty far flung accusations at recess from a couple of fellows that impugned my honesty and decided to take the hard and firm stance that "There ain't no alligators in Idaho...in or out of trees!"

Archie Matthews

I like to think I softened their obstinate behavior what with a tenderizing blow or two to their delicate noses, which were quite apparently bent out of shape at my crowd awing display at show and tell. No doubt both miscreants must have had tales of their own they were about to wend, and hearing mine, felt utterly shut out of the competition, which happened as Mrs. Bee called a halt to "Show and Tell" for that morning.

After a long and rigorous morning of learning useless drivel, we were soon rewarded with the lunch bell. And sitting with my classmates in the cafeteria, to my dismay, in filed the kindergarten kids, of which my little brother Ike was at the head of the line. Thus with several looks from my friends at the lunch table, another barrage of questions began to zip around me, doing their best to knock me over with a well-placed "Kill Shot", for it seemed when you're on top of the "Tell" billboard as the most "Brilliant Showman", everyone wants your head as a trophy.

"I thought you said Ike was eaten by that alligator from up in that tree?" Brute Worryton asked, giving me his "Low brow" stare.

Brute Worryton's name wasn't actually "Brute", it was Bruce, but since he was the biggest kid by far in our school, everyone just called him "Brute". Yet, unlike his formidable size, his demeanor was that of a big teddy bear, and therefore Brute was a friend to all….even me, despite his not quite understanding fiction at its best.

With a look over my shoulder, holding my sandwich in both hands, complete with my mouth full of the single huge bite I'd just taken, I mumbled, "Welp…I wonder how he got out of that alligator?" and wrinkling up my nose and sniffing the air….I mumbled, "Pew….I suppose I can guess".

The round of laughter all but silenced my critics on the matter for the rest of the day, although I got some mighty disgusted looks from the girls from the table beside us….for Ike was and always had been popular with the ladies….the little nit….

Show and Tell

And thus went my opening act in first grade at "Show and Tell". But I quickly came to the conclusion every stage performer must eventually arrive at, one can't forever ride the rainbow of stardom without fresh material. So in short order as my fame diminished and my class mates started looking at me normal again, not to mention our illustrious teacher Mrs. Bee, I once again found myself in need of either a Show or a Tell.

That's when a catastrophe happened at the local livestock feed mill where my father worked. It seems one of dads best employee's, Mr. Espo Garza stuck his finger where it didn't belong and thereby lost that particular digit, much to my dad's consternation, not to mention the finger's owner. I found out about it over the weekend by carefully eavesdropping on my parents late one night as they watched the late show. I had carefully positioned myself down the hall and peered around the corner to watch half the television screen, the other half being obscured by the arm of the couch.

I was laying there with my fist shoved in my mouth trying my best not to snicker at the jokes and wild escapades of the late night host, when dad told mom about the horrible accident. It seems Mr. Garza lost his finger, meaning not only did it come "detached" from his hand, but was nowhere to be found afterwards, as they rushed him off to the hospital some forty miles away.

It seemed the fellow and his finger had been cleaning the all but empty silo, when he got his hand in some kind of mechanical contrivance that quickly sent his finger to parts unknown. Dad as the foreman of the feed mill was responsible for supervising several of his employees to search the large silo that was normally full of sliced potato pieces, but was now harboring a missing finger amongst the still scattered remaining potato pieces.

Dad elaborated to mom that they had searched around and coming upon what he was sure was the finger, dad picked it up

Archie Matthews

and announced, "I've found it!" That's when Philip Raza, one of dads best workers, suddenly took one look at the white wrinkled up piece of finger like potato, and immediately passed out. This seemed to set off a quick panic that rippled through the remaining crew. Evidently, as dad explained there is a huge fear of methane gas in such places; thus the other finger searching employees seeing one of their finest fall over, evidently succumbing to methane gas, liked to have killed one another trying to fit seven grown men out of a normal size door all at once.

The long and the short of dear old dads harrowing tale was, some poor fellow lost a finger and everyone that worked at the mill knew about it, therefore I immediately calculated that it would be a hot topic at school that next day. And thus my fevered brain, if not rapidly dwindling stage career, immediately struck upon the perfect "Show and Tell" ever.

That morning I was up extra early rifling through the pantry and then dad's workshop. First I found exactly what I had been searching for and dumping its contents out, I found the perfect container for my "Show". With a few more preparations, entailing a knife and a particular condiment, I soon had my road to fame paved and hidden in the mail box just outside the front gate ready for pick up when I left for school.

After a quick breakfast of sly knowing looks towards my unsuspecting mother, let alone the veiled snickers imagining the reception I was going to get from my class mates at this morning's show and tell, I was soon off with my lunch box in hand and headed for the school. Oh, but of course, I'd made that quick little stop at the mail box and picked up the most amazing "Show" my class had ever seen....or so I assured myself with a diabolical chuckle as I made my way across the street towards my unsuspecting audience.

And soon I was filing into class with the rest of the inmates and forced to go through the morning rituals of putting our coats, hats and lunch boxes up. Then came the morning "Flag Salute" and afterwards, having to listen to our esteemed warden over the loud speaker give us his morning speech. Then after what seemed like half the morning wasted, Mrs. Bee announced it was time for "Show and Tell!"

To say my arm was in the air and waving like old Glory in a hurricane, would not have been exaggeration, for I not only waved high and proud, but I hooted, "ME…..ME….Mrs. Bee….pick me!"

And forever to her eternal dismay, poor Mrs. Bee did pick me…. "Okay, Archie….you may go first."

Zipping to the head of the class, for there was no sauntering or waving at the crowd this time as I passed, I went up the aisle between the desks in the blink of an eye. Oh, but the look upon their faces as I suddenly appeared at the head of the class, with my red handkerchief draped over my one hand, and the smug look upon my face, just anticipating the crowd's reaction to my Academy Award performance. And therefore, I took a moment for the tension to build and the mystery of what I had under the handkerchief to become unbearable, which it quickly did, as Mrs. Bee quickly urged me onward.

"Go ahead Archie, show us what you have and tell us all about it…." The absolutely clueless teacher encouraged.

Years later the woman was still heard around the holidays as she was a bit deep in the punchbowl, to say "I not only let him go first…..but urged him to unveil his Show and Tell…..lord help us all!"

I learned much later in life, well after she had retired and was enjoying her later years that with counseling and medication, she'd finally gotten over the nightmares. Although her daughter did mention, she never could face a box of matches again and would only light her scented candles with either a zippo or disposable lighter…..couldn't even stand to have the box in her house, full of matches or otherwise.

Archie Matthews

But I get ahead of myself......

After getting everyone's attention and being urged by Mrs. Bee to "Go on with the show!" I pulled my handkerchief away and displayed an everyday match box atop the outstretched palm of my hand. And holding my matchbox and it's mysterious contents, I began my "Tell".....which happened to be the very excitement filled tale of how Mr. Garza had his hand mangled by an "Alien controlled potato chopper" at my dad's feed mill; complete with gory details of bone separating, tendon tearing and blood curdling screams, all of which were my own additions to the story.

Not to put down dad's version by no means, but every story re-write has a bit of leeway for the Author to embellish. I'd learned that from my several Uncles as they told and retold hunting and fishing stories at hunting camp or around the BBQ, when the women weren't around. In my family the women have a way of huffing and snorting and throwing dirty looks around during even the most excited tales. Therefore, the Uncles didn't usually tell their tales until at the very least, their own wives were busy elsewhere. (But that went without saying....it went without saying, no matter how my mother tortured me as to where I'd ever come up with the idea of "stretching, embellishing, inflating, or as she called it, "heaven forbid......LYING". To have divulged where I had learned such things, would have meant "sick'n" her on my beloved story telling Uncles and becoming a pariah around the campfire....thus I kept my mouth shut.)

And just at the very height of my gory description, Mrs. Bee recognizing the somewhat green color, sweaty brows and rolling eyes of some of the more delicate girls in the class for what it was, quickly came around her desk and stepped up to my side, evidently with the good intentions or helping me with my display.

But little did the woman suspect, I not only had everyone's attention, including hers, right where I wanted it, which happened

Show and Tell

to be right on that closed match box, but I had everything completely under control.

That is right up until I quickly slid the match box open and holding it up high for everyone to see, I displayed the red ketchup drenched finger I so deftly poked through the hole in the bottom of the box and announced, "I found his finger!"

And as if two girls in the crowd wasn't enough swooning, I gave the finger a little wiggle, and away went Mrs. Bee with a gasp right straight over backwards and to the floor, quickly followed by Carl Sweezy's breakfast.

After that first brief loud hail of screams from the female crowd, not to mention a few groans and a loud oath or two shouted from the lads, as Mrs. Bee hit the floor with a loud crash, you could have heard a pin drop. Or at least for a few seconds, for the very next moment Brute Worryton pulled the fire alarm and all hell broke loose.

I'm not going to bore you with the details of filing out of class, down and outside as had been constantly drilled into us in direct response to a fire alarm bell. Once outside there was a bit of confusion by the rest of the teachers as to why Mrs. Bee's class although in their proper place, was not accompanied by their teacher. After a brief huddle of the teachers, Mrs.Hanson returned inside the building and shortly a scream from our classroom announced Mrs. Bee had been found.

After several minutes of standing outside casually visiting and waiting for the building to either burn down or be cleared and deemed safe, out marched the warden with a rather determined look as he walked up and down the rank and file as if searching for someone, which soon turned out to be me.

I have to say, I quickly realized the benefits of being a star, for I was swiftly given an escort to none other than the principal's office, by none other than the principal himself. Although I must say, my going wasn't cheered and celebrated as one would have

Archie Matthews

thought should be given to a now famous stage performer, but no matter, I was after all......just breaking into Stardom!

Of course Mr. Peterson, the principal, was extremely curious about both my Show and my Tell, but particularly ...... "Just exactly....where is the finger?!" he asked. And asked, and asked, despite my trying to explain it was on my hand.

The poor fellow was just too dense it seemed to comprehend the marvelous bit of "Magic" I had performed by thrusting my own finger through a hole in the bottom of the box, let alone the semblance ketchup has to blood.

Yet, quick as my escort and bodyguard could take me back to my classroom, (and when I say bodyguard, I mean it, for I got many an ugly look from pupils and teachers alike on our little march down the hallway) I quickly produced the matchbox in question and yet again, the poor dense old fellow known as our principal, demanded to know where the finger was.

Therefore, I once again thrust my finger through the hole giving it a little wiggle and was immediately awarded with a momentary encore as Trish Long sitting right next to my desk, watching everything, rolled her eyes to the back of her head and once again her mind departed for sunnier parts unknown.

Oh, sure, there were a few more screams and groans from this or that onlooker, but suddenly the whole thing seemed to make sense to our kind old principal, thus under full house arrest, I was immediately marched back to his office.

Needless to say, there was a quick phone call and instantly my mother appeared and was quickly informed of my show stopping, if not complete school stopping "Show and Tell" act. After a lengthy inquest that would have put the Spanish Inquisition to shame, I was tortured into spilling the beans about eavesdropping that past evening and hiding in the hallway, not to mention my secret construction of "The Finger In The Box", ketchup and all.

As a kid, you'd think parents would have more scruples than to punish you for every little detail of a crime….you'd think. But I assure you, as mother mentally checked off each and every violation I had gone through not only at the show and tell, but back into the night before, I could tell, when she said, "You're going to get it when your father gets home!"….she meant it. The list of charges were as long as my arm and I knew if convicted on every account, I would be put away and grounded for a very long time…..perhaps even until all the hide on my backside grew back…..maybe.

Once again, I won't bore you with the embarrassing details of mom's apology to both the principal and days later to Mrs. Bee. It seems my poor teacher had to take the rest of the week off to tend to a sick relative. But if the groveling and unabashed apologies mom gave the principal were anything close to what she gave Mrs. Bee later, I'm sure glad I wasn't present for it. At first mom had insisted I was going to accompany her to Mrs. Bee's home and apologize in person, but at Mrs. Bee's insistence, I didn't have to partake in that little meeting.

Oh, and boy howdy…..talk about "Get It" when I got home! Mom had me sitting down in a chair right handy just inside the door when poor old dad came in from a long day at work. The poor fellow seeing me sitting in the "Punishment chair" sadly shook his head and began pulling his belt from its loops about his waist. But before he could even open his mouth to inquire as to my latest offense, he was immediately set upon by a hysterical arm waving sports announcer, complete with full volume audio and stadium echo capabilities.

And just moments into moms very well told tale of excitement, woe and betrayal, dear old dad snapped…..and began laughing his head off. Which momentarily halted mother's tirade, not to mention her animated arm waving and all she could do for a few moments was stand still with the dumbest look on her face that I've ever seen. Yet just as quickly as her tirade stopped, it fired itself back up again, but this time it and her animated arms,

Archie Matthews

seemed to be directed at poor old dad as he fell over on the floor and continued to laugh his head practically off, all the while kicking his legs, while holding his midsection.

There was a point in time, that I was actually afraid mom was going to help him off with his head, for she got right down on her knees and kept insisting, quiet loudly, that my behavior and his was unacceptable. Although she didn't use those exact words, let alone those long phrases, for it seemed dear old mom and dad communicated in some kind of grunted four letter words. Thus I was seized by the collar by my infuriated mother and sent to bed without dinner.

I never did get a whip'n for the "Finger In The Box", or so it was forever named. Mom and dad discussed the matter long into the night and for several days afterwards. Every time the subject was broached, mom seemed to sway a little more dads way and eventually chuckled about the whole affair. Of course that was just the other day at a family gathering, some forty years later, but she smiled all the same.

The next few months my "Shows"….let alone my "Tells" although somewhat suspect, were still allowed until once again, an act was "miss-judged" as to cause and effect, and immediately went south; (Which doesn't happen to be a good direction for an act to go, if you get my meaning.)

Since I had been fishing with my Uncle Bob and my cousin that past weekend up to Jacks Creek, I'd returned home with a container full of huge tadpoles, smuggled home completely under my parent's radar; which every kid will tell you "is a good thing".

Putting my newfound little friends in a bread bag full of water, held water tight by a rubber band twisted at its opening; I decided to stash my amphibian act for a brief time in the mail box. Of course, as kids are wont to do, I made a minor miscalculation and put them in the mailbox Saturday afternoon, which of course meant they sat all that night, Sunday and

Show and Tell

Sunday night in the warm metal mailbox. Well, at least the good thing was, they went undisturbed by the mailman, who didn't deliver on Sunday, "Thank God" for little miracles.

What kid notices little things like the elapse of time, let alone depletion of oxygen, not to mention how detrimental a couple days in a hot mailbox can be upon tadpoles? Let alone actually looks at their exciting "Show and Tell" item while sneaking it out of its hiding place and into a small metal lunch box on his way to school? Nope.....not me....I quickly made the magicians shuffle and even little brother Ike was totally unaware, I was now loaded....for Bear....or should I say, "Show and Tell".

Once at school, and after the long morning ordeal of Flag Saluting and Warden Announcement's, soon came my chance at another award winning performance at Show and Tell. This time I felt confident my toned down animal act would thrill even my skeptic teacher Mrs. Bee, for what could go wrong with a plastic bag full of water and fifty or so thumb sized tadpoles?

But oh, how fickle fate tortures even the most prepared performers, let alone Magic acts, for I had it all worked out ...how I was going to suddenly pull a bag full of "Amazing Amphibians" from my Lone Ranger lunchbox!....My only concern about the whole affair was, that I had to leave my thermos in the mailbox. I just hoped the mail man was honest and wouldn't steal it before I got home...how I'd explain that weighted a bit heavy on my mind.......all of three seconds.

And then the unthinkable happened and Mrs. Bee announced we had some kind of assembly or some such thing and "Show and Tell" was cancelled! It was also at that moment; I came to the stark realization a "Riot" with only one person, was absolutely ineffective and with a stern look from Mrs. Bee, my one man protest was promptly put to rest.

We were quickly formed into lines and marched into the gymnasium as lemmings herded into the sea. But I fixed them, for I not only grumbled all the way, I grouched right up until the

Archie Matthews

guy with the "Amazing Yo-Yo" came out and gave a performance that enthralled each and every one of us.

After the assembly, long was forgotten any thought of my paltry "Magically Appearing Amphibian Act"…let alone the cancelled "Show and Tell". Thus the morning lessons passed quickly and before I knew it, we were paroled by the bell and marched off to the cafeteria for lunch.

Upon taking my seat amongst my friends at our favorite table, which was next to the girls table; which we all disdained, but to no avail for the teachers all being female themselves couldn't be reasoned with or made to understand how detestable eating next to giggling girls was. Thus sitting next to the girls, we all opened our lunch boxes and everyone began to visit excitedly and relive the "Amazing Yo-Yo" demonstration that morning.

Carl Sweezy was doing his impression of the Yo-Yo guys twirling both hands in the air, flinging the Yo-Yo's far and wide, when looking down; I realized I still had a bag of tadpoles in my lunch box. Looking around and making sure a patrolling teacher wasn't lurking near; I lifted up the bread bag and quickly realized they were exceptionally warm, and smelly. I was just calculating trash can distance versus teacher patrol speed, when Carl's arms went wide for the Yo-Yo finale, and once again…..All HELL BROKE LOOSE….as did the bag of tadpoles.

.

Looking back at the situation now, it's amazing how many times in life, I've witnessed single tragedies, horrors, sadness and even death, but none of those individual episodes could ever equal, the nightmare of an entire school coming to its knees retching at the smell of half decayed tadpoles.

Even to us boys, the stench of a scattered bag of heat liquefied dead tadpole remnants, had an amazing effect. Who's to say whether it was one of the girls who first defiled the cafeteria floor with their recently devoured sandwich, or perhaps it was their freshly drank milk…..be that as it may….someone lost their cookies.

104

Show and Tell

The effect, be it the sight, sound or smell, set off a domino effect that rippled across the cafeteria with alarming speed. It would have easily captured the Guinness Book of World Records, if they'd had one for vomiting, but as the principal assured me, they didn't.

Once again, I won't bore you with the gory details of absolute pandemonium, but once again Brute pulled the fire alarm and saved the day, for everyone was quickly hustled out the wide double doors to the outside. Thus, some of us fellows were spared the torture of seeing our comrades in arms; suffer the fate almost every single girl endured, including teachers and cafeteria personnel, not to mention most of the fellas.

Now I don't blame the little kids, say like in Kindergarten....but really? ....the older kids, in second, third and even fourth grade? Come on, what kind of wieners were being raised in the world that couldn't stomach a bit of Amphibian destruction at meal time? Needless to say, the older kids not only had extremely weak stomachs, but absolutely no sense of humor....which they displayed by picking on me over the next several years. It seems, people have long memories when it comes to making them loose their lunch in front of and amongst their school peers.

Long story short, once again I was singled out and escorted to the principal's office, due to the treachery of "Snitches". Where I was doomed to await my mother's arrival, which wasn't long......what with her taking those huge fast strides coming across the street and the school yard, as I watched through the principals window. I imagine it's the same feeling a prisoner upon death row feels watching the executioner approach.

After being once again remanded to my mother's custody, and after a very long wait, all the while hearing the death knell from dear mother as she threatened me with dad's arrival home from work. Hearing dad's car pull into the drive, I'd like to say, I felt confident that dear old dad was going to laugh this little fiasco off, like he had the last..... I'd like to say that, but can't.

Archie Matthews

It seems dad had no sense of humor that day after a long day at work. I never really understood if it was because everyone threw up in the cafeteria, or the gruesome untimely demise of a bread bag full of tadpoles. Either way, it was a moot point, especially to my backside as dad exercised me around the living room like a race horse on a hot-walker at the end of his belt.

To say my award winning performances were somewhat suspiciously scrutinized from then on would have been to say the least. I couldn't approach the school grounds with a lunchbox, package, or even my coat draped over my arm, without Mrs. Bee or some other faculty member frisking me down, not to mention search and seizure of even common items, such as horn toads, pocket knives, beanie flippers, not to mention......match boxes and ketchup.....let alone tadpoles.

Believe it or not, even my "Tells" were suspect and only told with Mrs. Bee close at hand with her soft teachers palm ready to clamp my audio box at the first mention of "Gory details". More than once my poor classmates were cheated with only portions of my exciting and detailed "Tells" as Mrs. Bee's soft, quick, teacher's mitts would instantly muffle the best parts of my tales.

But as you can tell, later in life, I began to once again astound my audience with "Shows and Tells", for if you've ever been to one of our family reunions or "little get togethers", be it around the campfire or around the BBQ, I am always ready with at least a "Tell….if not a complete Show and Tell"….much to my poor wife's chagrin.

(Did I mention she's a "Para educator" and works in a grade school? And just like Mrs. Bee, has not only extraordinarily soft hands, but quick ones to boot!)

Show and Tell

The Idaho Alligators

"ALLIGATORS!... ALLIGATORS!" was the scream that suddenly stopped all the laughing and carousing that hot summer day along the crick bank back in the summer of 1971. When my six year old cousin Micky came tearing down the muddy crick bank like a four wheel drive truck spinning wheels and all, it stopped everyone in their tracks; everyone that is, but my brother Ike, who was mid-swing on the rope over the water. As if the blood curdling screaming of "alligators" wasn't enough, nor the evident running for his life, but one look at poor Micky's bloody chewed up legs as he raced by sent every kid out of the water in a mad rush.

I had just hit the bank myself when I looked back and saw my younger brother Ike let go of the rope amid stream, splash down and come swimming over to the steep bank like a mad man. Although we usually only used the high bank on this side to board the rope swing, we usually just drifted or swam downstream to get out along the gentle sloped side some sixty yards below, but Ike realized the need to get out of the water as quickly as possible. Therefore, he came directly to the steep bank, and he came out so fast he looked like a rock a skipping across the water, only actually hitting the water every several feet and just churning air in between. If there had been an Olympic Swimming Coach there, I have no doubt he'd have been signed up for the next Olympics quick.

Micky churned up and out of the crick bottom and I could tell by the sound of his fast retreating screams he was either through the old pasture barb wire fence, or over it, and as fast as he had been traveling, I doubt he remembered to use the old stile that went up and over. Far more likely, he'd just run right through the barbed wire, the way he was running in fear.

I knew fear well, for I was deathly afraid of the dark and had found myself more than once, rushing headlong for a distant patch of light. Yes, I knew what fear was, as well as blind flight, and therefore I had instantly recognized Micky was running for his life in blind fear. And since fear is extremely contagious, I and everyone else that had seen it had immediately been infected and began running for our own lives.

I was doing a double take over my shoulder and half trotting up towards the little hill that led out of the crick bottom and up to the pasture. I was right behind my cousin Dean, yet halfheartedly trying to lag enough to see Ike make it out of the water safe, but not wanting to lag enough to actually get ate by those "gaters" Micky was screaming about. When all of a sudden Isaac

Newton's theory of relativity kicked me smack dab in the back of the head and the worst possible thing happened at the worst possible moment as Ike screamed, "ARCH...IT'S GOT ME!"

Any other time wild horses couldn't have drug me back to that crick after the warning I'd heard from Micky. Not to mention the sight of his gashed and bloody legs. It would've taken a big string of those huge draft horses to even have stood a chance of dragging me back. But as an older brother, hearing my younger brother in trouble was like pitching an anchor out of a speed boat, it stopped me dead in my tracks. I stopped so fast, I almost went head over heels...Almost...

Recognizing our only chance, I shouted at Dean as he was just chugging his large, chubby, snow-white frame up the distant bank. "DEAN! HELP!" I shouted as loud as I could. I will say this for Dean, as chubby as he was, he stopped on a dime and turned around with his eyes the size of dinner plates and his mouth puffing like a freight train and back he came. Bless his heart, for the boy was as loyal a cousin as God ever gave a fellow. In all our days of palling around together, Dean was family and when it came to kin, he was solid as a rock. A bit spongy around the middle and prone to huff and puff and wind easy he might be, but when the chips was down, Dean always stood solid.

"Arch, it's got me....it's got me!" came Ike's mournful wail as he set to churning the water into a white froth as both his arms began to beat the water. One look into his eyes further chilled my bones. I'd never seen my little brother more terrified in my entire life and we'd shared many a sleepless dark night sweating under the covers waiting for the monster in the closet to come devour us. I'd thought I'd seen terror, until I saw Micky's face as he'd raced by screaming "Alligators!", but it was nothing in comparison to Ike's eyes as he fought for his life a few feet from the steep bank in the veritable jaws of a monster.

"Arch, it's got my leg...Arch, it's got me" he wailed again so mournful that it all but broke my heart as I quickly ran to the

Archie Matthews

steep bank and dropping to my belly I reached out for his hand. I had just realized I was about a foot short as Ike stretched out with a grimace on his face, when suddenly something grabbed me around the middle. I'd have wet my bathing suit right then and there if it hadn't already been wet from the swimming, for I was sure I'd been snatched around the middle by one of those gators. When suddenly I realized it was Dean and he was standing astride me, pushing me forward so I could reach Ike.

As my hand grabbed Ike's, once again he let out a horrendous scream and if my hat hadn't been over there lying on the bushes already, it would have been shot off and over there that instant. My hair stood straight on end and I began to howl along with my poor little brother as we both pulled with all our might. Dean began screaming too as he began doing his best to heave me and my burden back away from the crick bank.

Then just as it felt like something was going to break, for my joints were screaming at the strain, Ike began to come forward slow but sure. And just as he came closer, Dean gave a wail, "I see it Arch....it's a huge alligator!" and suddenly he let go of me and began to barrage the huge shadowy shape in the water attached to Ike's leg. A rock chucker there never was that could best good ole' Dean, for both volume and accuracy, that boy could flat lay down a field of fire that would have made a World War II machine gun veteran green with envy. And the water above that shadowy form looked as if it were taking rapid machine gun fire as Dean poured on the coal, or rocks, I should say.

Then, slowly, Ike began to sink back as the huge shape began to once again drag him deeper. Again Ike wailed with fear and I dug my elbows and toes into the soil trying my best not to let my little brother turn into alligator poop without a fight. Dean suddenly changed tactics and began grabbing ever larger rocks until the splashes from the enormous fusillades threatened to drown both me and Ike.

The Idaho Alligators

"Dean....Help me! It's pulling us in!" I screamed as I began to slowly slide forward.

Dean immediately stopped and reaching down, grabbed my legs in a vise of muscle and fat and throwing himself backwards, once again we slowly began to haul Ike up and out of the water. This time I saw the muddy shadow heave up as my heart nearly popped out of my chest and through my mouth, as I saw how big the thing looked in the normally clear water. The mud on its back began to murk up the water and just as it disappeared in a cloud, it released Ike and all three of us shot up the bank.

How a chubby kid like Dean can move so fast is beyond me, but before I could gain my feet, he was half carrying and half dragging both me and Ike away from the crick. It was like being drug behind a large draft horse without any reigns to pull him up or slow him down, all I could do was keep stumbling along doing my best to try and get my feet under me and hold on to little brother Ike.

Finally after several yards of being drug, Dean slowed down enough that I got my feet up and under me and seeing Ike's bleeding foot all mangled and muddy, I quickly scooped him up "piggy back" and we lit out like our tails were on fire. We come out of that creek bottom as if a whole herd of alligators was after us. We made it to the pasture fence and seeing the bulls that were always in that pasture at this end, we quickly began to make our way around the wire fence, the long way to safety.

We were about half way around when we saw several people coming towards us from town, and I recognized Grandpa and Grandma leading the pack. It wasn't until I saw the adults coming that I realized I was spent and couldn't go any further, and my knees just buckled and down I and Ike went in a heap. Dean must have heard the pile up, for I went down with a groan, and Ike gave a yelp as his bloody, mangled foot hit the ground, for he too stopped.

Archie Matthews

I won't bore you with the retelling of the "Alligator Attack" as we quickly explained to Grandma and Grandpa, Eddy Mehan the café owner, Ed Shotz the general store owner and wild-eyed George Wellner. There was no need for embellishment, for they had seen Micky's skinned up bloody legs and were even now gingerly inspecting Ike's bruised, skinned and torn foot. George's wild eyes kept going from Ike's bloody foot to the crick and back again as he kept mumbling, "Gators….there's gators in the crick….crocs maybe…maybe there's crocs too….but the boy did scream 'alligators', so must be gators…but then again, what about crocs?"

Well I never was sure the difference between an Alligator and a Crocodile, I figure if you've been bit by one or the other, there isn't much difference, and I'd sure not try and argue the finer point with either Micky or Ike at the time, either. Trying to figure out if they were Alligators or Crocodiles, would be like trying to figure out if you'd just been run over by either a Ford or a Chevy, even a kid understands the stupidity of that, but evidently it mattered to old George, for he kept working on it.

Grandma insisted that Ike needed to be carried up to the house which was still a good quarter mile away, and after the telling of what had happened, Dean offered to piggy back Ike, while I showed Grandpa and the other men where the "Attack" had happened.

I have to admit, I wasn't very anxious to return to the swimming hole I'd known and grown to appreciate and enjoy the past couple of years, what with it being an Alligator infested death trap now, but grandpa was with me, and old George was packing his huge bear rifle and besides that, he had his two biggest dogs with him.

Now I never did know if they were Russian Wolf hounds or Irish Wolf hounds, for George admitted he didn't know either and half the locals claimed they were one and the other half claimed they were the other. But I will say this, both those dogs were dern near as tall as I was and huge dark burley rascals with wiry hair and huge heads full of teeth. They were the most stand offish dogs in George's herd of dogs, for their size and those teeth didn't throw out the "Welcome Mat" like most of the other furry frolicking dogs did that comprised the pickup load of dogs George always traveled with. These were the dogs George claimed were his "bear killers" and one look at the pair, with their size and no nonsense attitude; they looked like they could do the job. But right now, I'd wished someone had said they were experienced alligator killers, because the size of that bugger that had Ike, looked about the length of two or three bears, from what I'd seen.

We proceeded back down the fence headed back towards the crick, when two of Ace's biggest bulls came wandering over to the fence and followed parallel with us to the end of the pasture. George halted as the bulls did and looking over at the bovine with a serious look, he said, "You bulls best just head back over yonder, there's gators swarm'n this part of the crick, and although they been thwarted eat'n them two kids, I doubt this barb wire fence will stop them ...if'n they get hungry for the taste of beef....you best just run along now....yup, run along old bossy...there be gators here abouts..."

Eddy and grandpa just shook their heads for they were used to George and his peculiarities, but Ed Shotz the general store owner let out a loud snort and stopping, turned around and gave George a hard stare.

"George you chowder head....what in the hell are you doing talking to bulls about the dangers of Alligators and barbwire fences? Sometimes I swear they ought to lock you up!" Needless to say, Ed Shotz wasn't George's biggest fan, by a long sight. When it came to poor old George and his high jinx, Ed had very little patience for crazy people or "Nuts" as he called them.

"Wall now," George stammered with his eyes rolling around from Ed to the bulls and then narrowing to slits as he peered long and hard towards the crick. "I'm just say'n, them bulls ain't got guns

Archie Matthews

and see'n that you don't neither, I'd ask the question right quick, who's the chowder head and who ain't the chowder head? And if them gators gets a hold of you and them un-armed bulls, me and my boys here, aim to rescue the lot of you from man eat'n crocs!" and with that, George stepped lively with those big old dogs one to either side on towards the crick bottom.

Grandpa and Eddy just chuckled for although George's reasoning was a bit off, he had a point about having that rifle and those dogs, and Ed being at the mercy of man eaters. That's when I began to realize I was out in front and I was even worse off than the unarmed store keep, for not only was I also unarmed, but I was a third his size as well. And at that realization, my leadership abilities began to fade as did my enthusiasm as I shifted into low gear, in hopes that the adults would forge ahead before me.

"George,you dern nut! There ain't Alligators or Crocodiles anywhere nears here. This is Idaho, not the Florida everglades! There ain't gators nor crocs within a thousand miles of here!" Ed wailed in disgust.

"Ho there you dagnabbed know it all..." George grinned raising one shaggy white eyebrow and pointing a finger at Ed." You don't know what you're talking about....I seen me an Alligator down to Boise one time at the County Fair. They fed it a big pumpkin on a stick....had the biggest dern mouth full of teeth I ever did see....could a swallowed you whole!"

"George...." Eddy Mehan chuckled, "That was a hippo....not an Alligator."

George looked puzzled for a few seconds as he concentrated real hard staring straight at Eddy and then his eyes began darting around and his broad smile appeared and he slapped his knee and said, "Eddy, that weren't no hippy! I seen one of them down to Boise too, but they weren't feeding her no pumpkin on a stick!" She were a big gal alright and practically wore a pup tent as a dress, a smoke'n that funny tobacco and sing'n about free love. Yup, I seen that hippy lady that very same summer."

Both Eddy and Ed shook their heads in disgust and grandpa spoke up, "No George, not a hippy, a hippopotamus, it's a big animal from Africa and shares the same waters as those African Crocodiles. There are no Alligators in Africa, and I'm pretty sure there aren't any here in this crick either. But I know them boys seen something and we need to figure out what, or pretty soon we'll have all kinds of problems around here once the rumors start flying."

That was grandpa, patient with the children and the childlike, always the peace maker when it came to someone "haranguing" George, and patient to explain to George where the misunderstanding lay.

"You saw a Hippopotamus at the County Fair George, but remember you also saw an Alligator at the Boise zoo. The Hippo was the big fat thing eating the pumpkin and the Alligator was the big long lizard looking thing with that mouth all full of those sharp teeth." Grandpa explained.

George had stopped and was focusing on grandpa with his puzzled look and then as if what grandpa had said suddenly shed light on the dark subject, George smiled and nodded slowly. "Yup, that's right, there was that long slender critter with that long snout full of teeth at the zoo.....yup, I remember. That's a gator....yup, I recall now, so we're looking for one of them long slender things eaten people, and not that big fat pumpkin eaten woman?"

Ed Shotz quickly slapped his forehead with a dumbfounded look and then throwing both arms into the air and growled, "For crying out loud.....and he's the one with the gun!"

Eddy once again just chuckled and shook his head and mumbled, "I wished I'd have brought one, come to think of it..."

Archie Matthews

Now it was grandpa's turn to shake his head as we all proceeded on towards the crick. Before we'd taken another dozen steps, we were on top the little knoll looking down at the crick and I pointed and said, "That's where the big one is, right up agin the steep bank below the rope tree."

I've got to hand it to George, the men might have always teased him and claimed he wasn't just right in the head. But no one to my knowledge ever doubted the man's courage, for he never slowed up for a second, and just stepped right up to the clawed up crick bank where I'd pointed.

"I see where them boys come out of the water and clawed their way up the bank here" George remarked, pointing at the tore up ground where we'd pulled Ike from the jaws of death. "And I can see there along the bottom that something big had laid there in the deep mud", Then George slowly began to walk down stream with both his huge body guards close to his side.

"Hey,....you better looky here..." he called after a few minutes from a good hundred yards downstream as the big deep swimming hole began to shallow up into a swift set of rapids. "Wow, that's a big one....and it's one of them long ones and not a fat pumpkin eater!" He shouted as he began to dance around pointing into the rapids with his rifle. My hair once again lifted straight up at once again seeing the huge shadow that had tried to devour my little brother.

I noticed right off that grandpa took the lead and headed down stream to join George, while it looked to me, like Eddy and Ed weren't either one stepping to lively or in too big a hurry despite all their assurances about there being no Alligators or Crocodiles in Idaho.

Grandpa stepped up next to George and then Eddy and Ed with me slowly bringing up the rear.

"What in the heck is that?" Eddy asked as all four men began mumbling and pointing at the huge long dark shape just under

The Idaho Alligators

the shallow water against the rocky bottom. Although visible, it was hard to see any details as the water was swirling up and over the huge shape that was laying length ways against the current, one end pointed towards us and the other towards the far bank.

"Well, I aim to find out," Grandpa announced and began to wade into the swift knee deep water, which to me and everyone else was in itself a spectacular feat of bravery, for everyone knew my grandpa couldn't swim a lick.

Now when I say grandpa couldn't swim, I not only mean he couldn't swim, I mean he couldn't float or even bob along. The man was like a walking anchor, when he went into the water, he just walked along the bottom as if his butt was full of lead. I'd seen him enter one side of a deep fishing hole and come walking right out the other side, how he kept from drowning was anyone's guess. And despite the man's swimming handicap, he had absolutely "no fear what so ever of the water". I've seen him fishing out on the very tips of logs hanging over many a deep watery abyss, in order to take full advantage of a fishing hole, without even blinking an eye at the watery death that awaited him if he ever slipped and fell in.

And as he began to slowly wade out across the swift water along the slick rocky bottom, both Ed and Eddy shook their heads in disbelief, for it was a well-known fact in our small community that Grandpa couldn't swim a stroke to save his own life. And right behind grandpa and just as incapable of swimming as grandpa went the nut, Grandpa's good friend, George Wellner.

"I'm with you Arch.....I'll keep you covered.....right behind ya!" called out George, keeping his rifle pointed squarely at the submerged shadow, all the while doing his nervous dance and his legs going a hundred miles a minute, splashing water in every direction with each kick and stomp.

"You go back to the bank George and keep me covered from there....."Grandpa instructed firmly as he stopped and turning his

117
Archie Matthews

head urged George back to dry ground. He knew George couldn't swim either, and although he had all the confidence in the world in himself, he had very little in George's ability to stay upright and un-drownt. Seeing George slowly wade backwards to the bank, grandpa nodded, "Good fella George, you just keep me covered from up there."

Grandpa slowly edged along and was right up to the top of his knees in the frothing water and right in front of the "Alligator" and bending down, he reached below the water surface and with both arms slowly raised the shadow to the surface of the water.

George was standing there with his huge rifle leveled with deadly aim, although his aim was steady and true, his legs and feet were dancing an Irish clog as fast as any fiddle could play; all the while his eyes scaned to and fro, from grandpa to the shadow, up and down the crick, darting a thousand miles an hour. But with George that was how a person could tell he was nervous or ready for a fight. I just hoped his trigger finger wasn't as twitchy as his eyes and feet were, or even scarier yet, his aim. If he wobbled too much to the left, he'd hit grandpa for sure and I said as much.

"Don't you shoot my grandpa George!" I warned….

And Eddy just reached over and put his arm around my shoulders and pulled me close, "Don't worry, old George won't shoot your grandpa…." He whispered…"He ain't got any bullets in that rifle…."

Well that was news to me and if I hadn't been so worried about grandpa being so close to that huge gator, Eddy would have been hard pressed to explain that, but as it was, I just kept my mouth clamped shut and my eyes focused on grandpa.

Then as grandpa pulled the enormous dark shape to the surface, Ed and Eddy gasped as grandpa let out a big sigh of relief.

The Idaho Alligators

"Well I'll be.....it's a huge chunk of tree bark.....that's all it is!" grandpa shouted as the old mud covered rough surface of the water logged chunk of tree bark came to the top. After several seconds grandpa let it go and the current caught it and it went over the shallow ripples several feet then once again hung up on the bottom, half in and half out of the water.

At the sight of the large dark shadow breaking the surface and grandpa's shout, George began dancing around with his rifle still leveled at the tree bark. Although his aim was steady, his legs and feet were dancing around as if someone had given him a hot foot, ducking and dodging this way and that trying to keep a good aim on the suspected Alligator.

"For crying out loud George.....it's just tree bark.....it's not an alligator, stop pointing your rifle and dancing around as if you were facing a pack of mountain lions...." Grumped old Ed Shotz in disgust.

"No alligators?!....It ain't a Gator? Are you sure Arch?.....Just a chunk of tree bark? Well how come did that tree bark bite that kid? And how come that kid to pitch a fit and call that tree bark an Alligator...Do you suppose it's a crocodile?.....Is that it? Could it be one of those crocodiles?" George rattled off questions almost as fast as his feet were dancing around.

Grandpa slowly waded back to the bank and gave me a quick smile, then walked over to George who was still dancing around like an Irish clogger. Putting his hand up on George's shoulder grandpa murmured a few words and suddenly as if flipping a switch, George calmed right down. He quickly lowered his rifle, his feet began to slow down and soon stopped their quick shuffle then just as the tension seemed to ease out of his body, he grinned broadly.

"Wow, that was a close one.....I never did shoot an Alligator before....I shot plenty a Ba'r.....shot some mountain lions ....but I never shot an Alligator before....no sir.....and can't remember ever shoot'n a crocodile either.....I thought about shoot'n a hippy once.....but didn't do it.....nope, that rascal got away.....but nary an Alligator.....nope, not one...."George grinned and then wiped his sweat beaded brow with the back of his hand, his feet almost still now.

"Well you still haven't shot an Alligator...or a crocodile...you halfwit....it was just a chunk of bark." Ed Shotz snorted.

"You figure them kids just seen that old chunk of bark and panicked, Arch?" Eddy asked.

"Well, I don't know......"Grandpa began, "Micky was pretty scared and kept screaming he'd seen 'baby Alligators'....." and then grandpa turned to me, "What happened here, tell me everything that happened and start from the beginning."

I explained how we were all swimming like we always did here in the pool. How Ike was out on the rope when Micky came tearing up the bank screaming "Alligators"! How everyone swam for this side of the crick bank and how Ike came up to the steep bank and then started screaming he was "Got!"
I quickly told of Dean and I struggling to pull Ike out and the dark shadow having him by the foot. And then suddenly Ike had come loose and we'd run for home.

Grandpa nodded his head and chuckled, "I seen a 'V' shaped notch in that bark. I'm figuring Ike got his foot in that notch and panicked and when you boys pulled that water logged bark up, your imaginations took off and a man eating Alligator was born."

Ed and Eddy both began to chuckle, as did grandpa, who was then quickly joined by the hilarious high pitched giggles of good natured George, who kept bending over and slapping his knee and wiping his watering eyes. Then seeing and hearing George's giggles set everyone into deep fits of laughter for several minutes.

When the grownups began to once again contain themselves, I asked,

The Idaho Alligators

"But grandpa, that was after Micky started screaming "Alligators"……What do you think Micky saw?"

"Well, we won't know that until we get back and talk to him about what happened. No doubt he seen something, and as barked up as his shins and feet were, it wasn't just his imagination nor a bit of tree bark." Grandpa said with a sobering look. "Let's go back to town and nip the rumors in the bud before they grow any bigger…we stay down here much longer and they'll have the National Guard rolled out, tanks and all."

And with that, I retreated to the bush where several sets of clothes and my cowboy hat lay and gathering them up in my arms, followed close behind grandpa, Ed and Eddy. All the while George brought up the rear and followed us at a distant, for he kept stopping and looking back at the crick, with his two hulking hounds close to his side.

"Your safe now…..We got rid of that Alligator….No beef on the menu, you dern bulls, go back to grazing and stop fuss'n about it….no gators…no crocs either….nor any of them pumpkin eating hippies….neither! " ,shouted George as he waved his rifle at the two bulls watching us from the pasture.

"The nut!" grumped Ed "It'll be a miracle if he doesn't have everyone in the county thinking he shot and skinned an Alligator by the end of the day".

Eddy and grandpa just chuckled as we made our way back up to the road and then up into town. As we passed Ed's general store he peeled off and stepping to the boardwalk, he waved and called out, "Let me know if you need anything for that skinned up boy!"

"We will Ed, but Clara's got buckets of mercurochrome and bandages a plenty. Thanks for your help!" grandpa called back as we crossed the side street and approached our gate.

Archie Matthews

"Thanks again Eddy, for the help…..be sure to spread it around, it wasn't anything to be concerned about. Oh, and we've got an arm load of kids clothes if anyone's missing some." called grandpa as he waved to Eddy and then tussled my drying bedraggled hair with his large callused hand.

"Let's go see how Micky's doing" grandpa suggested as we headed into the house.

After dropping my armload of clothes on the back porch by the washing machine, we went in the house and into the parlor. There setting on the old horsehair sofa was the most pitiful mummy I've ever laid eyes on. Well at least from the knees down, for their sat Micky wrapped with red blotched bandages making each foot look the size of a gallon bucket, what with all the gauze. Once again the Medicinal Maniac had struck again with her germ killing cure all.

Micky's eyes were bloodshot and I immediately recognized the lava hot mercurochrome blotches through the gauze bandages. Poor Micky still had tear streaks down his cheeks and I felt sorry for the little guy, for I had felt the searing hot daubs as grandma had slathered my open wounds many a time with her flesh scorching germ killing medicine. The woman had it in for any and every germ on the face of the earth and evidently given an oath to see that every germ was scorched and/or scalded to death with the fiery antiseptic. I'd been blotted and tattoo'd with that bright red germ killer for years now. It took weeks after a daubing for the red blotches to slowly fade to pink and disappear long after the scratch or even a large gash had healed over.

 If you were even remotely related to grandma, and have ever experienced as much as a scratch that broke the hide, you've been daubed, dashed or splashed with her mercurochrome. And even if you weren't related to her, many a wayward visitor has meet the misfortune of being doctored by the Medicinal Maniac. God love her, and we usually did too, once the soul searing mercurochrome wore off, but there were usually a whole lot of

The Idaho Alligators

other feelings hastily thrown her direction while she was applying the scorching liquid.

I will say this, just knowing you would get daubed with the flaming antiseptic kept many a kids wound from becoming public knowledge. I for one, when hurt, would run as far from the house as I could get to howl my head off in pain, just knowing that if grandma got wind of it, I was in for even more pain. Therefore many of us kids would rather lay hidden out, bleeding and crying with our own handkerchiefs stuffed in our mouths to keep grandma and her medicine at bay.

"How you doing Micky?" I asked stepping into the room and seeing grandma sitting in her chair knitting, keeping a watch over her poor, pathetic little mummy boy.

"Did you see em?..did you see the baby Alligators?...They was everywhere....everywhere in the water...it was horrible...baby Alligators everyyyyy where." Micky began to stammer his eyes getting wilder and bigger, more and more like old George Wellner's wild eyes that it gave me a little shudder.

"Now you don't worry about the baby Alligators....I told you Micky, you just lay back and rest.....stop worrying", grandma said in a soothing voice as she looked up from her knitting.

"Well, we wanted to ask and get some more details from the boy about what went on...."Grandpa explained.

"Alligators!!!.....there was baby Alligators everywhere!....They was everywhere grandpa, they was everywhere!!" Micky began yelling and bawling and shouting, his eyes growing the size of dinner plates and the tears just running down his cheeks.

"Whoa now....you just settle down, just calm down..." grandpa said, trying to sooth Micky as he realized he'd fed coal to a fire that was about to blaze up and out of control.

"Now you boys just go on outside and let Micky just relax, I just got him to stop ranting and raving like a crazy man and you two come in and get him all worked up again." Grandma scolded as she stood up and put down her knitting, then sat next to Micky and began crooning softly to him about everything going to be alright.

Grandpa gave a nod, looked at me and said, "You best go get your clothes on and let's go see the boys on the front porch."

I ran upstairs and changed out of my bathing suit then into my jeans and a tee shirt, topping off my summer wardrobe with my straw cowboy hat. I then hurried back downstairs and joined grandpa, Dean and Ike out on the front porch.

There sat porky Dean in grandma's chair filling it up from arm to arm with his large bulk, and I gave him a big smile and he gave me just as big of one back.

"Wow, Dean....we'd have been goner's today if you hadn't come back for us", I said proud of how Dean hadn't kept running as the others had, abandoning us to our fate.

"Oh, shucks.....I couldn't leave you and Ike, to the alligators...." Dean grinned, embarrassed and turning red in the face. "You boys are kin, and like grandpa always says, if we ain't got kin, we ain't got anything."

"I'm very proud of all you boys, you stuck together and you're all here safe and sound." Grandpa praised us.

"Who else was down there to the swimming hole...other than that redheaded Sexton boy? He's the one came running into my shop screaming the alligators was eating everyone down to the swim hole." Grandpa asked.

"Well, there was Jimmy Sexton and Milt Sexton," I began to explain, "Milt's the redhead and Jimmy's the black haired....then there was me, Micky, Ike and Dean".

The Idaho Alligators

So grandpa asked questions and cross examined each one of us trying his best to sort out what had gone on. Everyone came back to the same beginning, that we were all swimming peaceful enjoying the day when along came Micky screaming "alligators". And what with Micky getting all worked up, grandpa decided we'd just better let him calm down a while before he pressed him again for information.

Grandpa gave us each a dime and suggested we wander over to the store and grab a soda then spend some time playing in the scrap yard. Although Ike's ankle had been daubed with grandma's liquid fire, and wrapped up, he was able to put his sneakers on and hobble along with me and Dean to the store.

As we entered the store, Ed was standing at the counter with a concerned look on his face and talking to a large dark figure standing with his back towards us. Hearing us enter, the tall dark figure turned about and right away I knew we were facing one of the Second Fork Sextons.

There were two families in our neck of the woods with the last name of Sexton, neither family was related, or at least if they were, they vehemently denied it, and being a rough sort, they weren't the type to argue the point with, so nobody did.

The Second Fork Sextons lived on the Second Fork Crick, while the Third Fork Sextons; you guessed it, lived on Third Fork Crick. The other huge difference was each family had a very unique distinctive look, for the Second Fork Sexton's had jet black hair and one immense bushy eyebrow that run from one side of their brow to the other, women included. Although I'd never seen one of their babies in swaddling clothes, I'd even heard tell when the wee'est tot was born; he had a full head of jet black hair, eyebrow included. My good friend Jimmy was a Second Fork Sexton, uni-brow and all. The other outstanding feature the Second Fork Sexton's had was, at least with the men that is, they all had huge bushy mustaches and beards, most of which just blended together into a huge black bush hovering in front of

Archie Matthews

their faces. Half the time, I couldn't even tell them apart, there just wasn't enough of their face exposed to tell one from another.

The Third Fork Sextons were just at the other end of the spectrum, for they all had red hair and freckles....although they had two separate eyebrows, even their eyebrows were red. Now when I say red, that's just what I mean, they weren't what's known as Auburn, no sir.....them folks had RED hair. I'd even slipped and said it was as red as Bozo the Clowns hair and been soundly punched in the eye by Milt Sexton. Milt happened to be one year older than me and evidently devoid of all humor when it came to either his hair color or mention of Bozo the Clown; I never was sure which. After the black eye incident, I made it a forced habit to never mention either within his hearing again, just to stay on the safe side; even though I wasn't rightly sure which reference had sent his fist into my eye.

I'd also seen Milt's older sister Mary at the age of sixteen beat the living day lights out of Matt Kinkaid who was in his early twenties and of a mind he was a rough character. Matt had made the huge mistake and asked her with a big sly grin, "Er you a 'Natural' redhead Mary?....."

She'd all but chewed him up and spit him out, and it was only with the help of two of Matt's cowboy friends and old Ed Shotz coming out and pulling Mary off Matt that saved any hide he had left. Which as they'd helped him get to his horse and into the saddle, wasn't much from where I'd been standing on the boardwalk out front of the store with my half drank soda pop. I'd vowed then, never to mention their hair color to any of them Third Fork Sextons, especially them girls. They was man eaters from what I'd seen, even if they only chewed and didn't swallow, but spit out what remained. And after seeing Matt all chewed up for his simple question, I counted myself lucky for just getting a slug in the eye from her little brother Milt. It seemed them redheaded girls was mighty touchy about questions involving their hair color, natural or otherwise.

So when that fellow turned around to face us as we entered the store, his steel gray eyes peering beneath that black bushy eyebrow a holding up his black hat brim, not to mention that's all of his face that wasn't covered by the biggest blackest bushiest pile of whiskers I ever did see. I knew right away this was Bart Sexton of the Second Fork Sexton's; Jimmy's dad. I could tell it was him from his big old crooked nose poking out just atop his whiskers. Jimmy was one of more than a dozen kids all calling Bart Sexton, "Pa". Jimmy had told me how his pa had gotten that nose in a "rough and tumble" in a scrape when he was a lad in high school many years ago.

My great grandpa "Grumps" had also elaborated since he'd been at that same "Barn Dance" the night those three big city boys thought they was going to have some fun with one of those redheaded Third Fork Sexton girls.

Grumps and a couple other fellows had heard the ruckus and gone out to find three "raggedy Andy's" all draped around the countryside looking like they'd been chewed up and spit out by a mountain lion. One of the redheaded Sexton girls a crying and everyone fit to fight old Bart, who'd done all the ravaging, except to the girl, who quickly told of being saved by a young black headed tiger.

The story went, he'd whipped them three city boys down to their foundation, but his own nose had taken a fierce toll and they'd had to sew it back up with a hide needle and a quart of moonshine. Seems the one doing the sewing had a week stomach what with all the blood and exposed nose cartilage, he needed the shine, for Grumps said, Bart hardly twitched a muscle but stood there and had his nose practically sewed back on from scratch.

As granddad always said, "You gotta hand it to them Sexton's, Second or Third Fork, they are prolific...tough and prolific!

Which I come to find out later, meant they all had bunches and bunches of kids. For the longest time when I was a kid, I thought

Archie Matthews

the majority of the world was populated by one side or the other, redhead or black haired with one eyebrow. And anything with the name of Sexton attached to it was tougher than "Wang leather", women included. In fact, it was often joked that if you needed something stuck together, you didn't need glue, you needed a Sexton.

"Just throw a Sexton in there and she'll stay put...." They were the mountain man super glue, as the joke went. It was the only joke that neither family would wail the tar out of you for telling within their hearing.

Seeing us come into the store, Ed and Bart turned around and Bart's whiskers moved slightly and a deep booming voice called out, "Hey thar ! Your Arch's kin ain't you?" and then as his steel gray eyes met mine, "Hain't you the one old Grumps called the "Henchman?"

It was like we'd been suddenly nailed feet first to the floorboards for all three of us kids stopped dead in our tracks and just stood there like dumbfounded deer caught in a vehicle headlights.

"Speak up boy....my Jim tells me you're a lad to hunt the hills with, but he didn't say anything about you being a mute!" boomed the baritone voice from behind the rustling black whiskers.

"Um....yup, I'm the one Grumps called the Henchman" I said about three octaves higher than I normally spoke and about seven pitches higher than I'd have liked to have answered the deep talking giant.

"Well....now we're getting somewhere!" roared the fellow as his eyes narrowed and his eyebrow lowered his hat about an inch...."I'm look'n for Jim....he was down to the crick when all this talk about gators cropped up, but now nobody's seen him.......you know where he's made off too?" and the hat hovered up there atop that eyebrow as the question hung awaiting an answer.

The Idaho Alligators

"Well, Sir, I did see Jimmy, we was down swimming, but come to think of it, he bailed out of the crick and went running off, but I didn't see where to." I stammered.

"Well, he was supposed to meet me here at the store, while me and Ed been shoot'n the breeze, and here comes that kin of your'n all tore up and scream'n about alligators. Then that Third Fork boy come hot on his heels shouting everyone's getting et' down to the crick.....now you boys say you ain't seen my Jim?!" asked the black waggling whiskers as the hat dropped along with the now furrowed eyebrow.

"Oh my gosh......"Dean exclaimed, "The gators got him sure...."

And with the dimes, let alone the soda pop quickly forgotten, both Dean and Ike did a quick about face and back out the door they went. Dean waddling his heavy frame back up the boardwalk as fast as he could and Ike hobbling along close behind, leaving me standing still fastened to the store floor.

"GATORS?!......What the heck is all this talk about alligators...I ain't never heard tell of such nonsense in all my life!" ,Boomed Bart as he raised both his arms exasperated and shot Ed a look of consternation.

"There ain't any Alligators Bart, the boys ran afoul of a huge side of tree bark and one of them got a foot tangled up and they all panicked. You know how young kids imaginations run amok......We'll find your Jim, he's around here somewhere." Ed explained in a calm cool authorative voice.

Then turning his head Ed looked at me and asked, "Archie, have you seen Jim since we come back from the swim hole?"

"No sir, I ain't.....last time I seen him, he was running like everyone else. I lost sight of everyone when I went back to help Ike." I quickly explained.

Archie Matthews

"Well he's gotta be around here somewhere, if he's supposed to meet you here, he'll be by. No need to rush off, Bart." Ed said assuredly.

"That ain't like my Jim to wander around. I'm a feared something's happened to the boy. He's a solid lad and comes and goes as he's told't, if he ain't come, something's happened and I aim to find out what." And with that, Bart walked around me and started out the open door, "My Jim shows up, you tell him stay put......I'll be back." Up the boardwalk, then down the street the big fellow went towards the other end of town.

Since Ola was a small town, comprised of the general store, the blacksmith shop and the café', there wasn't much in the way of places my friend Jim could be, and I was of the same mind as his dad, Bart. Jim was a solid lad and if he was supposed to meet his dad after swimming at the store, something was wrong. And Dean's astonishing statement that the "Alligators got him", was still ringing in my ears. So I quickly followed behind Bart Sexton as we headed up the street and was almost to the blacksmith shop when out came Dean, hobbling Ike and Grandpa.

"What's going on Bart?" Grandpa asked as he stepped up and shook hands with Jimmy's dad.

"Well Arch, I'm looking for my boy Jim. He was down thar swim 'n with these boys and the Henchman there says he seen Jim run, but nobody's seen him since", Explained the large baritone voice with a touch of concern.

"Hmmmm....I seen Milt, he come shouting alligators right along behind my grandson Micky, but I ain't seen your Jim.....Milt's over to the café with his older sisters Kay and Mary, they just rode in. Let's step over and ask them." Grandpa quickly offered.

And we all headed over to the café, close behind Grandpa and Bart Sexton. We entered the café and there sitting at the counter was Milt sipping a soda and his two older sisters Kay and Mary. Both the girls were visiting across the counter with Elaine Mehan. Milt gave a grin as he saw us come through the door and then he too noticed there was no Jimmy to be had with the crowd and you could see his brow furrow.

"Hello ladies…" Grandpa hailed the females at the counter, "We're looking for young Jim Sexton, have any of you ladies seem him around a bout's?"

"We're afraid the alligators got him!" blurted Dean from beside me.

"OH NO…the gators got him!" Milt wailed, spilling his soda pop over the counter, sending Elaine scrambling for a dish cloth to catch the liquid before it trickled off onto the floor.

"Now….just hold on there, there isn't any alligators and nobody is "Got". Grandpa assured everyone calmly.

"Well, maybe the baby alligators got him?" Dean excitedly offered, his face turning red from all the attention he was drawing to himself. Everyone's eyes swiveled to him, big Bart Sexton spun around to gaze intently at him beneath that big intimidating black eyebrow supporting his enormous black hat.

"Young man, this is Idaho…….There ain't any Gators in Idaho!.....Adults, babies or otherwise!" boomed the deep voice as Bart's whiskers waved in the breeze, never once revealing anything beneath. I couldn't even see a mouth opening, let alone lips or a chin. It was just a pile of moving whiskers that never ceased to amaze me that it produced sound, deep, loud and authorative.

"Well sir, one bit me on the foot and chewed poor Micky's legs up…."Ike began to explain timidly, "Although they said the big one that got me was tree bark, it bit hard like a gator,…..But Micky got all chewed up by baby alligators….Micky ain't smart, but he don't lie….."

Archie Matthews

"That's enough Ike ", Grandpa said as he patted Ike's head, "These boys have been scared and all this talk about alligators isn't helping. If Jim isn't here and he's not over to the store, we best go back down to the crick and look."

Where George Wellner had been during all this conversation is a mystery to me, but suddenly he "Popped up" right beside me and threw in his two cents.

"Hey now, I got my Ba'r dogs and my shoot'n iron with me, we fended off that big gator and saved them cows, I reckon we can come along and fight off a passel of little gaters.....if'n there's anything left of your boy Bart, we'll get it....I got a gunny sack in the truck....maybe they ain't et much of him by now.....maybe...." railed George excitedly as he shook and waved his big bear rifle and his legs began to dance around as his eyes darted from one person to another.

"Oh, great......might as well take Ole' George with us if we're a going gator hunting!" boomed Bart with a scowl so deep his eyebrow dropped his hat down pert'ner to his nose, all but obscuring his eye's completely.

"Now, now, George you go ahead and bring along your dogs, we can skip the gunny sack. We might need a flashlight because it's getting late in the afternoon, and who knows how long this'll take." Grandpa patiently explained. "Dean, you and Ike go back to the house and tell grandma what's going on. Don't say a word about alligators, just that we are going back to the crick to look for Jimmy."

And as the boys scooted out the door, away went George outside as well.

"Kay and Mary, I hate to ask, but could we borrow your horses for a bit?" Grandpa asked.

"Yes sir Mr. Matthews, they's both good horses and not nags. They got good solid bottoms and both been born and bred in the

The Idaho Alligators

woods and will stand solid for anything put on their backs, but a ba'r or a wolf....they'll not stand for that." Kay offered with a smile.

"Give me a few minutes to go back up to the store to get my hoss and swing by and get me." Bart boomed and out the door he went and up the street.

"Can I come grandpa?" I quickly asked, not wanting to be left behind while the search was on for my good friend Jimmy.

"Yes, you can come, but I don't want any more talk about alligators. You go over to my shop and grab the big flashlight off my work bench in the far corner, then pull the shop door shut and meet me back over here.

And I was off like a shot, leaving Grandpa talking to Kay, Mary, Elaine and Milt, and as I left I heard him say, "We'll find him....."

I ran over to the shop and found Grandpa's big flashlight on the bench in the corner and coming back out. I set the flashlight down and grabbed the big sliding door with both hands then slowly pulled it closed flipping the hasp into place. There was no lock, just a hasp, Grandpa always said, "If'n someone wants to steal tools, he can have ever one he can carry off.....seen many a man steal many a thing, but tools to actually work with, ain't one of them." Thus he never locked the shop and as far as I know he never missed as much as a nut or bolt, let alone a tool.

I came back across the street and there was George sitting atop Mary's spotted horse and Mary was standing by George smiling and encouraging him.
"Now you stay calm George and don't get all worked up.....you're going to make sure these other fellows get home safe now. You be careful with your rifle and don't you go off and get hurt." She gently urged.

 Mary was one of the kindest girls I'd ever known next to my cousin Trish, when it came to George Wellner. They both knew

133
Archie Matthews

George's wife and daughter and women will stick together. Both understood although George was nutty as a fruit cake, he was a kind and gentle nut that just wanted to help, even when he got in the way more than he actually benefited. Besides, Mary had a very calming effect when it came to George.

Mary was talking and encouraging George while Grandpa swung into the saddle and motioned for me to step up and taking his foot out of the stirrup, I swung aboard.

Kay and Mary both stood waving and smiling and Milt called out, "Don't get et by the Gator's.....Arch!" I looked back and was going to wave at Milt to assure him I was going to do my best not to get ate, but he was too busy ducking and dodging his two sisters.

We rode up by the house and Grandma stepped out to the front porch, "Archie....do you want your pistol?" Grandma called.

"No Clara, we're fine......we'll be home as soon as we find Jimmy. We'll be hungry when we get back, so keep dinner warm." And Grandpa smiled and waved and Grandma smiled and waved back.

That's how Grandpa always assured Grandma he was coming back safe and sound. Grandpa would always say he was coming back hungry and to keep dinner warm. My Grandpa never came home but what there wasn't a hot meal waiting, although a time or two, I can remember it wasn't the same day or the same meal he'd left behind, through no fault of his own.

But those are different stories, the man was an adventurous sort, and many has been the theory he's where I got my adventurous spirit, although the votes still out on where I got all my mishaps from. For Grandpa lived a charmed life in comparison to me his grandson, for he always came out on top smelling like a rose, while I'm usually at the bottom of the dog pile and smelling like I'd been there a while. Although many a person has pointed out,

I must have an over worked guardian Angel, for I'm still alive and with all my parts......mostly.....

We rode to the store and there sat Bart Sexton on a huge black and white draft horse that towered over the two horses we'd borrowed from Kay and Mary. Bart was setting astride a large black bear hide draped over what looked like some kind of saddle. As we rode close, I also saw a long barreled shotgun hanging from a string around the saddle horn.

"That's probably why he has to ride such a tall horse" I thought, "to keep that long barreled shotgun from dragging the ground."

And then we were off, headed down the street around the church and across the road headed for the crick. George and his dogs bringing up the rear, for both those huge wolf hounds were loping along easily staying up with the horses.

And before I knew it, we were back down to the swimming hole. If you'd have asked me any other time, I'd have said, "I never get to come down enough," but today, and now, I'd have said, "I'd visited it more than I'd wanted to that day."

We dismounted and both Bart and George began wandering around both intently looking at the ground, for both men were remarkable trackers, especially George Wellner. Bart stopped and called out to George, who quickly joined the big man and they began slowly moving up through the brush alongside the crick upstream.

Me and Grandpa staying back a ways, "To keep from messing up the 'sign'," Grandpa had explained. It seemed that's what trackers called following a track; it was called following "sign". Why they didn't just call it tracks was beyond me and when I asked, Grandpa went on to explain.

"Tracking a critter or a man ain't just following the foot prints in the dirt. A man and an animal can step on rocks or hard ground and you won't even see a track, but you'll see a stick or grass

Archie Matthews

that's been stepped on or broken, or moved or pushed out of place, so it's called "following the sign". Grandpa explained in low tones as we followed.

After traveling several hundred yards up the crick, we heard a faint shout and everyone's attention suddenly turned from the ground to a huge fir tree a hundred yards up the crick.

"What the heck...Is that my Jim in that tree a shout 'n?" boomed Bart the baritone.

"That's a good place, to get away from that big old she ba'r" George smiled and nodded, "Yup, I've sat in that tree a time or two. That's a good place to be.....she's a cranky one this time'o year....."

"What are you talking about.......George?" Bart asked as he stepped up the pace and was walking with long strides towards the distant tree, where now we could see a hand waving a hat out of the thick fir needles.

"Paw....look out ....looooooook ooooouuuut!" we heard just as Bart stopped and looked back at George incredulously.

"What did you say about a ba'r and that tree?" Bart suddenly boomed with a note of suspicion.

"I said, that's a good place to sit so's that she ba'r don't get ya...she's a cranky one what with those cubs and all...."George began to explain, just as the brush began "Popping and Cracking" coming towards us through the thick brush from under that big fir tree.

I was just trying to get my brain shifted into gear and decipher what I'd just heard, doing my best to add everything up, when I was suddenly being drug from behind and skipped along the ground like a sack of potato's by a spud starved cook. I'll say this about my Grandpa, he couldn't swim a lick, but the man could cover ground like a gazelle all the while dragging a dumbfounded grandson. The other thing I will say, is being drug by the collar from behind the way I was, I had a dandy view of that bear as she broke cover.

That big old black sow came shooting out of the brush so fast, it's a wonder she didn't catch everyone flatfooted, but she didn't. Bart went towards the crick as fast as a race horse, "Popping and crashing" through the underbrush every bit as noisy as the she bear had come.

George on the other hand, he was a dashing around the other way in a zigzag pattern screaming his head off and working his rifle action. Although he'd run close to a mile all total, it was around and around zigzagging back and forth over his own tracks aimlessly.

If that big she bear hadn't been so puzzled as to which one of the three groups to follow, she'd have caught George easy. But as circumstances would have it, she pulled up quick and stopped, her nose in the air, trying to decide which way to go, and she was still standing there when two dark shapes came hurtling out of the brush right smack dab on top of her.

Now, I've seen plenty of fights in my days. My Grandpa's brother was a professional boxer and from all I've heard and read, he was a scrapper from day one, although he was long since retired when I came along. But my family has been and always will be scrappers, we lived amongst scrappers and we scrapped with scrappers. So when I tell you, those two big wolf hounds of George's piled into that big sow bear and the fight was on, you'll know I'm not carve'n a chip off the blarney stone. It was a fight!

All George's yelling and shouting had brought those two "Ba'r Killers" as George was always fond of calling them, before any and all that would listen, and let me tell you, they went right into that Ba'r. It was just a huge ball of flying hide and hair, yowls and howls, no telling who was getting or who was giving It was like trying to watch the old "shell game" and keep track of the

Archie Matthews

pea, while the shells was being swished around by lightning fast hands. All the while being drug backwards as fast as a short legged blacksmith running for his and his grandson's life can go, which was amazingly fast come to think of it.

Then before I knew it Grandpa dropped me a "Ker-Plop" and as I tilted my head and looked back up over my shoulder, I saw grandpa grab that big old double barrel shotgun off from Bart Sexton's saddle, break it open and seeing it was loaded, he snapped it shut and stepped right up to me. "You stay smack dab behind me.....or you'll get snatched up and turn into a pile of bear poop in an instant....do you understand me?"

My head bobbed, "Yup, yes, absolutely, right smack behind you....yes sir" and if I'd been any closer behind him, I'd have been ointment on his backside. I'd seen bear poop, and I didn't hanker to turn into any, in an instant or otherwise.

Back down the trail we went towards the sound of the "Fight". Oh, it weren't any task at all to follow that sound, that was a heck of a ruckus, what with the bear squalling and those two dogs growling, and all the while George was yelling encouragement at both the dogs and the bear. Which at the time only would have re-affirmed Ed's opinion of George as a Nut, for he kept screaming for the dogs to "Get em....sick that Ba'r!" and then he'd begin to shout "Don't let them dog's get the best of you ma' ma ba'r, hang in there.... whip em down!"

And it was to this sight that I and Grandpa broke cover and stepped into as we saw the old she bear up on her back legs, half hunched forward, her glistening claws held out in front of her, her mouth wide open and full of huge teeth, roaring her defiance. The two huge dogs were several feet apart, each between George, their master, and staying that way, despite the knot head dancing around and around, yelling encouragement to all contestants equally. George was like some kind of demented circus ringmaster, wanting all spectators to have a glorious sight to see. Even if all the spectators had run off doing their best not to get ate and turned into bear poop, but that was George for you.

Dogs, bear and old white haired George circling and everyone trying their best to keep their distance, but not let their guard down either. Then grandpa tilted that shotgun into the air and fired one extremely loud round off. The startling result was the two dogs jumped right straight in the air, as did the bear, but they turned their heads towards us, while the bear jumped and slowly began to back away. The effect of the gunshot was just the opposite on George, for he didn't jump, but suddenly stopped jumping and dancing around he looked at me and Grandpa. Upon recognizing us, a dawning realization seemed to come over him and he smiled broadly, his eyes darting all around, he calmly walked towards us.

I never did see dogs act so protective as those two massive wolf hounds did, for as George walked towards us, both dogs slowly backed up keeping one eye on the retreating bear and the other on George, as they kept between their master and the danger. And then as if knowing George was safe and sound alongside us, they both slowly backed away and came galloping up beside George.

"Well, now.....I'd say that was a show! Did you see my boys, Arch.....did you see the boys? I told't you they was Ba'r dogs, yup......I told't everybody, these here dogs is ba'r dogs.....did you ever see such a show? They love to dance with that big ole fat ba'r sow.....especially when she's got those cub up a tree....she dances fine then....don't she?" George laughed and began dancing around excitedly again.

"George, you mean you knew that she bear was down here with cubs?" Grandpa asked incredulously, "How come you didn't say anything George? We almost got bear bit."

"Well, Arch.....we was alligator hunt'n.....you don't start talking about alligators on a Ba'r hunt and you don't talk ba'rs on a gator hunt.....that's crazy talk Arch. Besides, I and the boys been

Archie Matthews

down here many a time and danced with that old girl, she's never bit me once, Arch....nary even once....the boys won't let her, they won't let no ba'r bite me. These here is my ba'r dogs Arch, they don't let no ba'rs bite me. Alligators, I don't know......but ba'rs I know.....ba'rs don't bite me." George explained grinning the whole time and pulling up his long shirt sleeves as if to show, no bear bites, dancing around, all the time still clutching that big bolt action bear rifle.

"Okay, George..." Grandpa said a bit exasperated. "I know your bear dogs are dandies, and a dern good thing they were, or someone would have gotten ate for sure." And Grandpa gave me a look that assured me it would have more than likely been "The nut" as Grandma and so many other's called him.

Then as we began to call out trying our best to find which way Bart Sexton had gone, we heard a shout and saw a second hat waving through the branches of the big fir tree back the way the bear had retreated.

After several more minutes of yelling and shouting, we heard Bart and Jimmy coming through the underbrush both of them no worse for wear. Jimmy gave me a grin, "Hey there Arch, whew, so the gators didn't get you....the bear purt'near got me, but I ain't seen an alligator one from up in that tree and I had a real good look up and down the crick."

"Alligators.....alligators.....where in heaven's name did all this talk of alligators come from?", blared the loud voice of Jimmy's dad. "I'm so fed up with alligators....in all my born days of living in this country...I've never heard such talk as alligators as I have today!"

"Well fella's, it's getting late and by my reckoning we got just about enough time to get back to town before dark. I say, we all go back to my house and we camp overnight on a soft bed and don't give anymore thoughts of alligators!" Grandpa smiled.

The Idaho Alligators

"Nope, Not me and Jim, we're off up the crick for home. My woman will be wait'n and we ain't for leave'n the wimmin folk helpless while the men wander around like loafers......we're headed home.....come on Jim."

And with that the Sexton's loaded up atop that huge black and white horse and was off. But not without a word from Bart as everyone got aboard their horses and were about to depart.

"Young Henchman, I knew your Grumps from when I was a kid, he was quite a character and a braver man I've never known, except maybe your grandpa there, but you done alright today. The way I hear tell, you went back for your brother, and you come a look'n for my Jim. You're welcome to our place anytime.....anytime atoll.....and YOU..."and Bart's eyes swiveled above his twisted mangled nose to old George, "You... George, if you don't take more care around Ba'rs, you'll turn into a pile of Ba'r scat one of these days and that will be that!.....I'd either get a bullet for that rifle or give up the rifle, it instills confidence in other's that they shouldn't fathom, for it's a lie!"

And with that, off into the evening dusk they rode towards their home up and over the distant hill and several miles across country at night, a horse back as the crow flies.

When I remarked about it as we rode back towards town, grandpa just chuckled, "Those Sexton's are an odd bunch, but they respect and hold in high regards a friend, so seems like your welcome anytime. As far as riding home in the dark, Bart Sexton was born and raised in this country, he knows ever switchback and ravine for many a mile around. I'd not worry about him, especially atop that monster draft horse he's riding. I've shod that horse many a time, and its feet are big as dinner plates and he's as sure footed as any two mules, besides, he'll stand stock still and won't spook at nothing. Did you notice how we run up here and every one of them horses stood still and didn't buck or jump around? Them's mountain horses, good and solid, and if they'd been anyone else's horses, I'd have never borrowed them, but both Sexton's, Second and Third fork alike,

141
Archie Matthews

are mighty fond of their horses and they all got good ones. That's good to know, you ever have to borrow a horse or do any swap'n with them. Just remember though, Sexton's is just as good at swap'n as they are at fighting, so don't get in over your head or you'll find yourself standing alongside the road in your birthday suit and with a black eye, more likely than not."

As we were passing the general store, Ed came out on the board walk, "Did you find the boy?"

"Yes, we found him....and one of George's waltzing partner's too it seems". Grandpa laughed, as we rode on leaving Ed to scratch his head over that tidbit of information.

We rode up to the café as Kay, Mary and Milt came outside along with Eddy and Elaine. George bailed off and began dancing around and describing the bear and dog fight step by step to Mary as she kept trying to calm him down long enough to actually make sense out of what he was babbling about.

Eddy, smiled and asked, "So you found the boy, and no alligators?"

"We found Jimmy up a tree, after being treed by a sow.....come to find out she's been there before with cubs as have George and his dogs." Grandpa explained shaking his head with a smile.

"I will say this, up until now, I have always worried about that rifle he carries, but never again as long as he's got those two big bruiser's with him." And everyone looked over at the two huge dogs that stood close to their beloved master.

"When the old boy claims their ba'r dogs, by golly he ain't just a kid'n. That old sow was stopped cold, and although George dangled himself closer than bait ever ought to be and not get bit. I'd have to say, them dogs wouldn't let him get hurt, they stayed right between him and that old sow despite George's best efforts."

The Idaho Alligators

Grandpa and Eddy both just shook their heads and Elaine gave a snort and went back inside, she was a strong supporter of the "Put the Nut in a Home" committee, and didn't care who knew it either. But she knew she was way out matched, with Grandpa, Kay and Mary, for those Sexton girls thought the world of George, despite his good sense deficit. Mary was quietly giggling as George was dancing around, she held his hand keeping him close all the while trying to calm him down.

After offering a bed and a hot meal and being firmly, but politely turned down, Kay, Mary and Milt saddled up and up the crick they went towards their home. After Eddy had explained George's truck was being worked on by one of the Dobson's down in Sweet, the small town down at the beginning of the long valley, and George's wife would be along directly to pick her husband up, we headed across the street for home.

After eating dinner and Grandpa telling everyone about finding Jimmy and dodging the sow bear, it was soon pronounced bedtime and everyone was sent to bed. I, Dean and little brother Ike, were all sent upstairs to share the big brass bed, while poor injured Micky, the mummy boy, was doomed to spend the night on the old Horse Hair Couch.

I don't know if the couch was really made of horse hair or not. Everyone called it the old Horse Hair Couch, and although it was a beautiful piece of furniture and was prized by my grandma, it was a veritable "Torture Rack" when it came to trying to sleep on it. I know, I'd been doomed more than once to sleep on the itchy infernal torture rack when company came, especially female company.

Not having sisters or understanding girls at all, had left me strongly suspicious and standoffish of the opposite sex. And when I had been sentenced to sleep the night on that couch in order to give up my comfortable bed upstairs, it left me with deep seated negative feelings towards females. Argue as I might with my Grandma, (who also happened to be a female herself, and I strongly suspected more than a bit jaded on the subject) I never

Archie Matthews

could talk sense into her and keep my bed and have the female interloper, sentenced to "The Rack".

Needless to say, I was counting my blessings for getting to sleep upstairs in the comfortable bed, and with company. Don't get me wrong, it wasn't that I liked sharing, especially my bed, but what I did like was the company upstairs. There's just something comforting when you're terrified of being snatched in the darkness and eaten by a monster, knowing that there's someone else in the room. I don't know if it's the idea of knowing your death screams will be shared with a loved one as you're going down the monsters gullet, or the feeble hope that the monster might actually snatch and begin devouring one of them, while I make my get away and run for help. The coward in me often imagines it's the later.

Being the oldest, I of course had seniority and quickly assigned places in the bed to my two guests, for as the oldest and the one that had far more tenure in summer vacations spent in this bed, I felt self-elected as the Bed Dictator.

I quickly summed up the risks and calculated the odds and decided since Dean was the biggest, he'd sleep on the side closest to the stairs and the adjoining room's door. Ike would then sleep in the middle between Dean and I, for the following reasons. First of all, Ike was skinny and Dean was fat, Dean generated a lot of heat during the night and sweated profusely. I know, because I'd slept with him a couple of times without a "little brother buffer zone"; besides, Ike was skinny and needed all the heat he could get. The second reason was, if an attacking monster gobbled his way through Dean without choking, Ike was my back up defensive plan, for although Ike was small, he was scrappy. Besides, I felt my best chance of survival was on the side facing the outside two story window. The way I figured it, if there was an attack from Dean's side of the bed, I'd just jump through the window, land in the yard and then jump in through Grandpa and Grandma's downstairs bedroom window to safety. Oh what fear filled minds will conjure just before bedtime in the way of monster attacks and survival tactics.

The Idaho Alligators

I won't bore you with the long free for all kicking contest that three boys sharing a bed together engage in, or the early untangling of limbs and covers, not to mention then trying to sort out whose clothing was whose.

I will say we had a wonderful breakfast and were soon all outside about our daily adventures, everyone except Micky, the mummy boy, who was still laid up with his scorched flesh and bandages itching from top to bottom after a night on the Horse Hair Couch. And that's where we'd left him, scratching from top to bottom, still sitting there with his wrapped up feet, sad little Micky the mummy boy.

The next couple of days went along pretty smooth with minor adventures and a few mishaps, most of which resulted in one or two of us being doused and daubed by the medicinal maniac and her red liquid germ killer.

There was a brief instance where a handful of cookies had mysteriously disappeared from the kitchen while Grandma had been artfully distracted. But since there were no "Witnesses" as to the actual theft, and only one of us three kids could be eliminated from the line up as being the "distraction", the other two kids just got a verbal warning. Everyone was quickly reminded of the willow switch orchard Grandma cultivated down by the little stream behind the outhouse.

Thus it seemed like everyone had all but forgotten about the "alligators", that is, until grandma unwrapped Micky's legs and pronounced he could once again start visiting the outhouse and stop using the "Chamber Pot".

The chamber pot being that little porcelain pot Micky had been "Watering his Mule in, and occasionally pitch'n em some hay......" and grandma had been emptying out in the outhouse. But now, what with his legs healing up and grandma's mercurochrome taking all the credit, Micky was expected to go use the outhouse like everyone else. Which once his bandages

Archie Matthews

were removed, he was wont to do and headed out the back door towards the outhouse.

I and the boys had been present during the unveiling of Micky's bandaged legs, for what boy would miss seeing another battle wounded veteran's scars? There was a fine set of scabs on both legs and we all "ew'd and awe'd "at the sight of nice scabs if picked off properly would leave wonderful tall tale scars that every lad envied. But as Micky headed out the back towards the outhouse, the rest of us were "shoo'd" off by grandma and headed out the front door. We headed out the front gate and down to the shop and dropped in to visit with grandpa and help him with a few chores.

Dean grabbed the coal bucket and he and Ike headed out the back shop door to the large coal bin to get a bucket of coal to fill Grandpa's forge reserve, while I grabbed the big water bucket and headed right behind them. I went on through the scrap yard towards the outhouse on my way to the little stream behind it. I was coming to the outhouse and turned to the left to go down to the little stream, when I saw Micky standing off to my right, just outside the yard gate on the outhouse trail with a look of horror on his face, anchored like a statue.

Now when you've grown up with the insight as to the kind of monsters this world has, the look of terror on a person's face as they look past you, has the same immediate effect as a starters pistol at a foot race. Seeing Micky's look of terror as he stared over my shoulder towards the little stream, told me I was about to be overtaken and devoured from behind, unless I took immediate action.

I had once been shocked by a cattle prod and it had sent me off as if my tail was on fire, and at that moment, so had Micky's look of terror. I dropped the water bucket and shot into overdrive and came flying up the outhouse trail right towards Micky, with what I imagine, was my own look of terror. Suddenly something startled Micky and he jumped about two foot in the air and bolted back through the gate with me close at his heels. I was only a half dozen steps behind him, when all of the sudden the gate closed between us and I smacked full bore into it and rebounded as if a Hun crashing into the great wall of china. I could hear Micky screaming "Alligators... Alligators!" as he tore through the back porch and into the house, as well as grandmas welcoming scream at being startled.

Taking a moment to shake the cobwebs out of my head, having recently been thrust there by the hard firm gate, I instinctively looked back towards the stream to see what my chances were of surviving the masses of attacking alligators. But all I saw was the empty trail, empty that is except the water bucket I'd so quickly abandoned. After a few more minutes of a self-diagnostic exam to make sure my crumpled legs still worked, I gained my feet when I heard a shout from the back door of the shop and turned to see Grandpa.

"What the devils going on up there?"

"Micky's started running for the house screaming 'alligators'.....again.....but I don't see any." I replied shrugging my shoulders and holding up my hands.

I saw Grandpa shake his head and disappear back inside the shop. I also shook my head and wandered back to the water bucket, and slowly proceeded on down to the little stream. I'd spent countless hours at this little steam over the past couple of years, panning out the glittering golden specs in the sand at the bottom of the small creek. In all that time, I'd never once seen anything that even remotely resembled an alligator. But I have to admit, all this talk and excitement about alligators, had me spooked, and I approached slowly and cautiously.

After several seconds of cautiously scanning, I couldn't see a thing to be concerned about and so I walked right down to the stream and filled the water bucket and headed back to the shop. I did see a horn toad or two quickly scamper across the trail between the outhouse and the shop, but never even gave them a thought as all of us kids, including Micky had caught several

Archie Matthews

each and every year for pocket pets. And then I knocked on the back shop door, went inside, walked around the far side of the anvil to the slag tank and dumped the water inside.

The slag tank was a huge steel tub that held water so that Grandpa could douse his hot steel and cool it as needed. It was big enough to dip a kid ablaze, as I'd found out early in one of my earlier years of vacationing with my grandparents. The slag tank and the coal reservoir were constantly needing to be resupplied and it was a chore us kids enjoyed to be helping Grandpa with. Grandpa always gave us a big smile and wink of gratitude, not to mention a nickel or dime every once in a while. But now as I dumped the water into the slag tank and returned the water bucket to its place of rest, Grandpa stepped away from his forge and asked me what the yelling had been all about.

I had quickly explained seeing Micky with the look of horror on his face, although I did leave out my hasty abandonment of the water bucket and my own mishap with the gate, but went on to explain Micky's screaming into the house and Grandma's own shout of "Heaven's Sake!"

"What in the heck is up with that boy? He's seen something or some things happened and we better get to bottom of it. He can't just go through life screaming 'Alligators', that's not the kind of thing that you can go through life shouting without repercussions." Grandpa exclaimed as he began raking the burning coal out of the fire to enable him to leave the shop.

After several more minutes of waiting for the coal to die down to just smoke, Grandpa leading the way, we all headed for the house. We had just come out of the shop when in the distance we could hear George Wellner's truck approaching. But this time, we heard it coming from the opposite end of town, we turned to see the huge cloud of black smoke, complete with loud barking and baying dogs, not to mention all the creaks, rattles and groans that the old rust bucket naturally emitted. And then as the black cloud approached the distant knoll the smoke ceased as the engine shut off, and slowly rolling to the top, just before the road dropped into town, the truck stopped dead still.

Everyone had boiled out of the café across the street, and when I say everyone, I mean everyone, for there came Elaine in her house coat and hair still in curlers, big fluffy slippers on her feet and a face full of cream that looked like she'd dipped her whole head into the milk bucket. As frightful as her whole get up looked, her face was twisted into such an angry grimace; I doubted George was going to survive the encounter, if she ever got her hands on him. She'd come barreling out the back door to the café where her and Eddy lived and instead of joining everyone out front, I saw her run for the outhouse they had in the remote corner of their back yard.

Everyone else that came out of the café had their clothes on and didn't seem nearly so put out with George for having come to town at that moment in their lives, like Elaine had.

There Eddy was coming across the street, with a tall thin stranger that still held a sandwich in one hand and a cup of coffee in the other, a napkin stuck in his shirt front. Eddy was walking along just chattering away explaining the need for everyone to abandon the café, "Just in case the local nut miss judges this time and actually hits the gas pumps and blows the café to high heaven", Eddy concluded as he stepped up next to Grandpa and gave all us kids a smile and a nod.

After a few minutes of watching and waiting for the truck to come rolling down the hill, we suddenly realized it had stopped and wasn't coming any farther. I can tell you, it was a first in George Wellner history, for old George had somehow miscalculated and shut the truck off too soon, thus loosing the momentum needed to roll down the hill.

Suddenly the dogs stopped barking as if on command as the trucks motion stopped, and then the driver's side door flew open and with a string of shrieks and oaths the like I'd never heard, especially from George, he ran around the back and began

Archie Matthews

heaving and pushing with all his might. After a full minute of pushing and straining, he finally dropped the tail gate to his truck and screamed another set of oaths at the canine occupants and what seemed like a "thousand and one" dogs bailed out and began milling around the once again straining pushing old man.

After a few more minutes, Grandpa cupped his hands over his mouth and shouted, "George......Take the truck out of GEAR!!!!....." and hearing Grandpa, George quickly ran around and jumped in the truck and then stepped out again and began pushing once more. That's when the unthinkable happened and the truck began rapidly coming down the hill headed right smack at the café', and poor old George running far behind, him and his "Thousand and one dogs", baying, barking and howling their guts out.

It seemed astonishing to me, that even though they weren't in the moving truck any longer, their barking mechanisms seemed somehow linked to the movement of the truck, for the second it had begun moving they had begun barking, even though they too were left running far behind.

Now, I'd seen the scenario play out a hundred times, what with George's truck not having any brakes, he'd coast to almost a dead stop atop that hill from either direction and killing the engine would then coast down to the café. But I'd never seen it done without him driving, and certainly not with him running behind. And from the look on both Eddy and Grandpa's faces, I quickly realized they'd never see the like either. You talk about throwing a lit stick of dynamite amongst a crowd, it would have had the same effect, for our little crowd disbanded just that quickly and it was instantly "Ever man, or kid, for himself!"

"RUN!" shouted grandpa, and up towards the house he went, as fast as I've ever seen him run.

I'd like to say I was close behind, but the sight of George's truck coming and him running behind surrounded by that huge "herd'o dogs", held me for the briefest of moments. But not the rest of

The Idaho Alligators

the small throng, and Eddy was off like a shot and he too ran down the street, but he didn't turn into the grand folks gate like Grandpa did, but shot past, headed for the general store.

I saw Ed Shotz the store owner standing out on the boardwalk with his mouth wide open and a look of absolute astonishment on his face, that is until Eddy shot by him and ran on towards the distant church.

Who's to say what snapped Ed out of his startled trance, whether it was some stray gravel kicked up by Eddy's fast churning feet, or just the snap and boom as Eddy broke the sound barrier on his way by. Who can tell, and who would stop to wonder, while the blue truck sped right for the café and the two gas pumps that held thousands of gallons of gasoline, if struck by the old truck would blow the entire town to the moon.

The stranger with the sandwich and the cup of coffee first started one way and then as if trying to decide if the other way wasn't best, just kind of jerked one way and then back towards the other, unable to make up his mind as to where the safest place to run was.

That's when I came to my senses and realized I was still standing within the explosion zone and winding up my main spring, I snapped the catch and was off like a shot myself. Yet something had happened to my steering mechanism and dern if I didn't just light out the way I was pointed, which was towards the end of town and the oncoming blue rattling disaster, complete with chasing mad man and a thousand and one howling dogs.

Who knows why kids do anything!? Even when I was a kid, I never did rightly understand why I did things, most of the time..... Sure, sure, as I was getting the switch and under full duress, I'd wail out this excuse or that excuse, but mostly, I didn't even know what possessed me to do the stuff I did. Such was the mystery now.......I just didn't have a clue as to which direction to run.

I could easily have fallen in behind Grandpa, who had been followed by both Ike and chubby Dean bringing up the rear, towards the house. I could have followed Eddy and headed clear out of town the opposite direction, even though I wasn't fond of going to church, I'd sure rather attend it than get blown to smithereens. Why I had lingered and gaped at the show of oncoming doom as long as I did, I just can't explain. Nor can I explain when my senses did come back, why I took off up the road towards the fast approaching un-manned vehicle. But I did and we passed one another as I headed out of town, and it headed straight for the café and gas pumps and evidently the moon.

I'll never forget the wild wide eyed look on George's face, as he came running behind the truck, with his white hair waving in the breeze, his arms flapping, and his mouth wide open shouting every kind of word known or unknown to man. Even though I was not a man yet, I'd recognized some, but most I'd never heard before or afterwards…..(Well, until I began working construction many years later, and then more than a few I heard once again, a time or two, mostly when men whacked their fingers with hammers and such.)

Why is it that when you're running, or riding a bike, skateboard, or other contrivance, when you stare and concentrate hard on a rapidly approaching obstacle you want to avoid, you will almost invariably run right into it? They got a word for that kind of a phenomenon, though the word eludes me, crashing headlong into George didn't. Thus we crashed into a heap, and then suddenly our heap was crashed into by the thousand and one barking, baying dogs. Instantly we had an enormous heap of growling, snapping and biting mostly by George, the dogs did a bit of it as well. I'd have to admit, I was doing my best to stay to the bottom of the pile and keep as many of those dogs between me and the explosion I expected at any moment.

Then and even now, vast is the number of my family members that will diligently profess that I am guarded by the hardest working, over taxed guardian Angel heaven ever spawned.

The Idaho Alligators

Many a family gathering has brought one after the other astounding remarks that I am still "Alive"!

After a few more minutes of wallowing amidst the deafening canine mass, suddenly every dog stopped and I came to the sudden realization that the truck must have ceased moving and with no explosion. Therefore I began to swim to the top of the pile so that I could look at where I expected to see a still standing café. Nor was I disappointed, and I expected both Elaine and Eddy would be just as happy, when they realized not only their place of business, but their home had not been reduced to rubble.

Fighting my way to the top of the herd, I stood up and saw to my utter amazement, that blue truck setting right next to the gas pumps as if it had been expertly parked by a master valet.

George also sat up and began to mumble, "Oh NO….it's gone, blowed up and gone…..what's gonna happen to me?! I'm a criminal for sure….I'll be hung….yup, they still hang criminals."

And then I realized he had been turned around and was staring out across the street at the distant pasture far behind the café. "George, over there!", I urged "Looky over there!" and getting his attention, I quickly pointed and smiled.

"OH LORDY…There you are!" The old fellow howled with glee as he jumped to his feet and ran the hundred yards to the side of his truck and began dancing merrily around it hugging first one old fender and then the back tailgate.

To most, hugging a truck would have been an awkward affair, but good ole George made it look mighty easy as he dropped and even hugged a back tire. He just kept mumbling and cooing and petting his old blue truck, right up until the time that Elaine ventured out from the outhouse and came screeching up to the fence behind the café, screaming and deriding poor old George.

Archie Matthews

After assuring himself his beloved truck was intact, he then turned his attention over his shoulder to Elaine. One look at her, in that housecoat and those furry slippers and the half smeared, half wiped off cream she'd had all over her face, and George began howling with laughter.

It was no time before here come Eddy and Ed, as well as Grandpa, Dean and Ike, and right behind them came Grandma with as concerned a look as I've ever seen on her poor weathered weary face.

"WOW ARCH!" shouted Dean as he came running up to me and skidded to a halt his eyes big as saucers. "You're a HERO!"

Ike was also dancing around with a look of wonder on his face, "Wow, Arch, you saved the Nut!"

And then Grandpa was beside me, with his beaming smile and he gave me a big wink and taking my hand in his, he shook it, "Well now, that was a mighty fine piece of rescue'n I've ever seen myself. Let me shake hands with the hero of the day."

That's when Grandma pushed through and gave me a smothering hug right there in front of everyone. I'd almost rather have had her attack me with one of her willow switches as give me as disgusting a display of affection in public like that, but Grandma's are like that. Then she pushed me back and wailed, "Whatever made you do such a foolish thing?! Risking your life to save that old lunatic?! I swear sometimes you need your head examined!" and with that she turned around and was headed back towards the house.

What could I do? I wasn't about to let on like I had been an idiot and just stood there waiting to get blown up and had only fled like a chicken with its head cut off at the last minute and "Accidently" crashed into old George. Therefore, I did what a lot of heroes do, I imagine, and I kept my mouth shut and let the crowd puff me up into the two minute local legend I became.

The Idaho Alligators

Elaine seeing everyone giving her the "Eye" and suddenly realizing she was in public still in her housecoat and those fuzzy slippers, let alone her face all un-done, gave a scream and ran for her back door and disappeared.

Eddy walked over to George and began howling, "George! You dern knot head, you just about done it this time.....I swear if you don't get those brakes fixed.....I'm gonna have the sheriff lock you up and throw away the key! You're a menace to society!"

Since Elaine was no longer distracting George with her "get up", he had once again returned his focus back to inspecting his truck and wasn't giving Eddy or his rant the time of day.

Then Ed walked up to Eddy and putting his hand on his shoulder, he led the raving man over by Grandpa and said, "Eddy, you don't understand.....George's brakes were fixed just the other day, by Dobson, that mechanic in Sweet.....But the idiot's gotten so used to not having any, he can't, or doesn't remember how to even use them."

I thought Eddy was going to "Pop" a blood vessel, for his eyes did a bulging thing and he began to huff and puff and acted like a fish right out of water, opening and closing his mouth rapidly. Ed just kept patting him on the shoulder, "It's not his fault Eddy, he's just completely slipped his wing nut and the bolt is inexorably stripped, there ain't a bit of thread left on the old boy....." And that was the first time I'd ever seen Ed give a kind of sad look at poor old George, for usually he was ranting and raving like Eddy had been.

Grandpa just shook his head sadly at the news that poor old George actually had brakes now but didn't even have the good sense to use them. And then George suddenly snapped to and wheeled around and gave Grandpa a startled look.

"Arch, it got my dog.....it got my dog ARCH!" George began to shout and dance around like an Irish river dancer with his feet on fire. "Arch....the alligators got my DOG !" howled George mournfully. "Et him up and didn't even spit out the bones!" he wailed as both his hands grabbed his hair and his eyes instantly opened wider than ever an eye should.

The wail brought Eddy back to the right side of the mental road; he'd strayed across for the past few minutes. "What happened to your dog....?" He slowly asked, realizing George was all worked up about something.

"ET....MY......DOG!" George wailed again, but much slower, pronouncing each syllable as if he were trying to explain to a small hard of hearing child. And then suddenly all his dancing around stopped and he became as calm as I've ever seen him and with the meanest look I've ever seen on any man, let alone kind hearted old George.

"That alligator has et' my dog....Wilbur....and I aim to get me that gator, come hell or high water....I need a bullet for my gun...Arch, a bullet for my gun...for Wilbur." He growled his face still twisted with hate.

I'd never seen George so calm and still, usually he was in motion every second, but there he stood, with his face all twisted with a look fit to kill anything and everything, with his hand thrust out and the palm up, he was staring straight into Grandpa's eyes.

I have to admit, I'd never been wary of, let alone afraid of George, for he'd only ever been kind to me and every other person in Ola. I'd never seen him harsh with man nor beast and he was especially kind with children, but I'd never seen him like this; although there had been a time a couple years past, when grandpa had to intervene between George and a stranger.

The fellow had stopped for gas, and seeing all George's dogs lounging around in the nearby shade, he'd made some kind of derogatory remark that George had heard as he had come out the café door at the wrong time, at least for the stranger. George had snatched that fellow by the shirt front and pulled him tip toe, right up close, until George and him were eye to eye and nose to nose.

That's when Grandpa, who had also been in the café at the time, had seen the encounter and quickly rushed to the poor fellows rescue, and I don't mean George's either. I was sitting amongst the dogs over by the shop, enjoying the shade and the dog pet 'n zoo; for I liked them friendly dogs. That is they were friendly up until George grabbed that fellow, and then as if flipping a "vicious switch", those dogs jumped to their feet and instantly turned from a friendly pack, to a pack of snarling devils with gleaming white teeth.

No one knows what that fellow had said, but everyone knew how George loved his "Boys", as he called them, although there were sure a lot of girls in the herd, he still called them "his boys" females and all.

Grandpa had calmed George down and gotten him to release the fellow so that he could pay for his gasoline, and leave. I had saw Grandpa walk that fellow into and out of the café. I always wondered if it was to protect him from George or that Thousand and one herd of dogs, for they had all slowly surrounded that fellows car and stood by George, with hair hackles raised and teeth bared, those growls gave me nightmares for about a week.

So when George had wailed that his dog "Wilbur" had been "Et", and he had come to town for a "Bullet" for his gun, everyone was surprised, but not astounded, for George surely loved his dogs. If something had attacked one, let alone actually eaten one, there was no doubt George was on the war path.

"Okay, George....." Grandpa said soothingly, "If'n you need a bullet for your rifle to kill something that hurt one of your dogs, you know I'll get you one." Grandpa assured the poor fellow.

That swiveled Ed and Eddy's heads around as if they'd been a six gun cylinder spun by a gun hand. Not to mention both their

Archie Matthews

mouths dropping so far open I could see both their "Hangy down" things to the back of their throats.

As for me, I was still trying to figure out why George was without a bullet for the rifle he always carried? This was the third time in almost as many days that I'd heard it suggested that George didn't have a bullet for his big bear rifle. I'd been meaning to ask Grandpa about it down on the crick when we had spotted the "Bark", but had forgotten, and then when the sow bear had chased us. Big old Bart Sexton had suggested old George "Get a bullet for his rifle, or lose the rifle", but now, once again, my curiosity was up to full mast and waving in the breeze.

"Let's go over in the shade and sit down and talk about what's happened George." Grandpa calmly urged his distraught friend. Then looking over at both Ed and Eddy, said, "Why don't you fella's come over and we'll sit in the shade and see if we can make head or tails as to what's happened?"

Ed and Eddy both nodded and did their best to fasten up their mouths again as well as straighten their puzzled looks. We all walked over to the shop and Grandpa seeing us kids tagging along, dug into his pocket and pulled out a handful of change, handed Dean and Ike each several coins and said, "You boys go over there to the café and ask Elaine real nice for a six pack of soda.....and bring us all back a pop to drink."

Since I hadn't been selected and given any money, I took that to mean for me to stick around, and so I settled down betwixt a couple of shaggy spaniels that were close to hand and comfortable laying in the shade, and began to listen to the men talk, while getting a pet in on them friendly dogs.

With very little coaxing, George explained he'd been out last night with "Wilbur", his coon hound running a coon down on the crick. Everyone's head bobbed at hearing how George loved to run a raccoon with his favorite coon dog, Wilbur. George explained that although they "run em, we don't kill em or nothing,

The Idaho Alligators

but usually tree em and then sit and rest a while then go off and get another".

But after running this particular raccoon last night, it run up and around, and George proceeded to go into intricate detail about every brush, tree, stump and bramble they crossed and had to be urged on by Grandpa to less detail and more about what happened to Wilbur. Anyways, George went on to say that they went up and down the crick bank and then the coon dropped into "That hollow, by the slow pool and that back water......you know, where all them baby alligators are.....then that coon jumped in the slack water and crossed that deep stretch with Wilbur right behind......"

"Whoa, wait a second George!" Ed quickly interrupted.

George startled and tried to stand up from his kneeling position, when Grandpa quickly put his hand on his shoulder and gave Ed a sharp look. "Easy now George......What Ed is wondering about, is what do you mean 'where all the baby Alligators live? Did you SEE something like alligators down in the crick?"

I'm here to tell you, you could have heard a pin drop, for everyone, I swear, even the dogs, held their breath looking at old George.

"Well, I see' d the whole big pool of baby alligators Arch, but I didn't know' d there was a big'un, I never see' d a big'un, unless you count that one down to the rapids, but that was a log, weren't it Arch?" George explained with his eyes darting around wildly.

That's when I got another good look at those "Hangy" things to the back of both Ed and Eddy's mouths again, for both of their mouths were hanging wide open. I could have trotted a small dog inside and out without nary touching a side, they was that far open.

Archie Matthews

"You mean to say, you seen a bunch of baby alligators?" Eddy gulped, which was quite a feat with his mouth open that way.

"Oh, sure….sure, they always come out this time of year….the little rascals…" chuckled George, "They is friendly rascals and you can even pick em up and they don't bite or nothing." And then he began fidgeting and jumped to his feet and shouted, "BUT THEY NEVER ET MY DOG WILBUR BEFORE!" and once again he was dancing around with an ugly look. "Et my dog, Arch, et my good ole' dog Wilbur….he was my boy…..I NEED A BULLET…Arch, I NEED one!" wailed the poor old fellow as he once again pulled his hair with both hands and gave a frightful look.

The three men looked at each other and I could tell they were about fit to be tied, and that's when Dean and Ike appeared with a cold bottle of pop for everyone. Grandpa had told the boys six bottles, and that's what they'd got, and grandpa shared his with George, for everyone knew George couldn't have a lot of sugar, because he got even more worked up than usual. The pop went down quick for it was a hot day, and I could tell from the silent sipping of the soda, that Grandpa, Ed and Eddy were doing a lot of studying on what they'd heard from George.

"Well, I say we go back down to the crick and take a look at where George lost his dog." Grandpa suggested after several silent minutes of sipping soda and deep thought; all the while giving George the needed time to calm down once again.

"I ain't going back without I gets me a BULLET for my rifle!" wailed George, "I ain't going to risk my boys by taking them with me, and besides, they is BA'R DOGS NOT GATOR DOGS!.....Arch, you need to give me a bullet, please Arch, just one bullet….." he began to wail loudly once again as his feet began to pick up speed.

"Don't you worry George; I think we better all go with bullets this time." Grandpa said with raised eyebrows looking from Ed to Eddy and then back to George again.

The Idaho Alligators

I won't bore you with the scramble for weapons, nor the excuses that were stuttered, let alone the down and outright lies each man told his respective wife, as he snuck into his house, armed himself and then all met back in front of the blacksmith shop. I only know what I saw and heard when grandpa went to his bedroom and fetched his long barreled pistol.

Grandma took one look at Grandpa and that big old pistol in its holster and belt strapped around his waist, dodging into the kitchen she quickly came back out with the "first aid kit".

"You best take this with you, Archie, and don't you get shot, but if you do, you come home all the same." She smiled weakly as she handed him the small canvas bag with its wide strap.

Grandpa handed the first aid kit to me, "Here, you carry this and don't lose it."

Of course this sent my jaw to the floor, for I realized I was going too. And then suddenly as if remembering something, Grandpa went back into his bedroom and returned with something wrapped in an old cloth and quickly unwrapping it, handed me a lever action BB gun.

"I'd hate for an alligator to get you for lack of having something to shoot back with. That was your daddy's when he was a kid.....do you know how to use it?"

And all I could do was nod, for I was so shocked that I got to actually carry a shoot' n iron with the men. Of course I could use it, both dad and grandpa had taken me out with the Daisy BB gun and I'd shot cans in the back field. I'd always been under constant supervision, but I knew how to load and cock and aim, let alone fire the marvelous hunk of manly metal. Yet, all I could do was nod and croak, "Yes sir!" Giving the rifle a shake, I could tell the barrel that held the supply of BB ammo was full, meaning I had about two hundred shots or so. I felt confident that I personally could handle at least two hundred man eating

Archie Matthews

alligators all by myself, and I'm sure my broadening smile showed it, for that's when Grandma's look changed.

"Oh Archie, now that boy is far too young to be off with "the wild bunch", let alone carrying that BB gun, you best just leave him and that BB gun here." She said as she gave me the proverbial "Kick right smack in the manhood".

"Nope, he ain't on the nipple anymore and we need a young set of eyes on this expedition, besides, I'd rather he was with us, than sneaking along behind us. He'll be safe enough with all of us armed to the teeth, besides, I'm still not convinced of what we're going to find, but something tells me we best go armed. Besides, we gotta go back down where that old sow bear and those cubs were, and a BB gun might be just the straw to tip the scales, especially if we're setting up in a tree with a mother bear below." Grandpa smiled and patted me on the head and kissed grandma. "Keep dinner warm, we'll need a hot meal when we come home."

We met Dean, Ike and Micky on the front porch and Grandpa stood the boys up and gave them strict instructions about how he wanted the yard guarded until he got back. He told them to watch the three yard gates and be sure not to let any strangers or anything "Strange" in. He explained to them that he was counting on them to be the "Men of the house" while he was gone and they were in charge of those gates until he came back. Then he added, "And now don't you men let me down." And with a pat to the head of each, we were out the front gate and met the rest of the "Wild Bunch" as Grandma had called us, out in front of the shop.

There stood Ed with as big a double barrel shotgun as I'd ever seen, including Bart Sexton's. It was a huge long barreled affair with large curving double hammers, a dark freshly oiled walnut hand carved stock and only later did I learn it had been all hand carved by Ed himself. Ed also carried around his waist a belt glistening with huge brass shot shells, that I also found out later, he hand loaded himself.

The Idaho Alligators

Eddy was also ready, he held a long barreled lever action Winchester with an octagon barrel that showed as much age and use as its owner, but you could tell it had been well oiled and taken care of over the years. Eddy also wore a large "Bandolier" that draped over his head and shoulder across his body. It too held a couple dozen brass rifle shells that come to find out, he also hand loaded.

And then there was George. George stood there decked out as if he were ready for war. He held his huge bolt action bear rifle, but it looked a sight different that it had in the past, for it glistened now with a fresh coat of gun oil, the back sight that always laid down flat along the top, was now sitting upright, ready for action. George didn't wear an ammunition belt, but he did wear as big a belt knife as I've ever seen, before or since. The belt knife was held across George's chest by a large leather belt within a black bear skinned sheath complete with glistening black hair and an impressive string of glistening black bear claws, the large white bone handle looking well-worn and well used. To top everything off, setting on top George's head was a large black Stetson cowboy hat with a handmade horse hair hatband that had bright red glass beads worked within it, a bright white eagle feather sticking up at an angle out of the band towards the sky. I recognized that hat as his good "Sunday go to meeting hat", instead of his old beat up gray hat he normally wore. And to top it all off, George was wearing a complete set of hand made, smoke tanned, leather shirt and britches, all beautifully hand beaded, complete with buckskin fringes. The old man was a sight to see in his "Alligator Kill'n" get up.

As we stepped up, everyone looked at me and grandpa and I saw all eyes slide to me and my own rifle, BB gun though it was, I imagined I was a sight holding it. Ed grinned and Eddy smiled and George perked right up and he gave me a determined look and said, "Well now....someone has gone and armed this young killer.....I just hope there's gator enough for the rest of us when he's done." Turning and looking Grandpa directly in the eye,

Archie Matthews

George thrust out his wrinkled old callused hand, empty palm upward.

With everyone looking on, Grandpa dipped into his pocket and reaching out, put a bullet smack dabbed into George's awaiting palm. The look on Ed's face, let alone Eddy's really puzzled me, for they were both dumb with shock. While George's reaction was one of immediate deep satisfaction, as punctuated by his clutching of hand to chest and closing his eyes, he gave a huge deep sigh.

There was a long moment of silence as everyone watched George slowly open his eyes as Grandpa said, "Now George, we all remember what happened the last time….." and everyone nodded, especially George. "And we don't want that to happen again……do we?", and once again everyone shook their heads in unison, including George. "So, don't put the bullet in your gun, unless you are absolutely ready to shoot an alligator……and only an alligator, Okay George?"

George nodded, "I'll just hold this bullet in this hand, until I get ready to shoot the alligator, and only the alligator, this is an alligator bullet…..not a bear bullet……but an alligator Bullet…..right Arch?"

"That's right my friend, that's just an alligator bullet, it's not for bears, or deer or an elk or a tweedy bird or even a snake. That's strictly for shooting a big alligator." And Grandpa gave both Ed and Eddy a stern look, for they were both still standing there as if Grandpa had just committed an unthinkable crime by arming the village idiot and they were all going to die by that one single murderous bullet.

"Let's go down to where you saw all those baby alligators George, you lead us there, we're right behind you. And we're all going to be careful and not shoot one another in a lead hail storm, no matter what we find." Grandpa said with a stern look all the way around, including me.

The Idaho Alligators

I won't go into boring detail about our mile trek out of town to the distant crick. I will say as we went out of town, there was such a mournful howl set up by George's two large wolf hounds as I've ever heard in my life. They were tied with ropes to the hitching post at the side of the café and resented every second of it and were letting the whole world know their feelings on the matter. I never did know where George's truck with the rest of his "Herd'O dogs" was, but I reckoned they weren't far; they never were far from their beloved master.

When we passed through the tall grassy pasture and entered the brushy creek bottom, everyone readied their shoot'n irons for action, including me. That was about the time Ed broke his shotgun open and checked his loads to make sure he had both chambers full. Eddy worked the lever action on his rifle and chambered a round, and then eased the hammer down. I also saw grandpa slowly take out his long barreled pistol and earring back the hammer to half cock, he rotated the cylinder and then set the hammer down easy over an empty chamber for safety. Seeing all this preparation, made me also want to be ready and so I hefted my rifle up and was just about to cock it, when I inadvertently pulled the trigger and shot Eddy Mehan, my friend and neighbor right in the foot.

You talk about instant pandemonium, when one fella shoots another in a small hunting party, accident or otherwise, it sure did spark a small explosion.

Eddy howled and jumped, and all I can say is, I'm thinking it might have been a lesson for everyone, for Eddy dropped his own rifle, grabbed his foot and hopped around howling and cussing. And dropping one's own rifle while alligator hunting, in my opinion is a very bad thing, therefore I felt like it was a good lesson for everyone to see what "Not to do". I'm sorry to say, it wasn't looked upon nor perceived by the rest of our alligator hunting expedition as the learning experience it could have been.

Archie Matthews

Grandpa gave me a stern look and said, "You're going to have to be a lot more careful than THAT, if you're going to keep your shoot' n iron….be careful where you're pointing that thing."

"Danged kid…." Eddy scowled as he pulled his shoe off his foot and rubbed the top of it giving me a hard look, he replaced his shoe.

Ed had his back to us and I couldn't tell if he was keeping a look out towards the crick and alligators or was blowing his nose, for he kept snorting and blowing as his shoulders hunched forward.

"Oh, yeah, just you laugh Ed Shotz…..wait till the little beast shoots your eye out….then we'll see who laughs!" grumped Eddy as he bent over and picked up his rifle and once again gave me a wicked look.

"Sorry, about that Eddy…..I didn't know it was cocked…..I won't shoot your foot again." I offered apologetically.

"Well just see that you don't…..watch where you point that thing." Eddy grumbled.

I quickly cocked another BB into the chamber and this time, kept my finger outside the trigger guard. And seeing everyone giving me a baleful stare, I smiled and nodded my head towards the direction I was keeping my rifle pointed, which was away from everyone.

George hadn't said a word but he kept giving everyone a strange look and nodding, as if these kinds of little accidents happened to everyone and shouldn't be held against a fellow. That's when I suspected, I might not have been the first one to accidently fire his rifle and wound a hunting partner….it seemed George kept nodding like it could happen to anyone…..at least I'd been allowed to keep my rifle….and my bullets……so far.

"That's okay…..it happens….happens to the best of em….yup, a man's gun goes off mighty easy it does….sometimes just like it's got a mind to itself....yup, mighty easy....don't worry....it happens...Poor fella.....poor fella....gun just went off...." George kept mumbling with that odd look in his eye.

And with the decorum restored to our little hunting expedition, Grandpa urged the party to spread out and form a line with everyone facing the creek. I thought that was a really good idea, since that way it seemed less likely anyone else might get shot. So everyone spread out and we were all about four foot apart as we approached the crick surrounded by trees and as we eased out of the brush, Grandpa cleared his throat and warned, "Watch out now for that old sow....no telling where she's at...."

"Oh no Arch....she ain't around anymore....nope ain't seen her....maybe she got et by that alligator.....but I ain't seen her.....she's gone, the cubs is gone, ever thing gets gone when them baby alligators come out.....yup, ever time, ever year.....gone." mumbled George his rifle in one hand and his bullet still clutched in the other.

Well now, I don't know about the others, but that news made my neck hairs stand up and be counted. I didn't know much about baby alligators, but I supposed if there were enough of them to eat a sow bear, let alone her cubs; I was more than a little concerned. That's when I decided to put my finger inside the trigger guard.....just to be on the safe side.

The news had the same effect on both Ed and Eddy, for their eyes had swiveled right around to give old George the up and down, all the while opening up a couple sizes bigger. That's when I saw Ed, slowly cock the hammers on his huge shotgun and Eddy eared back the hammer on his rifle. But Grandpa just kept focused on the direction to the crick as we continued walking.

We were just to the top of the crick bank and everyone was ready to ease down through the tangle of trees, fallen tree trunks and brush that surrounds every crick, when grandpa stopped and held up a hand in the air. "What's that sound?"

Archie Matthews

Everyone stopped and ears perked up and our heads began to swivel around, each of us trying our best to make out where the ever increasing rustling sound was coming from

"Look OUT...The Gators is rushing us!" howled George as he pointed back towards the way we'd just come.

Now if my neck hairs hadn't already been standing to full attention, the shout that we were being "Rushed by Gators" sure would have done it. As it turned out the only thing I had left to stand on end in the hair department, were my eyebrows. With the sudden news we were about to be set on by what I imagined was a whole herd of man eating alligators, both my eyebrows shot up so hard they knocked my hat to the back of my head.

Everyone turned to face the rustling brush that seemed to stretch several dozen yards side to side and a good hundred yards back, from my vantage point. Everyone took deadly aim and prepared to meet our man eating foe with a bloody fusillade of lead and gun smoke.

And then there was poor old George.....

George, having perceived that now was as good a time as ever to load his single, alligator killing bullet, threw open the bolt to his large bore bear rifle and putting in the bullet quickly closed the bolt. The startling result of which was to see the bullet come sliding out the end of his rifle barrel and drop to the ground.

I have to admit, it didn't have the same startling effect it had on me, as it did on George, when I saw the bullet come sliding out the barrel, my mouth just dropped clear open. But good old George never missed a beat, he just picked up the bullet and sticking it back in the barrel opening, he quickly tipped the rifle barrel up. Dropping to one knee, George was instantly ready for all comers and took deadly aim at the approaching horde. Totally oblivious to the fact that he was facing a man eating horde of approaching alligators absolutely defenseless.

The Idaho Alligators

If things hadn't been so tense, I might have laughed or even cried, to think of poor old George down on one knee defenseless; his bullet too small to even stay in the breach of his gun, let alone not slid out the barrel.

And then it suddenly dawned on me, I faced the same scary end what with me and only a BB gun.

Only these men, with nerves of steel, each one a hardened mountain hunting veteran with years of experience kept a lot of innocent creatures from dying that day, for not a shot was fired before the horde broke from the brush, and a good thing.

The wave of dogs that came boiling out of the underbrush was nothing more than George's faithful herd looking for their beloved master. As the first wave broke cover, and seeing their goal within sight, gave such a joyful baying and howling that it liked to set the whole country to barking, or so it seemed as the rest of the herd of dogs began to wail and sing George's praises.

I saw grandpa give a huge sigh of relief and then give George a wide smile as we watched the white haired dog lover disappear into a sea of loving frolicking dogs. Ed and Eddy were both a bit shaken, both turned back to face the crick and stood breathing deeply, trying to ease the tension that had worked up inside them.

I on the other hand was shaking like a leaf having just been rescued from the veritable jaws of death, by the happy scene of George's dogs. I was just lifting up my BB gun and had set it in the crook of my arm, when my finger once again accidently touched off the trigger. I saw Ed to my right, which happened to be in direct line of my rifle barrel, grab at his ear, give a shout and he too accidently cut loose a round.

The "Booming" effect, shocked Eddy into instant pandemonium and he dropped to one knee, quickly noted the direction Ed's shotgun was pointed, which happened to be towards the crick,

Archie Matthews

and he began to lever round after round into the trees along the crick bottom.

Eddy's rifle fire ignited the powder keg of tension and everyone was firing into the woods by the crick, including myself and Grandpa. Ed, too began loading and firing and loading and firing his big old shotgun. After a few seconds of rapid fire and the evident lack of knowledge of the more modern "Smoke-less powder", there was such a bluish white smoke cloud that the crick was all but obscured, when as suddenly as it began the firing stopped.

"What in the world were you shooting at Ed?!" wailed Eddy.

Ed reached up and began to rub his sore ear, "A dern ground hornet up and stung me on the ear...but I was shooting at whatever it was you guys were shooting at!"

Eddy quickly stood up and stepped over to Ed and said, "Lemme see that ear.....did he sting you or did he bite you....their bites the worst." And then reaching up and touching Ed's ear for a second ....Eddy shot me a look and said, "YUP, you been bit.....them bites hurt like the devil don't they....." and Eddy turned away from Ed and immediately got as big a grin as a man can hatch without his head bursting in two.

Grandpa also turned away from Ed and gave me a knowing look as Eddy walked by him with his palm open and stepping up to me, there in his palm was a small golden colored BB fresh from Ed's dimpled ear.

"Well, let's get on with it, and watch them dern ground hornets!" Grandpa warned, giving me a stern look. Everyone once again, including George began to quickly move towards the crick, dogs and all, through the bluish haze of gun smoke.

Suddenly we were all standing by the slow moving water that ebbed in this little back slough, for the main crick was still several yards off. Then with an exasperated shout, both human's and dogs stopped dead in their tracks and everything got instantly quiet. For there in the water in front of us lay a billion and one "Baby Alligators".

"Well, I'll be!" shouted grandpa.....

"Oh my lord!" whispered Ed

"Will you just look at that?!" sputtered Eddy.

I have to admit, I couldn't even say a word. All I could do was stand there and take it all in, for they were everywhere. In the water, some floating, some creeping along the bottom, a lot of them were laying up on the muddy banks, strewn over many a log and rock. It was the most amazing sight I'd ever seen at the time, and to hear George tell about it, it happened about the same time every year. He'd evidently seen the phenomenon for years and was the least surprised of anyone.

"Yup, there they are! Every year the rascals are here....baby alligators as far as you can see...." Wailed George....."But they never Et my dog Wilbur before.....the evil little devils.....which one you suppose did it?.....do you suppose there's a big'un?.....or one of these little buggers did the dirty deed?"

"Oh, shut up you nut......We'll be the laughing stock of the entire county...."wailed Ed.

"This is your fault Arch....it was your grandson started this.....baby alligators !" snorted Eddy and without another word from either he or Ed, they both stomped off back towards town.

"WILBUR !" screamed George as he spied his lost coon hound coming around the far end of the water inlet, "Wilbur.....you're alive!"

And a more cheerful reunion you've never seen, as when George laid eyes on his missing coon hound. There would have been a wild hugging session, no doubt, if it hadn't been for poor

Archie Matthews

old Wilbur's entire head being filled and swollen up with festering porcupine quills.

"What did that alligator do to you?" wailed George, "He's fit you full of porcupine quills......I didn't know alligators had porcupine quills?....don't you worry Wilbur.....I got you now, I'll git you home and we'll pull these quills out and fetch that nasty old gater some payback later...."

George picked up poor old Wilbur and with his herd now whole he and his "Boys" headed back to town, complete with two huge Irish wolf hounds dragging a hitching post.

That left just me and Grandpa standing there looking at the pool with all those baby alligators, and I looked at grandpa and he smiled back at me.

"Well Grandpa, what now?" I asked, being real careful where I pointed my BB gun.

"Well, my lad," Grandpa said as he reached down and picked up one of the baby alligators, "It's time to kill this rumor once and for all...we're going to take this fella back to the house and have a talk with your cousin Micky."

And after a long quiet walk back to town, with our wet little captive in hand, we stepped through the gate, up the walk and entered the house. There sitting at the dining room table were all three boys and grandma, having a piece of pie and a glass of milk each. Everyone with a blue berry smile as happy as you please right up until Grandpa pulled the slimy little captive out of his pocket and held it up for everyone to see.

"ALLIGATOR !" screamed Micky and shot out of his chair and out the back porch door as if his tail had been doused with gasoline and set afire.

"Hey, that's a newt.......oh....." said Dean with sudden realization.

The Idaho Alligators

"Yup…..That's a newt." Grandpa smiled.

In wrapping up my little story, I'd like to say that my cousin Micky soon forgot about "Baby Alligators"….I'd like to say it, but sadly, it wasn't to be. Poor Micky wouldn't ever go back to the crick swimming with us again after seeing that huge pool of newts. Fact is, he was as jumpy around any kind of water as you could shake a stick at, still is to this day.

His mother claimed he wouldn't even take a bath inside unless he had something firmly wedged in the drain hole and could see the bottom of the tub clear as a bell. Oh, and you might wonder what had chewed up his legs that first day of sighting the infamous "Baby Alligators"? Well so did me and Grandpa, and on our way back to the house, we'd taken a little stroll along Micky's escape route. And just as Grandpa figured, there was a knee high bramble of blackberry bushes with a trail cut right through the thorny entanglement. It seems blackberry thorns will chew you up just as quick if not quicker than baby alligators will. To this day, my cousin Micky swears that summer he saw "Baby alligators" and nothing will change his mind.

Old George, well, he never was right in the head, but a kinder soul there never was. He mumbled about gators for years and then as with many things, gators were all but forgotten by George and replaced with other concerns. One thing that did hang on and on and on, was that bullet, the one grandpa had given him. Yup, it was one of his much smaller pistol rounds, Ed and Eddy had noticed it right off and each had been just as surprised as if Grandpa had given him a rifle round. But as both will vehemently attest to, they felt a "WHOLE LOT SAFER" with George just having that pistol shell.

But old George carried that pistol shell in his pocket like ole' Barney Fife in an Andy Griffith show. Sure, sure, there were times that old George would pull his "Bullet" from his pocket and put it down his barrel, as if he were loading an old muzzle loader. And after a while, he even got past letting it slide back down the

Archie Matthews

barrel to drop harmlessly from the end......well, all except that one time, but that's another story.

And what about that coon dog Wilbur? Wow, talk about a head full of quills. Old George was as good as his word, he took good ole Wilbur home and "Pulled Quills for a week solid", or so George always claims.

I will say this, I seen the dog several days later and sure enough you could see where another quill had come up and surfaced and George would get it pulled out. In fact, as usually happens with dogs that tangle with a porcupine. Wilbur gained a vehement hatred for porcupines and never passed up a chance to get even with one alongside the trail, the only thing is, he never did get even. But from that day on, practically every time I seen that dog, one body part or another was full of quills and George was forever trying to pull them out.

We all just figured the dog and George got separated and what with Wilbur fighting that porcupine, he didn't hear his master calling. Who's to say if George heard the dog yelp at getting poked, or just couldn't find his prize coon hound, but he was genuinely sure that his "Boy Wilbur" had been "Et" by an alligator, and George was adamant for "Payback"!

And the pool of "Baby Alligators?" or "Newts" as they turned out, were just water salamanders, the kind that are found in many a mountain stream. That pool to my knowledge is still there, and for many a year every summer, us kids would go down to watch the newts congregate there in that back slew, by the hundreds of thousands.

But never was it as exciting to see as it was the summer cousin Micky saw them as "Baby Alligators".

The Idaho Alligators

His Name Was Dewey

It all began with my wife going back to work as a "Para Educator" at the local grade school. Since we had successfully raised our kids to adulthood, my beloved wife decided she wanted to go out into the world and help raise other people's children. (Ho-boy howdy, was it a learning lesson for everyone, and I don't just mean the kids either.)

I had just come home from a long day at my job, where I had been battling the injustices of the world for a local government agency, when I sat down in my easy chair recliner for a moment of respite. Kicking off my boots and preparing to ease back for some much needed relaxation, I spotted what appeared to be a paper cup setting on the coffee table next to my chair. If I had only known then what I know now, I'd have run screaming from the room, but hindsight does no good when it comes to "Dangerous Dixie Cups".

Reaching over, I picked up the cup and since I was in the reclined position in my chair, I brought the cup close to my face and peered within. There right under my nose was what appeared to be muddy water, with a strange little black dot "bobbing" around occasionally breaking the surface.

Being in my fifties and never seeing such a thing before, I curiously poked my finger into the cup of water and touched the little black dot, trying my best to figure out what it might be.

That's when my "beloved" came sauntering into the room and said, "Oh, you've found "Dewey's pet", which gave me a vague bit of insight, for just that morning my wife Suzy had told me she and her class of second graders were going on a "Nature hike". Furthermore, in past conversations she had mentioned several of her pupils' names, and one child had stood out as a bit of a character, and his name I remembered was "Dewey".

"What the heck kind of pet could be bobbing around in this muddy water?" I asked with a bit of a smile, thinking it appeared to be just a piece of black flotsam, a piece of bark or rotted vegetation, for it just seemed to "bob" along and not really move or exhibit traits of actual swimming.

"Oh, it's some kind of black swimming worm….." my unwitting wife slash educator began to explain, just as I began to take my finger from the cup and saw a long black wiggling tendril attached to the end of my finger.

"LEACH!" I shouted as I rocketed forward out of my reclined chair, the Dixie cup of water all but forgotten, until it rocketed

His Name Was Dewey

across the room and spilled its contents all over my surprised wife.

"It's a dern leach!" I shouted as I gained my feet and stood before my Dixie cup drenched wife and her fuming look of disgust. (It's rather annoying standing before your water soaked wife, with her pupils pet leach attached to your finger, while she glares at you in petty disgust for having splashed her.)

Running into the kitchen, I began rifling through the cupboards. It's amazing all the stuff my wife keeps in her immaculately arranged kitchen, it's even more astounding that I've lived in this house for years with the woman and still don't have any idea where anything's at. And need I say, it's not easy rummaging through cabinets with a leach attached to your dominant hands index finger.

"Why on earth are you destroying my kitchen and what are you searching for?" shouted Suzy following me into the kitchen.

Seeing an opening between me and my next victim, my beloved wife took the defensive line and thrust her palm out stopping my next attack on her organized cupboard.

"I need some salt!" I calmly explained, even though to this day, she claims I "Wailed" the answer, if not "Sobbed" it.

"What in heavens name do you need with salt? You're not planning on eating the thing are you?" My exasperated life partner blurted, totally unaware that salt on a leach is like a blow torch to an ice cube, which was just the result I was looking for.

"If you haven't noticed, I have a LEACH attached to my finger!" I announced, lifting my index finger for her inspection. The perceptively larger leach, had already grown from a one inch long, thin ribbon, to the size of my little finger, engorged on the blood it was sucking from the end of my poor digit.

Archie Matthews

"I want some salt to dash on this bugger so he'll melt and die!" I hastily explained, all the while waggling the ever growing parasite before my wife's still dripping wet face.

"Oh no, you can't kill, Dewey! Just take your pocket knife and scrape him off. I'll get the cup and put some water in it and you can scrape him off into it." My maniacal leach loving wife ordered, giving me her no nonsense glare. "Go on now; don't just stand there with that stupid look on your face! And please close your mouth if you're going to make those awful caveman grunting noises."

And there you have it, long story short, the Dixie cup soon once again held "Dewey the leach", although a much fatter, bloated version, while I and my somewhat drained index finger were soon back in my chair. But, needless to say, I was NOT reclined, nor relaxed after having been feasted upon. Funny how having a living creature attached to one of your appendages, sucking out your life's blood will do that to you, or so I explained to my wife all evening, as she kept trying to get me to "just sit back and relax".

I won't go into morbid detail about the disgusting dreams I had all that night, or several nights afterwards. I will say; that no matter how thirsty I got in bed those nights, I just couldn't bring myself to sip water out of the glass on my night stand next to the bed. Instead every night, I had to get up and walk into the bathroom, turn on the light and make sure there wasn't a vile leach ready and waiting for me in my water glass.

The next week or two slowly passed with declining thoughts and dreams about the evil blood sucker and soon life returned to normal, "Dewey's evil pet" was all but forgotten.

I and my beautiful wife Suzy live on our six acres, which I refer to as our "Big Montana Cattle Ranch", due to the fact I always wanted to own a big cattle ranch in Montana, but Selah Washington was as far as I got. (Although only six acres, trust me, when I tell you it's plenty "BIG", especially when your

His Name Was Dewey

working your backside off mending fences and the thousand and one other chores that must be done.)

I arose that next Saturday morning bright and early and went about doing my chores. I fed the livestock and filled the water troughs in both the sheep and cattle pens, and after feeding and watering the pig, I proceeded up the back walk towards the house. On the way back to the house, I passed by my wife's little "Lilly pond", which is really only an old cast iron bathtub sitting above the ground filled full of water and water lilies. I noticed it was a bit low on water too and the lilies were looking a bit sad for lack of a full pond.

Although not particularly a "Lilly pond" fan, I had grown quite fond of the convenient tub full of water. For more than once, while tinkering around in my blacksmith shop, I'd accidently set myself aflame, and that handy extinguishing puddle had saved the day, if not a lot of my hide. Therefore, I never minded giving my wife a hand with her gardening chores and grabbing a nearby hose, I topped off her lily pond. Thus doing my good deed for the day, I smiled with a bit of satisfaction at my "thoughtfulness". (As any married man will tell you, wimmen are always craving thoughtfulness from their husbands, and mine is no different.).

Stepping into the kitchen, I was immediately greeted by my devoted wife, with a hot cup of coffee in hand and a big smile, and right away I knew my helpful little tub topping off had been witnessed through the window over the kitchen sink and appreciated. And it was with coffee cup in hand and a fresh peck on the cheek that I went merrily back outside and into my blacksmith shop.

I won't bore you with the details of the stoking of the coal fire or the hours I spent that early May morning enjoying heating up bars of iron and working them between anvil and hammer. I will say, I had just fashioned a couple of gate hinges and was just making a slight modification to the latch, when I accidently knocked the red hot latch pin off the edge of the anvil and into the rolled up cuff of my pant leg.

Archie Matthews

Anyone with a lick of sense knows when red-hot iron encounters cloth, combustion in the form of flames is immediate, and thus, my pant leg was instantly on FIRE!

Now I don't know about you, but when I burst into flames, I instinctively begin to give the world notice, and scream at the top of my lungs, "FIRE"! I've never practiced this art of notification nor given it much thought, it's more of a purely instinctive act. I imagine it's to allow any and everyone between me and a water source, fair warning that I am coming and coming fast.

To this day all three of my younger brothers often tease me after having seen me on fire many times, and remark that there is no need for me to scream I am on fire. As they so jovially point out, the flames, smoke and the utter look of terror on my face, always give everyone ample warning to get out of the way. As I remind them, the screaming isn't really an act of thought or planning, as much as it just happens the second after combustion. I have absolutely no thoughtful control over it, nor am I going to give thoughtful consideration as to stopping or stifling the screams, for when on fire I have far too many other things on my mind. The main train of thought being, where is the closest water source and is it big enough to get what ever part of me is aflame, submerged and extinguished as fast as humanly possible.

It was thus, that I quickly proceeded out the shop door, shouting "FIRE," and good thing, for as I exited with fully engulfed pant leg, I almost ran into and over my astonished wife who had been coming to give me a heat up on my coffee. Unable, or unwilling to slow my speed and exchange pleasantries, I went around her like a drunken driver trying to avoid a telephone pole in the middle of the road. Or should I say, I "Mostly" went around her, for as I went by I side swiped her, sending the coffee pot sailing across the yard.

It's strange how even though my mind was busy calculating distance, speed and wind velocity in my desperate flight towards the lily pond, I had time enough in which to hear my evil queens prophecy of impending torture as she shouted, "OH, are you in trouble mister!"

As if having ones body aflame wasn't torture enough, and despite the flesh searing off my leg bone, I needed to be sorry for knocking a pot of coffee across the yard. (But as I have stated earlier, "WIMMIN!" Their odd creatures with strange priorities as to how a fellow should conduct himself while aflame......but enough of that and back to the story).

After traveling what seemed like several miles at break neck speed, all the while battling hurricane force headwinds, finally the large bathtub slash lily pond loomed in the distance. And with every ounce of remaining energy I had, I desperately launched my searing flesh up and into the puddle of salvation.

With an enormous "Splash" I landed with both feet, boots, flaming, pant leg and all, right smack dab amongst the lilies. And after quenching the flames, my fire notification system began to power down and most of the screaming stopped. But as you can imagine, this only allowed my wife's screaming to be heard as she came skidding to a stop at the bathtubs edge. It seems after her initial fit of my knocking the coffee pot a flying, somewhere along that several miles of my running ablaze, streaming a black smoke trail and screaming fire, she realized I was in trouble and had followed along.

After a full twenty minute "Safety Meeting", the brunt of the one sided discussion being, "How I should NOT catch on fire and scare my wife to death", I promised to "Never do it again". Which just elicited another twenty minute "Rant" of how I always say that, but I "continually do all kinds of things again and AGAIN!"

(Note to self; Wimmen are soooo dramatic right after a person catches fire, geez. Might be a menopause thing, but I'd wait until she calms down to ask.....say in her seventies or eighties.)

Therefore it was almost an hour of sitting on the edge of the cast iron bathtub, before nurse Suzy decided I'd better roll up my pant

Archie Matthews

leg so she could assess the damage and the amount of burn ointment and bandages I was going to cost her. Taking my feet and legs out of the water and swiveling on my now, numb butt bone, I turned around and pulled my charred pant leg up to expose my scorched calf.

"Oh, it's not burned bad, it's only a little……" and I was about to say, "Singed", but upon seeing my now exposed leg, I screamed "LEACH"! For there, dead center in the middle of my lightly toasted calf muscle, was an incredibly large black leach.

"Oh, Dewey, so you are still alive!" my demented significant other called out.

"DEWEY!? " I shouted unbelievingly, "You mean this is that same dern leach that you brought home a week ago and set on me?"

"Oh now, it wasn't like that…and you know it. I couldn't just let little Dewey die, could I?" The Fiend, (also known as my wife) so innocently asked with her big blue loving eyes. "Every creature has a right to live, eat and breath…..don't they?" she asked so sweetly.

It was at this juncture, that I actually considered hitting her over the head, but all I had within reach was a large blood engorged leach. I must admit, I did fantasize about the newspaper headlines reading, "Wife beaten to unconsciousness with bloated leach, husband acquitted of all charges". But as tempting as it might have been, I knew the crooked legal system in this state would never acquit me, male or female judge. After all, I'm not stupid enough to overlook even the male judges have influencing wives.

"Rights…..Rights?! What kind of "Rights" should a leach have?!" I shouted more than a little bit exasperated.

"I don't know about the civil liberties of parasites, let alone a leach! I do know the bugger's eat'n me again and I am NOT

His Name Was Dewey

HAPPY!" I said with as much disgust as I thought safe to use around my wife, and not end up mysteriously drown't in my own lily pond with a leach, stuffed you know where.

Being married to my wife is like being in the Mafia; one has to be very careful you don't offend the "Boss" and risk getting "Whacked". It's a scary thing to be married to a woman that travels with a shovel and a bag of lime in her trunk, not to mention the little "Map" she keeps in her cars glove box of "Pre-dug holes".

Once again, I will spare you the gory details of scraping a fully engorged blood sucking leach off my leg. Nor will I describe in detail the fuming anger at watching the "Freak Show Zoo manager" march off with her pet leach "Dewey". I will say, it's a good thing we had some large red plastic cups left from the last BBQ we had, because the monster leach wouldn't have been comfortable in a little Dixie cup any longer.

After she so lovingly bedded down "Dewey" in his red solo cup'o water, I was hastily smeared with burn ointment and given a wrap or two of bandage and sent back to my blacksmith shop.

Authors note; (Any husband reading this, it is NOT against the rules to beat on iron while thinking about specific individuals and the injustices that you've had to endure.....wives included.....no matter who says what, the wife cannot read your mind, even though they give you THAT look and say, "I know what your thinking!"......it's a bluff; if it weren't I'd be laying in one of those "lime lined holes" if my Mafia Boss actually knew what I had been thinking.....and I don't just mean that particular time either.)

Another several days of shivered thoughts and sweat filled nightmares complete with blood sucking leaches, life eventually returned once again to normal; or as my wife would say, "As normal as life can be while being married to me".

After another week of working and toiling "for the man", once again I and my beloved wife were home again spending a quiet weekend together. That is right up until I heard the blood curdling scream from Suzy coming from the back pasture. Being in my blacksmith shop again, with iron in the fire, waiting for the intricately wrought piece of steel to heat up, I instantly dropped everything and ran for my wife.

As I flew through the shop door, another loud terror filled scream echoed from between the hay barn and sheep pens and I was quick to follow the horrendous reverberations. Even our large guard dog Chester had heard the screams and was just in front of me as we rounded the corner, each of us ready to fight what ever was threatening our beloved Suzy.

Why is it dogs always get right smack dab in front of a person, and then stop? Here we were making remarkable progress together, ready to tackle wild Indians, grizzer ba'rs or even attacking aliens, what ever the case may be, when "Man's Best Friend" stops and decides to throw a monkey wrench into our rescue.

And once again a wild scream broke out, but this time it was filled full of "expletives" that I can't mention here, as I crashed into and over my big red Chesapeake Bay retriever, in a tangle of arms, legs and snapping jaws. (As in the past, I felt immediately sorry for my snapping jaws, but I've never really bitten him, just snapped and cursed a bit....but again, not to worry, the curse has never taken effect and Chester still has his tail.)

After a short roll of flailing human and dog legs, I and Chester were immediately back upon our feet and there just a few feet away, looking somewhat haggard, was our beloved Suzy, her eyes wild, her finger pointing into the sheep pen.

Hurrying forward, I was astonished to see our large sheep ram "Buck" with an enormous swollen black nose hanging down like a short elephant's trunk. His head was down, his eyes rolling around like wheels on a slot machine, and his tail wagging back and forth, sheep scat flying out his back end as if it were an

His Name Was Dewey

immense pay off from a Vegas Casino. The other sheep were all cowered in the far corner as if instinctively knowing that their Male counter part had something seriously wrong with him.

To say that the situation was "strange and puzzling'", would be to say the least, and opening the gate, I stepped in for a closer look. But, Buck wasn't about to stand still for any kind of handling, and as he had always done in the past, we began to go around and around the pen, circling as two WWF wrestlers do trying to size up their opponents.

Long story short, with Suzy and Chester both barking their encouragement, it wasn't long and only after three or four failed tackles and only having been kicked like nine times, I got Buck down and lay panting atop the brute. When I said it "wasn't long", I meant in comparison to most times, when it can take me at least a dozen failed tackles, two dozen kicks and one or two charging head butt's from the brute before I can get him wrestled down.

Buck being the breed male, likes to think he's the dominant one, and therefore I rarely challenge his authority and try to let him have his little fantasy. Yet once in a while, about two times a year, I am forced to exert my own dominance and show him just which one of us is "Boss"; no matter how many bruises to his ego, or my body have to occur in order for his feet to get trimmed and his yearly dose of "Wormer".

After a few minutes of catching my breath, at which time, Suzy so lovingly handed it back to me, for I was way to exhausted to have caught it myself, I "scooched" up Bucks body and straddled his head to take a better look at his enormously swollen nose. That's when dear Suzy knelt down lovingly to take Buck's head into her lap as she usually did with our beloved herd as I doctored them.

My extraordinary wife has the remarkable ability of being able to sooth even the most savage beast, while I have to tend to all kinds of unsavory tasks about their anatomy. Her kind soft

Archie Matthews

hands and cooing gentle voice always not only calms the one we are directly working with, but also the nearby herd. That is right up until the point she screamed "LEACH!" into my left ear and nearly broke both my neck and Buck's in her panicked attempt to "Abandon Ship". For if you've ever seen a panicked seafarer that just realized they were in a sinking ship and about to be sucked under and into a devouring pool of blood, thus my helper abandoned not only her husband and the wild eyed Buck, but also "DEWEY".

Yes, for that's exactly what the huge black appendage hanging down from Buck's nose turned out to be. There hung the blood bloated leach my wife had so lovingly called Dewey. How long the blood sucker had been affixed to poor old Bucks nose is anyone's guess. But, since we feed and tend our animals both morning and night, it could've been attached all night long, and from the immense size of it, I'd say it had been feeding most of the night.

Once again, I will spare you the gory details of disengaging a blood engorged distended leach from a terrified ram's nose. A dose of antibiotic and a cold pack applied to the wound, no matter how under appreciated it was all received, and Buck was allowed up and back about his business. Which seemed to be trying his best to convince his "Ladies" he should no longer be treated as a "Parriah" and allowed back amongst them, but from their immediate hesitation, I could tell this next year we might have some mighty late lambs.

And this time, with Dewey lying upon the bottom of a galvanized bucket recently filled out of the trough, Suzy assured me, she was NOT going to once again turn the leach loose in one of our water troughs.

"Nor the lily pond?!" I quickly warned.

"Nor the lily pond!" Suzy remarked as she gave a little shutter and tromped off, bucket in hand.

His Name Was Dewey

"OH NO!!" I shouted, remembering I had left the final piece of my metal project still in the forge and still in the intense fire.

Running back into my blacksmith shop and to the blazing hot forge, I quickly grabbed the long end of warm steel at the far end away from the fire. Pulling out the steel, once again a loud agonizing scream echoed across the six acres, for the end that had been in the fire, was completely melted away and gone. Thus a week of hot, hard work pounding and shaping, reheating, and more pounding and shaping had been ruined and all because of the leach named Dewey.

To say I was beginning to hate that parasite, would have been a lie, for I had immediately formed THAT opinion of the leach named Dewey the first day I'd laid eyes upon it.....or should I say index finger.

But with the final assurance that Suzy had been just as appalled at our last encounter with the Devil Leach Dewey, as he so appropriately became known as. I felt confident my wife would dispose of the vile thing once and for all. (But little did I take into the account of female reasoning, let alone wife reasoning...and more specifically, "Suzy Reasoning".)

And life on the farm that summer, fall and winter came and went until the glorious holiday of Christmas arrived. I love Christmas, our savior's birthday, the family gathering, the sights and smells.

That Christmas morning was magnificent, the girls were home with their families, packages, a magnificent breakfast cooked by the loving hands of wife and daughters, the men sitting around visiting and the grandkids playing with their newfound toys. To say life was grand would have been but to touch upon the tip of the iceberg.

And then as instructed, us guys moved the dining room table into the bigger back room attached to the back of the house, the big room with sky lights and huge windows, the room we referred to as the "Solarium". The largest room in the house besides the living room, yet the living room held couches, chairs and end tables, while the solarium only held a couple thin book cases and a huge fish tank.

Ever since I was a kid, I'd loved and grown up with aquariums. I not only enjoyed watching the fish "bob" and swim around, but I also particularly enjoyed the thick large green plants that our four hundred gallon Plexiglas fish tank held.

Yes, those of you that have fish tanks will agree, although a bit of work to clean and maintain, there is nothing like a living green aquarium in a home. I especially loved to watch the fish in the evenings with all the lights but the tank light turned off. The bright tank light lit all but the darkest back regions of the tank, where only behind the enormous large Amazon Sword plant and big chunk of drift wood, could the shadows remain.

And it was when we were moving the table and putting in the leaf extensions to make the table long enough to seat all of us, that I noticed my beloved fish tank had some green algae on the prominent side facing the dinner table. Since it was still early in the day, I had lots of time to spread a cloth upon the table and remove plants and filters and drift wood and such and give the tank a thorough cleaning, and it was towards that end that I began to proceed.

Yet, it was not to be, for my dear wife caught me and lovingly convinced me it was in my own best interest not to make a mess, and that the "Fish tank is fine". Yet, as any aquarium connoisseur will attest, a little algae problem can turn into a big algae problem very quickly….as do a lot of other problems, but are so often over looked by husbands, as my wife so readily points out.

So it was just before dinner, while the women were at their busiest in the kitchen, mashing yams and mixing gravy, buttering the brown tops of their rolls as they came out of the oven with that little paint brush, that I seized my opportunity to go unnoticed and do a quick algae scrape. Taking an old credit card out of my aquarium cleaning kit and shoving a chair up to the tank, I quickly rolled up my sleeve and began scrapping the sidewall glass of its algae deposit.

Fate is forever fickle in it's dealings with me….or is it "Murphey's Law" that the worst possible thing will occur at the most unlikely time?....something like that. I am not sure, other than to tell you…..my whole life has been full of "Happenings, tragedies, instances and turmoil", most of which wasn't even my fault, okay, maybe "Most" isn't quite accurate, but some of it wasn't my fault.

And there I was balanced on the dining room chair, as the solarium doors were thrust open and the women swooped in carrying all manner of food dishes. It wasn't until several trips of the girl's comings and goings that I was spotted, and then it was a trip or two after that, before in swooped the queen bee, complete with the turkey in her clutches. Let me tell you, if you've never seen a massive queen bee buzzing around angrily carrying a dead turkey, it's quite a sight. (Don't tell my wife I said that).

Seeing me with my arm in the fish tank, precariously balanced on her good dining room chair, despite her death threat "Not to", my beloved wife was well into the depths of the Christmas spirit and only mildly growled for me to "Get down and wash for Christmas dinner". Which I couldn't help but chuckle, since I've got my arm all the way to my arm pit in water, how much more "Washing" could I accomplish….but you know how wimmin are.

I soon finished as everyone began to pile into the solarium and seek their seats for the feast. I quickly stepped down and taking up a towel I had so thoughtfully laid out, I began drying my hands and was about to dry up my arm and roll down my shirt sleeve, when an ear piercing scream almost shattered the windows and what was left of my ear drums.

I whirled around to my right, and there was our oldest daughter with her hand over her mouth, her husband ashen white with his own look of terror and disbelief clearly etched on his face. (And when I say etched, ladies and gentlemen, I mean you can still see those little lines in his face today)

And then again, right behind me another and another gasp, then loud hair raising screams, turned me swiftly around yet again. There sat our other daughters with their men, faces aghast pointing their fingers at me.

And then I heard my wife's distinctive high pitched wine glass shattering scream, "DEWEY"!

Whirling around to face her, she pointed an accusing finger, I slowly raised my right arm, and sure enough….there was the enormous black leach named Dewey, hanging by the back of my right arm, looking like a huge blackened over cooked yam. And then, as if the strain of holding on by just his blood sucking mouth were to much for him, he fell off with a "Ker-Plop" right into an empty awaiting white dinner plate.

Well, at least I wouldn't have to explain how I scraped him off that time, for I didn't need to, since he just fell into the dinner plate like that. I also probably don't have to tell you, that was the shortest Christmas dinner on record, for having seen Dewey, everyone but myself lost their appetites.

After everyone immediately left the room, some for bathrooms, while others raced to both the front and back doors, to attend to their gag reflexes, I scooped up Dewey and back into the fish tank he went. After all, he was as much a part of me as any other critter ever had been, seeing he'd feasted on me most of his life. Besides, my dearly beloved had started all this, she could just fish him out of the aquarium in the spring and get rid of him. And at least now, I knew where the filthy blood sucker was, and wouldn't be sticking my arm in there again without paying close attention.

It must have been the half gallon he'd drained me of, but despite all the gagging noises and whining coming from the back bathrooms and bedrooms, I was hungry and for the first time in a

His Name Was Dewey

long time, there was enough of everything I liked, and even more so.

I'd like to tell you the rest of the Christmas vacation went off smooth and soon everyone got over seeing a massive leach attached to the old man at the dinner table....yup, I'd like to tell you that. But lets just say for several Christmas's afterwards, everything went well and their were always plenty of smiles and good cheer....that is right up until dinner time. Some how the Christmas smiles always seemed a bit strained at the table, and moods sobered more than just a bit as people would take their seat. Even years after we'd finally removed the large fish tank from the house, there always seemed to be haunting looks towards where it once was.

Oh, and Dewey you ask? What happened to Dewey?......hmmmm....funny you should ask. The next spring I made a little trip with a bucket of water back into the little town where my wife works. The internet is an amazing tool...with just a smattering of knowledge; it's truly remarkable all the information you can glean about people.

In fact, in our small town, a remarkable statistic that stood out to me on the internet was there are only three individuals with addresses in this school district with occupants named "Dewey". One of which happened to be on the front page of our local news paper just the other day.

 I seem to remember the headlines;

"Family in Selah Washington Attacked by a Giant Leach!"

"The Dewey family while swimming in their back yard pool, were horrified to find Mr. Dewey had an enormous leach attached to his buttocks as he exited the pool". No one seems to know how the leach got there, let alone it's immense size."

Well, I guess one "Dewey" eliminated......two more to go....

Archie Matthews

His Name Was Dewey

Uncle Tick's Shotgun

"I ain't gonna shoot that cannon!" I had said shaking my head, with my hands up, palms out doing my best to fend off the ancient double barreled shotgun my cousin Monte was trying to get me to take. "That blunderbuss will kick me into the next county, and I ain't ready for a backwards visit into the place." I joked.

"Oh you big wiener!" growled Monte, "Just put the butt of the stock up agin the tree here and pull the trigger, thar ain't gonna be no kick that way!"

"Nope, not me, it's your daddy's gun, you shoot it." I dared him.

"Well of all the....Okay, I'll do it you old lady!" grumbled Monte as he wheeled around and placing the butt of the stock firmly against the tree trunk. Cocking the only working hammer, he pulled the trigger, first one barrel and then the other roared. An eight foot flame shooting out the end of an ancient old shotgun is an amazing sight, but then as the double barrel bucked straight up with nowhere else to go, what with the butt of the stock up against the un-moving tree trunk, the second barrel went off.

Why Monte had loaded both barrels is still to this day, beyond me, but he had. Even more baffling was that although one of the two hammers would pull back and latch, the second hammer was broken and not only wouldn't latch when pulled back, but the spring that pulled it forward had no resistance left. Therefore as Monte had cocked the working hammer and fired that barrel, evidently the violent bucking of the shotgun upwards had flung the broken hammer back and forward with enough force that it too fired. The result of which, was as the gun bucked up into a forty-five degree angle, the second shot went off and brought the gun barrel all the way back and slammed into Monte's face, his head slammed back into the tree trunk and down he went like a wet sack of oats.

One minute I was watching the fireworks, two eight foot bright orange and blue flames erupting out the end of the old antique that hadn't been fired in years; the next moment, my cousin Monte lay dead at my feet. Seeing my dead cousin suddenly lying like a doll rag at my feet sent a cold shiver up my spine, not to mention what it did when it crept up under my hat. I know my

Uncle Tick's Shotgun

hat rose about a foot off my head as my hair suddenly leapt straight up and practically sent my hat flying.

It's a startling realization that one pull of a trigger, not to mention the second round firing accidently, can kill a fellow even when he's supposedly at the safer end of the gun.

It seemed like I had been nailed to the ground and all I could do was stand there, my hat hovering above my hair standing straight on end, my mouth wide open. It seemed like I'd stood there for about a full hour, when Monte's eyes suddenly shot open and he jumped to his feet and threw his hand up to his even now, blackening eye and began to yell his head off.

If it hadn't been so sudden and what with me still in shock, I'd have derided him for being a "cry baby". But since I'd witnessed the whole surprising event and Monte had missed half of it, what with his eyes being closed, he evidently didn't have the appreciation for the spectacle that I did. And without a moment's hesitation off he ran for the house, wailing all the way.

Now since his parents were away, as well as all his brothers and sisters, I didn't know why he was in such a hurry to get into the house, let alone scream for help like he was doing. Watching him make for the nearby house, I just stooped over and picked up the old blunderbuss and ambled along behind him.

When I got there Monte had grabbed a big towel and was dipping it in the water bucket on the front porch and holding it to his face. When I caught up and asked how he was doing, he took the towel down and I had my answer.

"WOW, now that's a shiner!" I exclaimed before realizing what dire consequences such a black eye was going to present when we told his parents what had gone on.

"Oh man, it feels like it blowed half my head off, Arch!" wailed Monte, dipping the towel back into the cool water and once again

Archie Matthews

bringing the sopping wet towel to his face. "Oh wait till ma see's this, oh ....Pa is going to kill us!" Monte moaned.

"Hmmm, well now....about that..." I stammered, "It's your daddy's shotgun, you took it from the mantle, loaded it and shot it......I guess I don't understand what dire part of this adventure I partook in, unless it was standing by and refusing to shoot it and then watching you do it!"

"Why you dirty rat! Benedict Arnold! Why would you rat me out....what'd I ever do to you? Ain't we kin....isn't it supposed to be one for all and all for one...like that dern movie? You'd just stand by and watch me hung and stand and clap your hands and probably shout 'hooray!' You traitor!" reviled Monte in a wild dancing stomping rage.

"Whoa there, whoa just a minute, suppose we just put the shotgun back up there on the mantel and just act like the whole thing didn't happen?" I offered, with a more than hopeful tone.

"How in the heck are we going to explain this!" Monte wailed as he once again lowered the towel and showed me a huge black eye on one side and a quickly darkening eye on the other side, not to mention his nose seemed to be trying to turn a corner where there wasn't even a corner.

"Ouch....say Monte, I'm thinking you might have a broken nose, and that other eye is starting to darken up a might." I warned with a bit of a grimace.

"What?!" shouted Monte, sopping towel and all, quickly ran inside and into his parents room to look in their big dresser mirror. And then with a loud gasp and a resounding wail, Monte shouted, "Oh, my nose, it's all crooked, my eyes is swelling shut and we're dead men, ma and pa is going to kill us!"

I quickly took the old double barrel shotgun and set it back in its place atop the fireplace on the big steel hangers that had been fashioned by my great grandpa Grumps so many years ago.

Uncle Tick's Shotgun

The story went that Grumps had carried that shotgun for years and years and only upon his having to relinquish all his firearms at the ripe old age of ninety, he'd bestowed upon uncle Tick, his ancient double barrel shotgun. It had set on the mantle for as long as I could remember, along with the two solid brass shotgun shells that set right beneath it.

"Oh drats!" I groaned as I went to the mantle and lifted down the shotgun again, hitting the lever that broke open the breach, I pulled out the fresh expended brass shot shells. One look and it was obvious as the dickens they'd been fired, for the rolled under edge stuck straight up and jagged, and where there had been a hard cardboard end was now just a gaping hole revealing an Empty shell.

Monte came trudging out of the bedroom with his sopping wet towel, his second blackening eye, exposed trying to see where he was going, and he slumped into his dads old chair in the corner. "What'cha doing there Arch? Oh don't tell me we cracked or broke the stock!" Monte moaned.

"Nope, but just as bad Monte, we didn't think about the shells, looky here." I explained as I held the two fired shot shells up and towards Monte so he could see they were accusingly empty.

"Oh NO!" wailed Monte, "That's it, we're dead men! Pa's awfully proud of that shotgun Grumps give him, not to mention those shells. He's been claiming for years he was saving those shells to kill a bear with, out' a respect to Grumps. That was Grumps Ba'r rifle, he shot many a bear with that old shotgun, and pa was always gonna get one with those last two shells. Oh Arch, why didn't we think of that before we stole't the gun and ruin't the shells?"

All I could do was just shrug, for sure enough, I hadn't given it any thought as we'd taken the shotgun out on kind of a lark and spur of the moment. I couldn't say there had been much thought on the matter, and none what so ever about the resulting repercussions when uncle Tick found out we'd wasted his

Archie Matthews

precious two shells. And then suddenly a marvelous idea just shot into the side of my head and stuck to my brain.

"Hey, Monte, when do your folks get back?" I quickly asked.

"Well, I expect them tomorrow, or the next day. I can't rightly say, they was supposed to leave Aunt Bessy and Tom's in Yakima today, and it takes a solid day of driving, but pa ain't much at driving after dark so I figure not tomorrow but the next day", Explained Monte..... "Why?"

"Well then, we got plenty of time!" I shouted with a wink, "I'll go back into town and talk to old Ed at the store and see if we can't get two more shells. He's always got old stuff a plenty, I'll just bet he's got a shell or two around. Sure, that's what we'll do!" I laughed relieved we might not be facing the hangman just yet.

"But what are we gonna say about my face? How are we going to explain that?" whined Monte.

"For crying out loud, do I have to be the entire brains of this outfit?" I replied, "I'm headed back to town, you think of something! I'm taking your horse, unless you want to drive me back to town?"

"Take him, I'll pick him up or you can ride him back with those shells, good luck. If you don't think of something or come up with another couple brass shells, it's been nice knowing you." Monte replied from under his wet towel.

I saddled up Monte's horse and rode back to town, for I was only twelve and didn't drive. All the way home I thought more and more about finding a couple brass shells and then I realized if I couldn't do that, I knew Ed Shotz the general store owner reloaded his own shells as did Eddy Mehan the Café owner. The way I figured it, if I couldn't buy shells, I might be able to just reload the ones I now carried in my pocket.

Getting back to town early, I unsaddled Monte's horse and turned him into the back pasture and going into the house, I sat down and visited with Grandma.

Grandpa had passed a couple years prior of a massive heart attack and grandma was holding onto the old place as long as she could. The blacksmith shop lay closed and dusty now quiet beyond belief, with only a rare visit from me, with far too many memories to frequent often.

We sat out on the front porch that summer evening, grandma in her chair knitting and rocking her evil little dog Festus, getting old and gray but just as big a snitch as he always was. How that dog knew when I was up to something was just absolutely uncanny, for even now, his beady little eyes bore into me and he growled, just sensing I was up to something.

The next morning I watched the clock it seemed forever before 8am arrived and the store was opened. I immediately ran over when I saw Ed opening up the front door, I stepped beside him and pulled one of the brass shells from my pocket.

"Say Ed, I don't suppose you got a couple of these old shells laying around?" I asked hopefully.

"Whoa, that's an old eight gauge solid brass!" Ed said a bit excited, "I haven't seen one of these since….hmmm….seems like it was about ten years ago when your Grumps bought ever one I had, which was only about a handful I'd found in the back. Can't even order these anymore, I wouldn't even know who to talk to. But I can get the more modern shells, they'll shoot just the same", Replied Ed, after examining the shell and then slowly returning it.

"So, no chance of finding any around in the back or know of anyone else that shoots an eight gauge?" I asked woefully without much hope.

Archie Matthews

"Nope, the only eight gauge around was your Grumps, say now, I do seem to remember he left it to Tick and I thought he gave your Uncle Tick a couple of....Oh, I see..." Ed replied and then gave me a suspicious look, "Is this one of the two shells that Grump left with your Uncle Tick? Last I heard old Tick was saving them two shells for a tribute Ba'r hunt for the memory of Old Grumps.....Oh, and you've up and shot one?! Oh don't tell me you went and shot one off?!" glared Ed accusingly.

"Well, right now, I'd surely like to not have to tell you that, but come to think about it, I got even worse news, we accidently shot both off." I wailed and taking the shell back, threw my head down. "I just got to get two shells and replace them! Uncle Tick and Aunt Edna are due back day after tomorrow!" And then I broke down and went into what had happened with the shotgun and the shells.

Cousin Monte had come to town, talked me into going out and spend the night with him. As boys will do we got to daring one another to do dumber and dumber stuff until before I knew it, we had fired off the old antique eight gauge double barrel shotgun that hung above their fireplace. I went into how Monte had accidently fired both barrels and his resulting broken nose and black eyes and then our discovery and realization that we now had two Empty shells to explain to Uncle Tick.

"Yup, I'd say Monte pretty well summed it up....Your Dead!" Ed chuckled.

"Oh come on Ed, I know you got a reloader, don't you suppose you could help me reload these two shells?" I asked, twisting up my face as pitiful as a wrung out dishrag, "Please...for poor old Uncle Tick and if not him, for the memory of Grumps?"

"Well, got the powder, and wads and I think I even got primers that will work. Come on lets go in the back and see what I got", Announced Ed with a thoughtful wink.

Uncle Tick's Shotgun

And in the back of the store we went, sure enough at a big desk far to the one side of the back room, Ed stopped and sat down in a huge swivel chair. He began to slowly and methodically go through each drawer and pulled out a large brass die and a small hammer and punch. He also found a box of primers and a set of small metal measuring thimbles. Soon he produced a small pocket book that looked like it had belonged to "Methuselah" himself, the pages where so faded they were hard to read, but they had pictures and I could tell it was "Hand loader's Bible", or so the title announced.

"Here you go young Henchman, you take this book and those parts and pieces and carry them out front and I'll get you a can of powder", Ed instructed as he handed me the bundle and went down the far dark isle of the storage room. I carried everything out to the front counter and in a short time, as good as his word, Ed returned with a small can of Black powder.

"I'll loan all this to you with one stipulation!" Ed warned with a glare. "When this goes sideways and your Uncle Tick has you boys stood upon the gallows and is about to pull the lever to drop you into the noose, don't you dare mention me!", Warned Ed with one eye closed and the other piercing into my eye.

"Oh come on Ed, this ain't going sideways, besides you aint a bit afraid of Uncle Tick!" I snorted with a chuckle.

"There ain't but one way for this to end, just like any other deception… Bad! And as for your Uncle Tick, ain't anyone afraid of Tick, but everyone with a lick of sense is mighty cautious around your Aunt Edna, including me. If'n I was you and Monte, I'd just buck up and own up to what you done and die a clean death, because ever lie ends bad in the end, ever one. And when you're my age, you'll realize its better to just own up to your mistakes and learn from them. Trying to cover them up just leads to bigger and deeper holes. Dig' n deeper ain't any kind of way to fill a hole in, sometime you just gotta stop dig' n and only then will the hole stop getting bigger. You think on that young

Archie Matthews

man." Ed warned and pushed the bundle across the counter to me.

In looking back upon that very moment, I realize now just how right that kind old man was, for I had been right on the cross roads of stopping and owning up to my and Monte's mistake or digging us in even deeper. And like the dumb kid I was, I scooped up the bundle and shouted Ed, "Many Thanks" and off I went to dig that hole a bit deeper.

I dashed down the road and slipped into the blacksmith shop and closed the sliding door behind me. I followed the faint light coming from the far corner and going to grandpa's old work bench where the light from the two corner windows was best, I took my shirt sleeve and wiped the dust out of the window panes. I pulled up the old powder keg grandpa had always used and opening the "Hand Loader's Bible" I began to read the faded book to the best of my ability.

I won't go into the long boring details as revealed in the small faded book, or all the intricate instructions described in the book that needed to be strictly followed as "not to cause a dangerous discharge". What I will tell you was at the age of twelve, pictures were as good to me as a thousand words, or so the saying went, therefore I just did as the pictures showed.

Before the afternoon was over, I had two remarkably authentic looking brass eight gauge shotgun shells. Holding them up I was mighty happy with how I'd painstakingly rolled the ragged rim over to hold the upper hard cardboard wadding in place. I even went so far as to "Antique" the top a bit by rubbing my finger in the soot of the forge and carefully darkened the cardboard top of the shells.

Stepping back out of the shop and into the bright afternoon sunlight, I held the shells up and with a huge smile; I inspected them in the sunshine and if I'd been able to twist my arm correctly, I'd have gave myself a rounding pat on the back.

Uncle Tick's Shotgun

But just as I was contemplating my quick wit and good fortune in skullduggery and fooling my poor old Uncle, I suddenly noticed Ed, sitting at the café counter watching me and slowly shaking his head with a sad look of reproach.

That night, I'd like to say I slept sound and peaceful with no troubles or worries about the sneaky no account, under handed scheme I and Monte were perpetrating upon his kind hearted father, for Uncle Tick had always been the best of uncles. Well mostly.....and then I began to dream about all the times he'd played a trick on me. Like when he'd jumped out of the dark at me on my way to the outhouse one time, scaring me into "Watering my Mules" way before I'd gotten to the trough. Oh how I'd been so mad and embarrassed as I'd had to go back inside with wet trousers and change my pants.

And then there had been the time we'd been deer hunting and Uncle Tick had convinced me the big black shape down by the crick was a black bear. I'd shot it once and since it just stood there, I quickly levered another round in my rifle and shot it not only once but twice more in rapid succession only to be laughed practically out of the county by none other than Uncle Tick. For the rascal had realized it was but an old fire blackened stump and had convinced me it was otherwise.

Uncle Tick was a practical jokester from a way back and I had been the brunt of many of his jokes. Of course they had all been in good fun and none had been to slight or meant to embarrass me, as most had, but had not been intended as such. Therefore there was never any real need for "Payback" or any animosity between us. In our family we constantly poked one another and always in good fun with no harm ever intended. If we didn't poke a joke your way, even with our family friends, we didn't like you and it became rapidly apparent at our BBQ's and family get-togethers. Thus it was all those practical jokes that I dreamed about that night.

The next morning I saddled up cousin Monte's horse and made the several mile ride back up to their home deep in the timber

Archie Matthews

and way up the crick. When I approached of course their dogs wailed and warned company was coming even before I got within a half mile of the place. When I rode out of the timber and came up to the porch there sat Monte with two of the blackest eyes and swollen nose I ever did see. All you could see of his two blue eyes was little glistening slits on either side of a hard kicked red apple.

"Holy Smokes Monte… Buddy, you look like you been kicked by a mule square in the face!" I remarked as I slid off his horse.

"Oh Arch, it's been a rough night and I feel like I was kicked in the nose by old Bess our milk cow……wait just a minute!!! Of course….that's it, I'll tell ma and pa I got kicked by Bess our milk cow! Sure enough, they'll buy that whopper; the old rip kicked Mary nearly clear through the wall this past winter. That ring she got from town had turned green on her and she took a wire brush to it and knocked one of the stones out and left a sharp burr, and when she grabbed old Bess by the nipple, the fight was on! I'll just say a horsefly bit the old gal and she kicked and here I am, black eyes and can't breathe a lick out my nose!" Monte grinned slyly.

"Well guess what I got?!" I grinned as I pulled the two glorious brass shells out of my pocket and stepping up on the porch handed them to Monte to inspect.

"WOW, you got two that look exactly the same as the ones we shot! Spectacular! You're a lifesaver for sure…..we're not dead men after all! Whew, I ain't slept a wink just thinking about pa's disappointment", sighed Monte with a big smile beneath his crooked swollen nose.

"Well, they ain't new shells, I reloaded them….but they are done by the book, although I ain't sure I got everything just down to the grain, that dern book was mighty fine print and hard to read, but they sure look good don't they?" I smiled back and nodded.

"Why there ain't a feller that could tell the difference! I can't even believe they ain't the same un-fired shells that set forever on the mantle. Let's put em back up there and our backside is covered and we're free and clear on the home stretch!"

And with that we walked in and Monte place the old shotgun shells right smack dab center in the dust less little spots upon the mantle. We were grinning from ear to ear and slapping one another on the back for most of the afternoon.

And three weeks went by smooth sailing and everything was right and square and plumb in the world of Archie, not to mention Monte, and then here come Uncle Tick and Aunt Edna and things took a quick turn out of kilter.

Uncle Tick and Aunt Edna roared up in their old car and almost run right into the front fence, for Uncle Tick forgot to throw the car into neutral before bailing out and the car rolled right up to the gate post before he got back in and applied the brake.

I and grandma were sitting on the front porch eating a late breakfast when we saw Uncle Tick and Aunt Edna's car coming up the road fast. I remember grandma saying, "Oh my…oh my….they're coming right up to the porch!" Although close, they didn't quite make it through the fence, but for a minute there I wasn't to sure either.

Tick jumped back out of the car and for the first time in my life, I saw Uncle Tick forget to open Aunt Edna's car door, and I also noticed the immediate shock on Edna's face as she realized it too.

Uncle Tick ran through the gate and right upon the porch and I almost imploded with guilt for I knew our whole shotgun debacle had been discovered and I was about to die at the hands of Uncle Tick.

"Arch, Arch, quick grab your ba'r rifle and come a run' n! A black bear plundered our chicken house last night and practically mauled Monte and little Sid when they went out to see what the Dickens was going on! We got a rogue ba'r terrorizing the countryside and I need help!" rambled Uncle Tick so fast it was hard to take all of it in while realizing I wasn't going to die, at the same time.

"Oh my heavens!" wailed grandma, "How bad is Monte and little Sid? I'll get my first aid kit and can come along too!" and without a moment's hesitation grandma was out of her rocking chair. She scooped up my coffee cup and half-finished breakfast plate and whisked inside, the screen door banging shut behind her.

"Oh, he didn't rightly maul the boys, but Monte was off his guard when he throwed open the hen house door. That ba'r run right over the top of him on the way out and sure enough, he's re-broke that nose and his eyes is already swoll' up tight so he can't come with me to track that ba'r. Little Sid got off a shot with his twenty two and we got a blood trail and wounded ba'r. But Sissy's boy Sid is only a kid and your Aunt Edna won't even begin to listen about me taking him on a ba'r hunt yet, let alone a wounded blood thirsty rascal. So's I come a run'n, I knewed you was still here with your gram and you're a crack shot.....I need ya Arch",wailed Uncle Tick.

Sissy was Monte's older sister and her boy little Sid was still only about nine or ten and I'd no doubt Aunt Edna wouldn't let him go along on no bear hunt. I was mighty sorry to hear about poor Monte and his freshly broken nose. I'd seen him just last week as they came to town and his nose was just beginning to look like a nose again and not a huge red freshly stomped apple. I had also been encouraged to see that Monte's black eyes were all but healed up and a slight blotchy yellowish blue, but you could look him in the eye again and see all of his eyeballs, where before all you could see was little swollen slits.

"I'll come with you Tick; just let me get grandpa's rifle and my coat." I said as I got up and went inside, just as Aunt Edna had recovered over the shock of having to open her own car door, let alone the front gate by herself and come stomping up the walkway.

I went into grandma's closet that set up under the stairs leading up to the second floor. I reached in and pulled the light string and saw grandpa's old leaver action 30-30 with its long octagon barrel and well-worn dark walnut stock sitting in the corner. I also reached up on the little shelf and grabbed the old half box of shells and closing the closet door went back out to the front porch, where Aunt Edna was tongue lashing poor excited Uncle Tick like a hound dog caught eating a chicken.

"What on earth has removed you from your senses Tick?" wailed Aunt Edna, "The boys ain't et and hardly bitten, they just had a close call....you need to just settle down and not run off without a lick of sense or you will surely end up a steaming pile of ba'r drop'ns! You get ahold't of yourself or I will get ahold't of you! I never in forty years of marriage had to open my own car door, let alone a gate....heaven's, what would your pappy say? What would your dear mother say? I swar', they'd both roll right over in their graves and I bet their lying face down even now, ashame't!" Scolded Aunt Edna, wagging her finger and scowling at poor Uncle Tick, with his hat in his hand and his head bowed in shame.

I cleared my throat and stepped through the screen door just as grandma came along with her little medical kit, her sweater over her arm. Shutting the door and screen door, we all bailed into Tick and Edna's car then roared off up the road for their house.

Sure enough after the long ride and listening to Tick and Edna both bemoan not only having lost several chickens, but poor old Monte was black-eyed and broken nose anew. They went back and forth about how brave little Sid had fought off the wild ba'r as it had run over his uncle Monte practically mauling him on the way by. To hear them tell it, little Sid had gotten off a good shot that only by chance hadn't dropped the vicious ba'r in its tracks. All the while I and grandma just nodded and held on for dear life for Uncle Tick was almost the craziest driver in the county; next

Archie Matthews

to the town "Nut" old George Wellner with his old blue pickup that had no brakes.

After the hair raising ride up the twisting turning bumpy dirt road with its steep banks overlooking the crick far below, we finally arrived, believe it or not, safe and sound in their front yard.

We skidded to a stop and Edna quickly gave Uncle Tick a piercing look and Tick gave a gulp that bobbed his adam's apple all the way up and dropped it down with a loud clunk as he jumped out and running around, opened Aunt Edna's door. And then as Edna was getting out, Tick remembering grandma, Edna's sister was sitting in the back. Quickly stepping back, Tick opened grandma's door, with a flourish, his hat in hand.

"Well now, that's better Tick, there is no excuse for lack of manners" nodded Aunt Edna with a smile at her husband and taking grandma's hand, away towards the house the women went.

"This'a way Arch, I'll show you where the blood trail starts and you can get a feel for the track, I'll go grab my ba'r rifle and away we'll go!" Uncle Tick urged.

Uncle Tick lead the way to their chicken house as if it hadn't been in the same place for the past forty years. And sure enough, the hen house door was all askew, and there in the side of the wired yard was a tell tale opening surrounded by small black hairs showing where the bear entered.

As we got close, Uncle Tick pointed out the large bear paw prints leading out of the door and off towards the crick bottom, and there, just as Tick had assured me, was some drops of blood.

"I'll be right back, gotta get my shoot'n iron and my jacket, I'll be right back!" shouted Uncle Tick over his shoulder as he quickly sprinted for the house.

Uncle Tick's Shotgun

I began to carefully walk around first looking at where the bear had come in through the chicken wire. It had barged right into the thin walled hen house through the small door just big enough for chickens to enter and exit from yard to hen house. The bear had just pushed through the opening and enlarged the hole until it was practically big enough for a five hundred pound chicken to easily walk though.

I could see blood in the chicken house and I deduced it was more than likely chicken blood, and not a wounded bear at all. The way I figured it, if little Sid had shot and wounded the bear, those boys wouldn't be run over as much as they'd have been run through, and by that I mean, ate, digested and pooped out.

There isn't anything meaner than a wounded cornered bear and anyone with any experience with bears knew it. Nope, I didn't doubt little Sid fired a shot, but I strongly suspected it wasn't even close to the bear, more like in the air or into the ground. But I wasn't going to argue the fact to his grandpa Tick or his grandma Edna. Both of which were convinced they had an up and coming bear hunting hero in the family at the ripe old age of nine.

Uncle Tick good as his word came barreling back out of the house packing a suspiciously familiar shoot'n iron and sure enough as he came close I recognized the old ancient double barrel shotgun I and Monte had fiddled with weeks before.

"I'm ready Arch….I been saving these shells your great grandpa Grump give me with his old ba'r rifle and I been just a hope'n and a pray'n that the day would come that I could shoot me a ba'r with it one last time for old Grumps sake!" grinned Uncle Tick as proud as a blue ribbon winning coon hound at the national trials.

"Um….but Uncle Tick, don't but one hammer work on that old thing?" I quickly pointed out.

"I seem to remember Grump never did get that hammer fixed…..and how old is them shells? Do you reckon they'll even

209
Archie Matthews

fire?" I asked. For I was more than a little hesitant about wandering after a bear with only one rifle and a very questionable shotgun with a broken hammer , needless to say my hand loaded shells. The only thing I could think about was how hastily I'd loaded them and how confusing the black powder table in that book had been. I wasn't to confident when it came to just "How many grains of powder went in". And there had been the nagging at the back of my brain pan as to something was missing as I'd completed the job and presented the shells to Monte. I just had a huge nagging doubt as to their workings, let alone effectiveness against a large black bear.

"Oh, don't you worry about old Uncle Tick and this here Ba'r rifle. Whagh, I seen your Grump shoot many a ba'r with this here shoot'n iron, even with that old busted hammer and every one went a "Plunk!" right smack dab into the stew pot. Yes sir, we are gonna have Ba'r stew tonight!" grinned Uncle Tick

I just couldn't help but feel I was on my way to getting a big fat scoop of "Just deserts", as we began to follow the tracks of that big black bear.

Since I was younger and the better tracker, I of course took the lead, Uncle Tick close at my heels whispering encouragement the whole time.

We'd come about three miles from the house when the bear had finally stopped moving in a straight line away from Uncle Tick's place. That told me the bear must have been mighty shaken up and decided to put a lot of landscape between him and that hen house. I thought perhaps I'd been wrong and maybe little Sid actually had put a twenty two round in his butt. That would've made me run in a straight line for three miles before I began to amble around.

Then we came to where the bear had begun to settle down and search for food stuff. He'd rolled a log, eaten some grubs and then he'd headed for a patch of wild oaks and snuffled around underneath looking for acorns.

And then he'd slowly made his way down to the crick bottom and this was where I made motion to Uncle Tick to perk up and pay attention. We were starting to close in on our quarry, but there was little need, for Tick had hunted Bear even before I'd been born and new the signs as well, if not better than I did. One look at my uncle told me he was ready and loaded for "Ba'r".

We came around a big rock set almost next to the crick and as I stepped around I saw not ten feet from me, that big old boar bear just as surprised to see me as I was him. That bears head slowly swiveled around and when his eyes met mine, ever hair on him stood right straight up, and I have no doubt, ever hair I had did the same, for I felt my hat lifted plumb up and off from my head. I stopped dead in my tracks and I heard Uncle Tick stop and he whispered, "You see him Arch?"

I'd like to say I didn't answer verbally because I didn't want to spook my quarry, but I won't lie to you, I had such a lump in my throat, I'm surprised I didn't faint for lack of air to breath, let alone say something. But that old bear didn't have a lump, let alone fear for scaring me, he began to growl and any hairs that had been a bit slow to stand on end under my hat, suddenly snapped too.

That growl immediately got a response out of Uncle Tick, for I heard him say, "Shoot him Arch, let him have it, I can't get around you without falling in the crick, start shoot'n…" hissed my uncle about two inches from my ear, which was a remarkable feat as short as Uncle Tick was.

I had a round in my chamber, but all I could keep thinking about was that worn shell ejector in that old rifle I now held. Grandpa had always claimed he was going to have it fixed or trade that worn rifle in for a new one. The mechanism that pulled the spent cartridge from the breach and allowed it to be thrown out and make way for a new unfired shell to be reloaded was severely worn. And about every other shot, found the cartridge still wedged in the breach of the barrel when the lever was thrown

Archie Matthews

open; this meant digging ones pocket knife out and working the spent shell out. I can't begin to tell you the hesitation of shooting a bear just several feet away, knowing that more than 50% of the time you will only get off one shot. The beads of sweat on my forehead right about then were the size of coffee cups, handle and all.

The bear began to side step slowly edging away one slow deliberate step at a time, one foot and then another, growling the whole way and staring right smack into my eyes. That bear was just daring me to raise that rifle and try to put a bullet in him.

Right about then my mind was a human calculator and I was a figuring odds, and friend, no matter how I crunched the numbers, it looked like my best bet was just stay friendly and let the bear get away.

But I could hear Tick's hisses getting louder and more excited as he slowly began to push my arm up with the intention to take a "Look see" from underneath. He couldn't step around me without going neck deep into the crick, and my neck deep was about a good foot over his head. Therefore he slowly began to push up my left arm, so he could take a peek, but that bear evidently saw the movement and he stopped moving away and his eyes quickly told me, if I tried anything, he was going to make the first move in the "Great Archie Bear Mauling" and I surely didn't want that!

"Tick, he's not ten feet from me, sideways and he'll have me before I can even get the shot off…..", I hissed trying my best to keep the arm my Uncle was trying to lift up, down and still.

"Cut him a lick Arch…..trust to your rifle and just lever round after round into him, step up close to him and I'll come around and give him both barrels!" Uncle Tick assured me in a low tone.

And then the bear gave a jump and I fired, and before either Tick or myself knew what was going on, we were both in the water a tangle of arms and legs.

Uncle Tick's Shotgun

All I can say is Uncle Tick was lucky I'd already fired my rifle, for when I came up for a breath I was mighty tempted to shoot him then and there. But after I realized I'd shot and was giving some thought to levering another round into the chamber, my little dunking had cooled me off enough, I didn't shoot my uncle. But I can't honestly say I'd completely done away with the idea.

The bear had given a leap forward and sideways and I am very happy to say, the direction down the crick and away from me and my stumble bum Uncle. As I had accidently pulled the trigger and fired my chambered round into the crick, Tick had tried to jump around me and slipped and in his haste to catch himself amid fall, took me with him. Now as we both fought to get foot holds in shallower water and out of the deep hole we'd fallen into, I stood up and reaching back pulled my Uncle to my side.

"Why in tarnation didn't you shoot that bear!" wailed Uncle Tick with an astounded look on his face as he stood there dripping wet and poured the water from his shotgun back into the crick.

I quickly threw open the lever of the old 30-30 carbine and sure enough, no shell ejected and I held the breach close to Uncle Tick's face and said, "That's why, grandpa never did get that ejector fixed and I knew I only had one shot."

You could have driven a four door Buick in Uncle Tick's mouth and parked it there without nary touching a cheek. "Well, I'll be dogged….I suppose I can't blame you for that, I'd hesitate to make that kind of hasty move myself". Tick assured me.

After wringing out most of our clothes and wiping down our rifles with our still damp handkerchiefs, I looked at Uncle Tick and said, "I don't think little Sid hit that bear. We ain't seen nary a drop of blood track' n him, he didn't look hit and I think we just seen some chicken blood. I think we'd best just let this one go until we got better shoot irons. I don't fancy run' n onto him again in this crick bottom and having to make that decision again."

Archie Matthews

"Oh, now Arch, we got him and he can't make it out until he gets to the meadow yonder, the side is too steep. He'll either have to cross the meadow and you can pick him off or follow the crick on down to the far off bottom and cross over the top and once again, you'll have a chance to pick him off. Don't give up on me now, we almost got him!" wailed Uncle Tick.

"Okay, let's go and go fast, or he'll be across the meadow and we'll lose him sure." I said, against my better judgment, for I'd seen just about all of that bear I cared too. But I surely didn't want to let Uncle Tick down.

We quickly hurried down the crick and we could hear the bear doing his best to make it down stream and stay ahead of us. From the sound of him, he was going straight down the crick and we could see walls of sparkling water showers far ahead of us.

Finally we could see where the meadow was and I cut across the crick and up a rocky shelf and quickly took a knee, grabbing my pocket knife I dug the last spent cartridge out and levered another round in and lined up my sight. Sure enough, there went the bear straight up the center of the grassy meadow and I lined right up between his shoulder blades and let him have it.

The rifle recoil made me lose sight of my quarry in the tall grass of the meadow, and after a few minutes of looking close; I could see the bear a full fifty feet and off to the one side of the meadow, down.

"Did you get him Arch….did you get him?" Uncle Tick kept asking as I was trying to get my eyeballs focused after having my shoulder mailed back to me from the neighboring county. To say that old 30-30 lever action rifle kicked was an understatement, it was like holding a mule's leg to your shoulder and pulling its tail.

The old powder in the greenish colored brass shells and the whitish colored lead bullets hinted the ammo were probably loaded and crossed over with Christopher Columbus on the Mayflower, they were that old. It took a few minutes for the huge

Uncle Tick's Shotgun

bluish black cloud to diminish enough I could see the black lump up in the far corner of the long grass meadow.

"I can see him down, but he's moved a good fifty feet from where I hit him and I can't see all of him, we best approach careful or he'll snack on us yet." I warned as I slowly stepped down and quickly levered open the breach and this time out ejected the spent cartridge. Thus I quickly and effortlessly levered in a new one.

"Let's go, and if'n I was you, I'd be ready. I wished I could have got another round in him to be sure, but we'll be close up to him in this tall grass", I said as we quickly crossed the crick and stepped into the waist high grassy meadow.

We slowly crept closer and closer to the corner of the meadow where I'd spotted the bear, and then I saw a splash of blood on the grass. I clicked my tongue on the roof of my mouth, caught Tick's attention and nodded at the blood.

"You got him a good one", Uncle Tick whispered.

"Yeah, but did I get him good enough?" I hissed as we crept even closer.

We could see the dark shape laying where I said it was and once again, my hair stood on end and Uncle Tick gave a shout. For we'd both immediately recognized the old fire darkened log for what it was, and Tick had seen the movement of the bear as he made a dash for the trees from where he'd been laying.

I'll never forget Uncle Tick lifting that long barreled shotgun and firing it at the fleeing shape of the wounded bear. There was a two inch flame and a "POOT" and what looked like confetti flew out and celebrated the bears get away with a flourish of a New Year's party favorite.

Archie Matthews

For a moment all I and Uncle Tick could do was stand with our mouths open at the startling misfire of the old brass shotgun shell. And Tick groaned, "Well that old shell was a dud!"

But my rifle was up quick and seeing the bear almost make the tree line, once again I let go a round and once again lost him in the cloud of smoke and recoil. Yet this time I immediately worked the lever and seeing the casing half in and half out, reached in with my fingernail and tipping the rifle up flicked the spent shell out and levered another round ready to fire.

"You got him clean that time Arch!" shouted Tick, "You got him dead center, I can see him down for sure."

I quickly stepped over to Uncle Tick's side and sure enough, away from the bluish white cloud, there I could see the old bear lying where he'd fallen.

I won't bore you with our relief in seeing the bear down, or the two hours of bloody work skinning and gutting and boning the meat out and packing it into the half dozen plastic trash bags that Uncle Tick had brought in his pants pockets.

"I knew you'd get him Arch, I had faith in you…",smiled Tick when I noticed the plastic bags. "Now all we gotta do is fix us a travois and we'll tie the hide to form the bottom and lay the meat atop and home we'll be!"

On the long walk home all Tick could do was bemoan the fact that he'd " had a bear all lined up in the sights of old Grumps Ba'r Killer, but the old shell had just given it's all to old age and in the end, just didn't have it in it any longer."

I just played it smart and never said a word, I had an awful time trying to figure that powder chart out and evidently had been mighty light on the measure of black powder it took to do more than a "POOT" and throw confetti.

Uncle Tick's Shotgun

And home we we're and just about dark. As nice a welcome as ever there was one for there stood Aunt Edna, grandma, Sissy, little Sid and even poor old Monte trying his best to see in the failing light out those swollen up black eyes.

We quickly took the meat to their smoke house and hung it amidst the rails to be smoked at Uncle Ticks leisure. Tick quickly grabbed a large galvanized tub and put the hide in, laid in a bunch of salt and water then announced "We're done and into the house for a good meal and sip of whiskey! We by golly earned it this day!"

We went into the light of the house, which was still a marvel to me and grandma, not to mention Tick, Edna and family for they'd only had electricity for the past few months. It had only been a couple months back that they were still using coal oil lamps. The Idaho Power Company had brought a power line from the lower Ola valley and on up the crick. Now several families including Tick and Edna had found themselves with genuine life altering electricity.

Soon after as fine a meal as two "Ba'r Killer's" have ever been treated too, everyone wanted to hear the hunting tale and Uncle Tick being a "Whopper Swapper from a-way back!"
He began to spin a heroic tale of two men stalking a "Killer Ba'r" though swamp, thick brush and over hill and dale.

The "Great Stand Off" was described as the bear standing over us as we bared our teeth and all but committed suicide in one huge hand to hand encounter. Nary was a mention as to my hesitation to shoot, the ultimate accidental firing into the crick when startled by the bear, or our quick dunking in the crick, thanks to Uncle Tick. Nope, that tale of bear tracking expertise was painting both my Uncle and myself as genuine "Ba'r hunting extraordinaire's"

Uncle Tick in the excitement of the tale scooped up his shotgun leaned against the wall and stalking through the living room he described our sneaking up to the wounded grizzly growling and

Archie Matthews

cornered. Then as he described us jumping full into the face of death, Uncle Tick raised up his shotgun and shouted "BOOM! And we both let the rascal have it!"

Everyone cheered and all I could do was smile at grandma and roll my eyes, for we both knew Uncle Tick and his hunt' n tales were prone to being stretched here and there, not to mention puffed up and pulled out of shape like a wade of taffy. But everyone was smiling and with a flourish Uncle Tick up and set that big old shotgun with its wobbly hammer down on the hard floor. Immediately a loud explosion ensued, an eight foot fountain of flame that looked like a volcano erupted and out went the only light in the house. Not only were we instantly in the dark, not a sound was heard but the ringing in our ears and the smell of burnt gunpowder in our nostrils.

You could have heard a pin drop in a brief instant following the explosion, and then a squeaky voice announced, "Well Arch, that one wasn't a dud....."

It was only many years later at my beloved Uncle Tick's wake that Monte and Little Sid laughed and laughed and shared the realization the next day when Uncle Tick was replacing the blown apart light fixture, he noticed there had been a very strange amount of confetti or paper wads to clean up. Also while inspecting the ceiling, Tick remarked how strange it was there were no BB pellets!

Monte had been the only one to realize my mistake in reloading the shotgun shells and forgetting the shotgun pellets. But after a long moment of head scratching Uncle Tick had begun laughing and laughing and exclaimed "Ain't that just the last laugh old Grumps would have had!!! The old fart gave me two shells to go ba'r hunting with that just held confetti!!! "

Monte claimed never to have divulged our little fiasco with the shotgun and shells, but at the wake the story came out and everyone roared with laughter as we all had a drink and said

Uncle Tick's Shotgun

good bye to one of our families best "Whopper Swapper's"!
He'll be forever missed!

Archie Matthews

220
Uncle Tick's Shotgun

The Quarter Kid

There isn't a kid on earth that hasn't heard the term, "Worthless Kids!" Usually it's shouted by some old fart waving his cane above his head, as he narrowly avoids being trampled by a herd of kids stampeding by.

But in my family, immediate and away off into the far reaches of distant relatives, kids were, are and always will be highly prized, and never more so than the "Quarter kid".

Therefore it's to her memory, I write this story.

Away back in southern Idaho, in the dusty little town of GrandView, I lived with my parents and two younger brothers. There were eventually four of us boys, but baby brother was but a glimmer in my parent's eyes at this stage of our lives. And thus at this time there were but the three of us Matthews boys. If anyone had inquired at that time, they'd have been told, "That's plenty". But evidently nobody said such a thing where my folks took notice, for a few years later baby brother was born. The consensus then by everyone, including my parents, was four Matthews boys was "More than enough", and the worlds been trying to whittle us down ever since. But that's another story and I need to get back to telling this one.

We lived in a little red brick house across from the grade school right smack near the center of town. Well, almost, for town was but one street with buildings on either side, while the grade school was just a stone throw to the South, and the high school was about the same distance to the North.

I suppose there are all kinds of benefits to living across the street from the school you attend, but in my opinion they were all the "Wrong kind of benefits". Yet dear sweet mother and father often remarked otherwise.

"Oh, you kids are so lucky you only have to walk across the street!" dear old dad would remark, "When I was a kid, I walked twenty miles to school and back again, uphill both ways, fighting man eating bears and wolves with my bare hands....the other hand was busy dragging my kid brother along kicking and screaming through ten foot snow drifts!"

Now, I'd seen that school house dad was so fond of talking about, it was only about half a mile up the road from his childhood home. And since I'd only been up to my grand folks place in the summer, I never did see how deep the snow got. But, I also never did see any Bears or wolves. I will say, dad's statement did happen to ring true about uphill both ways. For sure enough there was a large dip in the road, and you'd go down into the dip on one side and up the dip on the other side, so technically, it was "uphill both ways".

And then dear mother would always rattle off how "nice it was to be close to the school in case she was needed."

"Yeah, RIGHT" I always thought, "Just close enough to come stomping across the street, grab me by the back of the shirt and drag me home for a "whip'n".

Like that time at recess, I rolled up as "sweet a slush ball" as ever was crafted by a six year old and pitched it with such speed and accuracy, if a baseball talent scout had seen it, I'd still be awash with fame and glory. But, "Oh, No", dear sweet mother had happened to be watching from our living room window and just as that ballistic marvel was launched, even before it contacted Mary Lee Bee's left ear, mother had been out of the house and across the street.

My first hint of impending doom had been right after, the anguish of receiving a slush ball in the left ear, turned into a sly smile of sweet bloody revenge on Mary Lee's face; just as a looming shadow was cast over me. No need to go into bloody detail of that event, let alone the many that followed over the years. This story is not meant as a Horror Story to frighten children into screaming fits, let alone giving reading parents any notions of moving closer to their children's schools.

Let me just point out that living across the street as a kid from the grade school seemed to have its advantages for some, but not others. (I, unfortunately being one of the others)

But shortly after that brutal winter, (and I'm not just talking about the weather), it was summer and school was out. Somehow, I remember the summer's as a kid much more fondly than the "School months". And so my story about the "Quarter Kid" actually happened one warm summer afternoon that following year, after the "Mary Lee Snowball Beating".

Archie Matthews

It's funny how kids remember things by association, most of my early years were broken into either glorious events, in which I avoided getting caught, or less glorious events where someone else got caught, or harrowing experiences where I not only got caught, but paid a severe price. The "Severe Price" being the currency demanded by either mom's hair brush or dad's belt as to how many layers of hide would be worn from my backside.

(Enough of the gruesome details and more of the glorious summer day....back to the story.)

It was late summer and although I was home, I wasn't happy about it. Usually, at this time of the year, I was still at my beloved grandparents place some four hours drive north in the little town of Ola. My parents had been off visiting some other relative in the northern part of the state, and therefore had swung by and picked me up. Of course it had been with "no prior notice" and a good thing, for I'd have hid out. They never told me when they were coming to pick me up. Not since that first time they'd made that mistake and I'd hid myself in the creek bottom. Of course, they'd eventually found me, and by "found", I mean as soon as evening approached and the creek bottom threatened its impending darkness, I'd scampered for the house.

Needless to say, as a kid, I was deathly aware of the darkness and all the foul, flesh eating demons and kid eating monsters that inhabited it. Therefore, all my folks had done was wile away the day and a wait for darkness. It was a trait that they often took unfair advantage of in my early childhood.

So I was once again home after having another summer vacation and the time of my life off in the wilds of northern Idaho. Thus I found myself once again in the little southern town of GrandView and far from having wild adventures any longer that summer, or so I thought.

I remember that long ago day had gotten off to a bit of a rocky start, for although it was Saturday morning and cartoons were

The Quarter Kid

supposed to be on the television, they weren't at our house that morning and that was the rocky point, I speak of.

Any kid will tell you, Saturday morning cartoons were what we strived so hard for all week long; sitting quietly, paying attention in class, being attentive students, not only making our teacher happy, but our parents proud. And in that definition and in those examples, did the "Rocky" part take root, for it seemed I had failed in all of those and thus was serving a Saturday morning without cartoons.

Although not quite sure of the terminology, I had seen a court house drama on the television called "The Perry Mason Show". It had been about "Inhumane treatment", and I felt confident if only Mr. Mason was there to represent me, I'd have been allowed to at least watch my favorite "Space Ghost" episode; not to mention perhaps a bit of the "Wiley Coyote and Road Runner". But alas, it was not to be and since dear old dad had rolled the set into their bedroom the night before to seal the deal, I was sitting outside on the step at the crack of dawn, with my two younger brothers growling at either elbow.

"You're a poop, Arch….a real poop!", whined first one and then the other.

"Yeah a real poop!" came the echoing of the other brother.

Their disappointing cartoon starved whines sounding exactly the same after the past thirty minutes of constant beleaguering.

"I hate living this close to the stupid school!" I growled in turn. "If we lived away off in the boonies like normal folks, my teacher wouldn't be able to rat me out. She wouldn't be able to just walk across the road and visit with mom and we wouldn't be in this fix."

As you can tell, I was an incredibly intelligent young fellow and had vast reasoning powers even at the young age of nine.

Archie Matthews

"But she could still use the telephone." Little brother Roy quipped with a quick sidelong sneer.

If looks could've killed back then, that branch of the family tree would have been immediately pruned back if not entirely lopped off and none existent thereafter. But even though nasty to see, my looks couldn't kill, no matter how much I practiced.

And then a bit of excitement occurred in the form of the old man up the street coming by along the sidewalk out in front of our white picket fence; the excitement being our large German Shepard "Lady Dog". Seeing her old nemesis approaching, she began to run along the inside of the fence, snarling and growling at the old man.

Suddenly we all forgot our bickering and fell silent as we watched the old man pass by. We called him "Shotgun Shorty", because while he hobbled along with an old crooked cane in one hand, he cradled an ancient double barreled shotgun in the crook of his other arm. As in every town with kids, there is always a mysterious old fellow that elicits all kinds of wild and scary stories and Shotgun Shorty was ours.

Shorty lived in a small run down old shack up and around the corner by the far southern end of the school. The old shack had once been painted, but was long worn and rustic with so much bare wood showing. What color it had once been was an argued topic amongst most adults, let alone us kids. The strangest thing about Shorty's house wasn't the infinite pile of clutter that surrounded it, nor the old wood and barbwire fence that encompassed it. It wasn't even the life threatening signs that hung all about it warning "No Trespassing, Violators Will Be SHOT!" Although scary and foreboding that they were, the strangest thing was the massive metal antennae that was screwed, bolted and held next to his old shack with all those cables and guide wires.

Late at night if you were crazy enough to get anywhere close enough to Shorty's house, it was rumored that weird alien radio

The Quarter Kid

sounds emanated from within. Of course, I can only pass on the rumor; for one thing, I wasn't crazy, especially not crazy enough to be anywhere close to such a scary place as Shorty's at night. Besides, back then as a kid, I was absolutely terrified of the dark, so much so, that even an entire herd of wild horses couldn't have dragged me outside at night, let alone within throwing distance to "Shorty's House of Terror"

Everyone in town thought Shotgun Shorty was odd, or at least all the adults, but the kids all knew Shorty was an evil demented kid hater that just roamed around disguised as a normal kid hater.

The clincher for our family was the fact that our beloved family dog, showed great disdain for Shorty. For every time he came walking by, Lady dog would walk along the fence showing her teeth and growling from one end of the property line to the other, letting Shorty know he'd better just keep shuffling along. And as he did once every now and then, Shorty stopped just outside our gate and slowly and deliberately turned our way and with his little "Popeye'd" squint, he said, "Yup, worthless danged kids". Then as if satisfied he'd delivered his "Sermon on the Mount", he slowly turned and back down the sidewalk he went towards town.

I'd like to say it tickled us kids and we got quite a laugh to see the old codger and his grumpy hobble, but to kids our age, candy, soda pop and brightly wrapped packages on Christmas morning "tickled us". While any and every encounter with Shorty was "Hair Raising", and I don't mean just on our dog either.

But just as he disappeared on down the street and everyone's neck hair began to lay back down, Lady dogs included, we heard a distant sound that brought us all up and off the front stoop. With a three stooges rush and shuffle, everyone ran to the white picket fence with excitement, for we could hear our Uncle Bob's truck coming.

Now Uncle Bob's truck was the talk of the town. Not that it was extra fancy, or flashy or expensive like the vehicles of today, but

Archie Matthews

Uncle Bob's truck had what most trucks of today don't have, and that is the poorest mechanical upkeep known to man. It was a well-known fact that although Uncle Bob was an excellent butcher and could make a chunk of rawhide taste like a sirloin tip steak; he was the worst mechanic in the whole county, if not the entire state. And the proof was obvious every time Uncle Bob drove that "old rust bucket" as everyone called it, for as he drove it, he was constantly stopping and picking up pieces that kept falling off.

Dad, like most men, just wrinkled his nose and squinted one eye in disgust as Bob's old truck went by. Back then practically every male from the age of ten and up was supposed to be somewhat mechanical. Every guy, no matter how skilled or lack thereof, was at the very least expected to keep his vehicle from falling apart as it drove down the road. Most of the women, my mother included, just looked on with quiet sympathy as Bob's truck ambled by, parts either dragging along behind or falling off completely. Most of the time Uncle Bob would hear the parts either dragging or falling off, he would stop and pick them up and put them in the bed of the truck.

(To say that Uncle Bob had a quite a collection, would have brought hysterical laughter from almost anyone, if not everyone, and usually did.)

But once in a while he'd miss a piece or two and if someone saw that he wasn't going to stop right away, they'd go out into the rode and drag the larger pieces off to the side, knowing Uncle Bob would be along on his return trip and pick them up later.

After what seemed like nearly a half hour and a dozen or so stops to pick up his truck parts, Uncle Bob made it down the half mile stretch of road and came to a loud screeching stop in front of our house. Dad came crashing to the front door his hair still exhibiting having only moments before being in bed, hastily wrapping his house coat around himself , still barefoot.

The Quarter Kid

Seeing Bob, dad halted half in and half out of the still swinging screen door, which happened to come back with a "welcoming smack" to the side of his head. I don't know if it was the screen door "Whacking" him or his stepping out on the jagged old concrete step that put dad in a cranky mood, but something did. And with one hand holding his fresh screen door face tattoo, the other hand holding the screen door, he shouted back over his shoulder to mom inside, "It's only Bob, Frieda, not a car wreck!....or at least not a fresh one...." He muttered with disgust, still rubbing his face.

Uncle Bob just grinned his good nature smile and opening his truck door he stepped out and stepping off to the side, we saw another smile within. There on the seat over on the passenger's side sat our spindly little girl cousin "Vera"; which was a bit of puzzlement at the time.

Our Uncle Bob had three sons and no girls and happened to be married to mom's sister Doris, and Vera happened to be mom's other sister "La'Vera's" daughter. So as you can imagine, it was a bit of a surprise to see our cousin Vera sitting with a smile in Uncle Bob's truck.

About that time mom came outside and mumbled something to dad about getting dressed and helped get him pointed back in the right direction inside the house.

Uncle Bob helped Vera down from the pickup and I swung the gate wide for both to enter. Lady dog gave Uncle Bob a quick security scan "sniff" and stepped aside to give Vera a big lick of "Welcome".

Everyone loved little Vera, including animals, especially Lady dog, and believe it or not, so did my brothers and I, even though we were considered "Rough Character's" by most people. (Most people being women, that is). And although we were "confirmed girl haters", like I said, everyone loved the thin quiet little Vera.

Archie Matthews

Of course our Aunt La'Vera, Vera's mother, had even rougher labels for us boys, but the woman had girls, mostly. She did have three boys, and fine fellows ever one, but out of seven kids, four of them were girls. By my way of thinking having all those women in the house tended to cloud parent's judgment into thinking even boys ought to be civilized.

"Thank God", my parents weren't under any kind of notions, nor were Uncle Bob and Aunt Doris. Families with all boys seemed a lot more grounded in their knowledge that "Boys will be boys" and didn't have fantasies about days devoid of adventures, harrowing experiences, mischief and other such "boyish" happenings. Don't get me wrong, I love my aunt La'Vera, but as I said, the woman had girls and expected less rambunctiousness from boys.

(Now don't for a minute think she actually got it, for my fellow male cousins on that side of the family were every bit as rambunctious as me and mine. It's just aunt La'Vera, always seemed to expect more simple and toned down behavior than she ever got out of any of us, her own boys included.)

Uncle Bob went on inside behind dad and in front of mom and with a "Whack" of the screen door closing, so did all hope of Saturday cartoons that morning.

It wasn't long afterwards that the momentary mystery of Vera showing up with uncle Bob was solved. It seems Vera's folks were off to the big city of Boise and had taken the rest of the brood off for school clothes shopping for the up and coming school year.

When questioned why she didn't go, Vera explained she was a "Hand me downer". Which we all knew meant, she had an older sister that was easy on clothes and she got her "Hand me down" clothes.

"I'm not a "Hand me downer", my younger brother Toad (his real name is Ike, but I always called him Toad) explained, "Arch is hell on clothing, so I get new stuff mostly."

"Yeah, lucky for you!" wailed little Roy, "I'm a hand me downer, Vera," little Roy said with a bit of a smile and reaching up took the older girls hand, in a display of shared clothing solidarity.

It was then, that I happened to notice Vera kept her other hand tightly closed, almost white knuckle tight. But being a boy, and surrounded by my younger brothers, I wasn't about to divulge the startling fact to my siblings that I had noticed a "girl's hand", fisted up or not. (That is rule number seventy six, in the "Infamous Boy's Book of Rules", which I and my brothers abided by religiously.)

"Oh, I don't mind being a hand me downer." Smiled Vera with her twinkling kind eyes, "I'd just like to go to town and see the sights once in a while".

"Well, you're here with us, and although this ain't Boise, it's not the boonies either. We can go over to the school and play." I offered.

"Yeah, I'd like to swing a might on real nice seats." Vera smiled excitedly, which meant, she would welcome sitting in the canvas seats our school swings afforded its riders, unlike the sliver infested old plank I'd seen at her house.

I'd tried to use my Aunt La'Vera and Uncle Rawl's swing, but that swing was a rustic affair where the rope came down through the middle of an old rough board and not only afforded a prickly ride, but a wobbly one at that. I'd been to Vera's house often and rode that old handmade rodeo rope ride her daddy had made. A rider was lucky to walk away with a mild case of butt rash if not a sliver or two, not to mention if you weren't careful, one leg or the other would come off that tippy board and a wicked crash would ensue.

(Author's note about rope swings; sitting astride a rough hemp rope had its draw backs and could prove injurious to either male or female, depending upon the logistics of a crash.)

That was one of the very few "nice things about living close to the school", the swings had nice canvas bottoms, and as long as you mounted them properly, you had a mighty fine chance of not walking home hunched up crying for your mother in a high pitched voice. Although rumor had it, girls suffered from other effects of straddling a rough hemp rope, especially in a dress, but of course being a boy, I can't confirm anything about those kinds of rumors.

And with a shout inside the front screen door, I sent word to the proper authorities that us kids were going across the street and behind the school to play on the playground equipment.

"You watch out for your brother's!" came a shout from the female warden, as we headed out the front gate.

"Oh yeah, I'll watch out for Toady and Wart", I grumbled, for that's how I used to refer to my beloved brothers. But just someone else call one of them that and the fight was on and I'd proved it more than once. I might call my little tag along siblings names, or even push them around a bit, but woe betide anyone else give it a try.

And just as we stepped out of the gate on our way towards the school across the street, suddenly there loomed Shotgun Shorty, with his gnarled old cane and that double barreled shotgun. I was close enough I could read the words "Made in Chicago" on his belt buckle, for I'd almost run smack dab into the old fellow. And right there not two feet away was belt buckle, shotgun and his cane, or better known to every kid in the county, as his "Kid Whack'n Stick".

"You dern worthless kids better watch out!" he shouted as he lifted his cane menacingly as if about to give me a hearty "Whack'n" over the noggin.

The Quarter Kid

Now, one thing about my little brother Toad that I need to mention, he was the quickest thinking kid you'd ever want at your side. Good little Toady could always be relied on in a pinch, and like I said, he was a "thinker, quick as lightning".

"Oh, Mr. Shorty......" Toad called out just as sweet as a slice of peach pie.

Everyone's eyes slowly swiveled from my impending cane whacked head, with soon to be spilt out brains, to where my beloved brother Ike softly called. That's when I heard the distinctive rattle of our gate latch and the hope inspired deep growl of Lady Dog.

The immediate look of terror on Shorty's face told me exactly what I suspected, but just couldn't turn my eyes to look at. My eyes although affixed to that nasty crooked cane just hovering above my head about to dash my "think'n basket" into a million pieces, caught sight of the frightened look on Shorty's face. It didn't take me but half an instant to suddenly realize although armed with both a wicked looking cane and a double barreled shotgun, that old man was scared to death of our dog.

"Now....just you wait....don't you do it....don't you open that gate!" came that scary, gun totting old man's shrill voice....."I'm goin.....just you wait....I'm goin", and Shorty began to hastily back away across the street.

"You go away and leave us alone, or I will open this gate!" Ike warned with a quivering finger on the gate latch the only thing between our lady dogs mouth full of teeth.

I recon little brother Ike figured as close as Shorty was to that gate and as quick as Lady Dog was, Shorty didn't have much of a chance to get his shotgun into play. Like I said, Ike was a "Thinker", and a quick thinker at that.

Archie Matthews

"I'm going.....I'm going......you dern WORTHLESS KIDS!!!" shouted Shorty as he hobbled off as fast as I'd ever seen a hobble performed. His cane making a ticking sound faster than my granddads pocket watch, as the old fellow made a "B" line for home.

"Why didn't he just shoot us?" Vera whispered her eyes as big as saucers.

"He only gots two shots, and there's four of us, Lady dog makes five", little Roy quipped up, mighty proud of his recently learning to count to five, holding up five fingers, one for each of us kids, and an extra finger on the other hand for Lady Dog. (Roy never did use his thumbs for counting, which always made it an awkward process when involving his hands to demonstrate any numbers past eight.)

Although I doubted little Roy's assessment of the shooting situation, I was much more impressed with Ike's quick thinking and magnificent rattling of the gate latch, and I was quick to tell him so.

"That was mighty quick think'n Toad!" I smiled, quickly wiping the fear induced sweat from my forehead with the back of one arm, all the while patting him on the back with the other.

"Maybe we should take Lady Dog with us, Arch....I mean, what if old Shorty comes back look'n for paybacks?"

Sometimes my idiot little brother Toady had stupid notions, but this was not one of those times and as the oldest, I was quick at realizing the benefits of this strategy. I quickly entered the gate and running up to the front screen door, I called inside, "We're taking Lady Dog with us!"

"Okay", came the female Wardens voice from way back in the depths of the kitchen.

And then as I turned and made my way back down the front sidewalk and almost to the gate, the screen door opened and dad's head appeared. "What do you mean you're taking Lady Dog?" Dear old dad asked suspiciously giving me his best lie detector test from afar. His eyes scanning my every facial expression, body stance and pupil dilation, scanning for any tell-tale sign I was up to something.

If you've never met my dad, I am here to tell you a more suspicious father, never graced the face of the earth. My dad could smell, if not hear or see one of us boys even considering something the least bit "Suspicious in Nature". Now if I'd have even hinted we were taking the dog to set upon an old man if he bothered us, I knew exactly what would happen, and it certainly wouldn't be an enjoyable trip to the playground equipment. I'd tried in the past to "Level" with my dad about my expectations as well as the results of my little "Adventures" and "Trust Me" when I say; it never ended with any kind of "Enjoyable Trip", but rather ended in "Un-enjoyable forays" inside the woodshed. (Need I say more?) But on the other hand, dad wasn't anyone's fool either, and I knew some cockeyed story of "Walking the dog" wasn't going to smooth down the old man's suspicious neck hairs, let alone pass the "lie detector test" I was now being subjected to.

"Well....Vera doesn't have a dog and wants to play fetch with Lady Dog while the rest of us swing and play on the monkey bars." I explained, as if selling dear old dad beach front property in Arizona.

I have to say, although he did swallow it hook and line, he did sputter a bit over the sinker, but after a few seconds of working that one eyebrow up and down, he quickly disappeared back inside. Having once again passed through security, it was full steam ahead and adventure ahoy!

I won't bore you with the details of three boys, a spindly girl and a huge German Shepards trip across the road and around the big brick schoolhouse. It was a mighty quick trip without any misshapes, but as we went around the far side, I did notice old Shotgun Shorty giving us the evil eye from the security of his wood and barb wire fence. I will also mention, seeing me looking at him while we rounded the school building, he shook his cane

Archie Matthews

in the air with dire future prophesy. But only a few of my neck hairs raised up, for I hadn't been the only one to notice Shorty watching us, and an encouraging deep growl from Lady dog let me know she was on guard and ready for all comers; shotgun totting old man and be danged.

We hit those swings with a vengeance and it wasn't long before we were all sailing through the air, legs kicking and each yelling his favorite wild shout of happiness. We sailed through the air and took turns bailing out at the highest appendix we dared, each of us making a mark far out in front where we landed. Of course my being the biggest and bravest, I always won, that is until Vera shot me down with her amazing acrobatics.

All I can say is, skinny girls must have a lot less wind resistance than burley boys. She didn't swing any higher than I did, nor did she even "squinch" up her face or throw herself violently forward with screams of "Banzi" and "Geronimo"! Nope, she just slowly worked up altitude with those spindly thin little girl legs and with a little squeal, she'd launch herself out of that swing and cut through the air like a hot knife through butter.

"Yup, skinny girl wind resistance", I'd grumble, each and every time she'd bested my mark, even with that one hand tightly held shut the whole time. Her little knobbed up fist curled around the swing chain as if she was a cripple, her other hand holding on and then as she'd launch herself, all the while that fist held fast, she'd let go and sail through the air.

Both Toad and Wart just shook their heads with awe, seeing their older brother continuously unseated as the families "all time longest swing jump hero". My defeat was utterly shocking and their faces seemed to show some surprise too, as once again Vera, in the semblance of an arrow shot from some kind of swing bow, shot far aloft and a good two foot past my farthest mark.

"Okay, enough of this stupid swinging......On to the Monkey bars!" I shouted as I abandoned the swings and ran for the neighboring steel bars that I knew my little brothers couldn't even get up on, let alone a wisp of a girl like Vera.

The Quarter Kid

The Monkey bars seemed my best chance of renewing my "Big Brother Hero" status, for although it had taken me a while to realize the futile efforts of regaining my fame on the swings, it had finally sunken in. Thus I was more than willing to abandon what everyone was clearly enjoying, for what I knew, no one could best me at, let alone compete.

Anyone who knows Monkey bars understands it's only the most sculpted physic of a mature nine year old that can climb up the metal rungs, balance on the topmost bar. Then with the agility of Tarzan himself, launch out and grab the bars, swinging from one to the other towards the far side. Of course, I had only just gotten the hang of it that very summer, after a series of disasters the previous year. The first set of trials, being once you climb up, keeping ones balance prior to launching out into the abyss and grabbing the bar that seemed about fifty feet out. (Or that's how far it felt to a short armed nine year old) Balance, as I first found out, was not one of my strongest suits. Many was the time I arrived at the top rung, taking a stance and quickly letting go to launch myself, I came immediately crashing down into the deep foul tasting sand below. (It's amazing all the nooks and crannies sand gets in when you come crashing from far above into it....repeatedly)

And then there's the long brutal arm over arm swinging one's self forward to grab the next and next bar in succession. Actually, the succession part used up most of my nine lives, for the first one was far the easiest. Only upon swinging myself forward and letting go, in hopes of throwing myself far enough to grab the next, did I even stand a chance of success. The hardest part of the whole ordeal was all the sand I had to eat learning just how far I had to launch, all the while also learning from the knots on my forehead, not to over launch.

But today, I felt very confident my skinny little female cousin was not going to show me up before the boys. (Especially with her curled up fist, there wasn't anyway she was going to Monkey those bars. I smiled to myself with the wicked thought of how much sand she was going to eat, learning that little lesson.)

Archie Matthews

Stepping up to the Monkey bars with a bit of a flourish, I climbed, balanced and launched, then on and on I went. I'd like to say, on and on and on and on and on, but my absolute world's record best was two bars before down I went with my face plant into the soft deep foul tasting sand below. The tricky part was jumping up with a mouth full of sand, and trying to make the spectators believe it was a spectacle of fascination. Which I could see right off, Wart was impressed, by the awe written all over his face.

"WOW, Arch, I never seen anyone with so much sand in their mouth!" little Wart pointed out fascinated.

"Oh, yeah, Arch....and nice nostril pack'n job too!" heehawed Toady, trying his best for comic of the year.

Vera smiled and gave a giggle as she began helping me dust myself off, while I was trying my best to dig a few more enormous sand boulders out of my nose. That was when I noticed old Mrs. Benson's tabby cat, scratching around the far end of the swings, finishing up his evil little "Cat Business....and I'm not talking buying or selling on the stock exchange". With the sudden realization as to why the playground sand tasted so horrible, I found it easy to expel every sand granule in both mouth and nose in an instant of hacking and coughing.

Then, after a few minutes of spitting and grumbling about "Vile cats and bloody happenings", I gave Vera a knowing smile, if not a foul breathed one.

"Go ahead and give it a try Vera!" I smiled smugly, just itching to see how much of the vile sand a girl could eat, not to mention pack up her nose. (I shot a knowing nasty look back towards Mrs. Benson's cat as it had covered up its foul little package awaiting some unaware kid at the far swing.)

"Okay, Arch", she smiled so sweetly that it almost made me feel like some kind of monster. (Almost...but not quite...remember there is that little book of rules and this happened to be about two hundred and ten. "When faced with female competition, do anything and everything to win, or face being labeled, 'Beaten by a girl"……cat poop and be darned.)

That's when Vera opened her tightly clenched fist and produced as shiny an American Quarter as I've ever seen. I remember thinking it must glitter that way from being rubbed and worked between those soft delicate little girl fingers. But then I caught myself and quickly pushed all those thoughts into the deepest darkest recesses of my mind, only to be loosed once again in my teenage years; much to the horror of many a girl's mother and father.

And quickly putting the quarter in her mouth, Vera climbed, mounted and balanced on the top rung like a circus performer, and then just as she had sailed through the air off the swing, she launched herself far out to the awaiting bar, cutting the air as a hot knife through butter.

The dull "Clang!" sounded just as loud in my ears as it did when my own head impacted an overshot Monkey bar, but this time although I winced for Vera, my forehead didn't hurt. Into the sand with as spectacular a face plant as ever was witnessed by three boys, went little Vera without another sound.

I remember Vera laid there face down as if nailed to the ground for what seemed like the longest time, before any of us came to our senses and ran to her limp body.

"Oh my gosh! I think you killed her, ARCH!" screamed little Wart, his eyes as big as truck tires, complete with shiny hubcaps.

"I didn't kill her…..she killed herself….." was all I could whisper, as I rolled her over. And sure enough, I thought little Wart was right, for Vera was limp as a wrung out dish rag, and just about as white. And then her eyelids fluttered and she looked right up into my face and began to take a long deep breath. But halfway through that long intake of wind, we heard a raspy little whistle and saw Vera reach up and grasp her throat.

Archie Matthews

Toad, ever the quick thinker and having seen the quarter go into Vera's mouth for safe keeping while she performed her Monkey bar acrobatics, began to shout, "She's choking, she's choking on the quarter!" all the while running around in a tight little circle with his arms waving above his head in sheer panic.

Like I said, Toad was the quickest thinker, but not the coolest of nerves in a crisis situation.

"I'm telling MOM!" shouted little wart as he beat as quick a retreat for the house as I've ever seen his little legs take him. And that was what little Wart was particularly good at, running and telling mom, but this time it looked to be a good thing, or at least my backside hoped so.

"Arch….ARCH!" screamed Toad, "She's turn'n blue Arch!"

And sure enough if she wasn't. It wasn't a nice pretty shade of girlish blue either, but more of a, "I'm in serious trouble breath'n" blue.

Vera was a spindly girl, tall and gangly, but as I picked her up I was a bit worried, for she must have bones made out of lead and I knew right away we were in trouble.

"Head for the house Ike, run fast and tell dad come a run'n Vera's turn'n blue.....we'll be come'n fast as we can." And with that, Toad was off like a rifle shot, across the playground and around the far corner, Lady dog barking right at his heels.

Now, my granddaddy was a blacksmith, so was his dad and his dad's dad, they was all blacksmiths and big burley men ever one. I'd seen my granddad pick up his huge steel anvil more than once and move it from one end of his shop to the other, it was quite a sight, even for grown adults watching, not to mention me as a kid. And he moved that anvil like it was a pocket watch he was merely checking the time, nary a strain or muscle twitch on his face. "Boy howdy", did I wish I was my granddad then, for that little girl felt like she was heavy as an anvil.

The Quarter Kid

(Authors note; although I wasn't there at the time, mom always chuckles when telling how little Roy came running into the house screaming "Vera swallowed a quarter, Vera swallowed a quarter!" And how everyone remained calm as Uncle Bob remarked, "Well, now she's worth a quarter." That is, everyone remained calm right up until Ike came crashing into the kitchen and shouted, "Vera swallowed a quarter.....and she's turn'n BLUE....Arch says come a run'n or she's dead for sure!")

Then I saw dad coming and he was coming quick, his face was a working like he was about to take on the world, and I immediately recognized for the first time I was seeing my dad actually scared. He came charging up and I shouted, "Dad, she's got a quarter caught in her gullet and she's turn'n blue!"

Dad snatched Vera up and back in them days, we hadn't heard about that foreign fella named "Hymlick". In those days we pounded a choking person's back. That "Wallop" dad gave Vera scared the dickens out of me. I was afraid a "Whack" like that and he'd have broken her right in two, but she gave a big "Gasp" and that "Whistling" of air started up again, but poor little Vera was still limp as a dish rag, albeit a blue one.

Then up rumbled Uncle Bob's truck and dad ran to the pickup with Vera still cradled in his arms and shouted, "I got some air in her Bob, but she's barely breathing, we got'ta get her to town and the hospital, that quarter's lodged in her throat!"

I'll never forget the look on Uncle Bob's face as he kicked open the passenger door and shouted, "GET IN!"

Since I was right at dad's hip pocket, he grabbed me by one arm and swung me aboard, right into the back of the truck bed amongst the pile of pickup parts.

Uncle Bob must have pushed that "Go Fast Pedal" all the way to the floor for that truck lit out of there like it had a rocket engine, albeit a smoky and rattling rocket engine. We flew back to the house, and it wouldn't have surprised me to know that our tires only hit every couple hundred yards, brother, we was sailing!

Archie Matthews

We skidded in front of the house and dad shouted to mom through his open passenger door window, "Frieda, we're headed to Mountain Home and the Hospital, Vera's choking!"

And before I could bail out of the back of the truck full of gouging, bounced about parts, we was off at break neck speed. (I remember very well it was break neck speed, because that's exactly what I'd have broken if I'd have been foolish enough to try and abandon ship.) Therefore, I hung on for dear life; which is quite a task when your nine years old, amongst a whole pickup bed full of old rusted truck parts trying to beat you to death. Most people don't realize just how "dear life" can be until you're fighting for it, amongst man eating vehicle parts.

After almost being beaten to death by what I now know was an ancient air cleaner with cover still attached, I somehow caught a hold of the bed rail right behind the window and peered inside.

There was poor little Vera whistling her ragged little gasps and still turning bluer and bluer, dad a holding her cradled in his lap and shouting for Bob to "STEP ON IT!".

All the while, poor old Uncle Bob was steering that old truck as if his own life depended on it. (Which upon reflection, it surely did, for if something happened to little Vera and her ma and pa found out about it, his life was surely on the line.)

That's one thing about my entire family, we dote on our kids, take more stock in them than money, or gold or even diamonds, even the shady characters like me, not to mention the even "Shady'r ones"

And then we hit a bump that not only sent my feet clear up past my head, but while clutching that bed rail between the bed and the cab, my fingers was pinched as if they had been caught in a bear trap. It's a hair raising experience to be violently bouncing around the back of a speeding rust bucket, even without your fingers being chewed off betwixt the truck bed and the cab. And then suddenly with an enormous "Clang", the back bumper fell off and clattered along behind, but it couldn't keep up and quickly fell behind in a cloud of grinding sparks.

Many a citizen of GrandView will tell you in those days that forty mile stretch of road into Mountain Home was a rough one, and many a citizen might complain about it, but not me, no sir. The way I got it figured, it was that rough road that not only saved my life, but the life of my little cousin Vera. Suddenly we hit another huge rut and instantly my bear trapped fingers were loose and I had just enough wind left in my scream hole to give a loud sigh of relief. Then with another loud "Bang!" the rear fender fell off and sparks commenced to fly.

Now I'm not a metallurgist, or any kind of a mechanic, so I can't tell you what kind of metal that old truck bumper was made of. But I can say whatever metal makes the brightest blue and reddish sparks, that's the one they'd made that particular truck part from. Not to mention the "Hanger" part, for that part holding it to the rest of the truck was determined to hold on, and that fender drug along for a good while; At least until she was ground pert'near down to the nub, the shower of sparks becoming smaller and smaller as did the violent death scream of the fender being ground into nothingness.

The whole while we were flying down the road, I could hear dad shouting inside the cab for Bob to go faster, and Uncle Bob replying just as panicked "She won't go any faster, I got the pedal so far down, I'm afraid of it not stopping now!"

And then we hit the bad bump!

I remember that bump well, for not only did it heap a pile of sharp jagged truck parts right atop me, but I heard dad give as scary a shout as I ever heard. "She's stopped breathing ….BOB!"

Fighting my way out from under those gnawing truck parts, I wiped a bit of blood from my gashed forehead, once again clawing my way back up to the cab I peered in through the back window. There lay poor little Vera, not only limp as a wrung out dish rag, but no longer blue as much as dark purple. Her sad

243
Archie Matthews

little limp body just laying there in my panicked dads lap, he and Bob exchanging scary glances and both of them sweating as it we were being chased by Hell itself. Then as if by a stroke of the good Lord's hand, my reprieve from the gnawing truck parts came in the form of "The Good Bump" that sent the whole truck into the air, and the next thing I knew, away sailed the tailgate.

If you've ever wondered just how the mighty salmon swims against the strong flowing current and makes its way up stream, brother, let me tell you….it's by nothing short of "brute force" and an overwhelming desire to "Survive". For as that tail gate went sailing off into the wild blue yonder, a powerful current of truck parts surged towards the bed opening and began to sail out and clatter upon the roadway. Thus I was left to battle my own way upstream and I swam with all I had against the current trying my best to survive.

I imagine an aircraft pilot would enlighten many a reader with his glorious tales of flight. The majestic beauty of the blue sky, the spectacular white fluffy clouds, so on and so forth, but let me tell you….flying ain't nearly all it's cracked up to be. Except for the landing, that is; And what a landing, let me tell you what….

We'd hit the train tracks just several miles short of Mountain Home, just before the turn off to the Air Force base. And back in those days, they didn't make long gradual approaches as they do now days, no sir! Back then, they believed a train track crossing should be considered an "Event" and taken with a slow savory approach, of nearly straight up and down. Therefore, anyone dumb enough, or crazy enough, to take a train track crossing anywhere near the speed we'd launched at, it wasn't so much the takeoff, as the landing that sent quivers up ones spine.

Two things happened when we touched down, some sixty seven feet from where we took off.

(Authors note; I know it was exactly sixty seven feet, for at the telling of this tale around town, a couple local high school kids took a tape measure and measured it, as well as took a Polaroid

The Quarter Kid

of the tire marks. It was the talk of the town for quite a few years, even made the local high school newspaper.)

For the first time in my life and but for a brief instance, I experienced the amazement of weightlessness, just before my tailbone came up and introduced itself to the back of my head; furthermore a shout of two men praising God, came from the cab.

Both Uncle Bob and dad we're shouting "Thank God, Thank God!" And as I slowly pushed my tailbone back down from under my shirt collar and back into the seat of my britches where it belonged, I drew my battered bleeding body up to the back cab window and looking inside. I could see Vera breathing with big gulps and her eyes slowly batted open.

And then yet another miracle happened and Uncle Bob's brakes worked and the old rust bucket truck rattled to a stop....well, almost. As luck would have it, not all the parts stopped moving, for as the tires and frame stopped, the front fenders just kept going, right on down the road, grinding away sending sparks flying in all directions. Okay, so it mostly stopped, and by mostly, I mean to say, the other back fender fell off as well as one wheel. And with the truck listing in the front and settling down to the pavement on one hub, I saw uncle Bob slowly wipe the sleeve of his shirt across his brow and heard him whisper, "Thank you old girl for holding on this long". And right behind his thankful whisper, was dad's "Amen to that.....Amen to that."

But before we could say or do anything else, a loud siren came around the corner from the Airbase and an ambulance screeched to a halt, three men bailed out and ran to the front of the truck.

It seems mom had called ahead to the hospital and they'd sent the closest ambulance headed our way, and that happened to be the Air Force ambulance.

Archie Matthews

It was a happy sight to everyone when Vera sat up, blinking, smiled a faint little grin and said, "Welp, it went all the way down, it went hard, but it's down there."

After meeting her folks at the Mountain Home hospital, Vera was given a good bill of health and pronounced, "None the worse for wear", which La'Vera, her mother had a hard time accepting.

"Are you sure she'll be alright with that quarter in her.....what if it rusts, or blocks an innard?" La'Vera lamented.

"No worries madam, kids have been swallowing money ever since the days of the Romans, if she poops out two dimes and a nickel, bring her back, there might be a problem", Smiled the jovial emergency room physician, as he handed both me and Vera a lollipop for our troubles.

"Oh, Arch!", Vera's smile faded into concern at noticing all my Band-Aids, my dried bloody nostrils and increasingly swelling black eye, "What on earth happened to you?"

I smiled back and said, "Oh.....just play'n with girls on the Monkey bars, it's a dangerous game".

And that's the way it happened.....mostly.....and I'll wager my cousin Vera never put a quarter in her mouth thereafter, nor I dare say I or my brothers.

What happened to Uncle Bob's truck, or should I say, "Truck Parts?" Well, we caught a ride back to GrandView with aunt La'Vera and her husband Rawl and ever time we'd come up to a truck part, Uncle Bob would give a shout and we'd stop and he'd throw it in the trunk. Long story short, Uncle Bob kept that old truck rattling along for several more years....right up until it took his life. But that's another story.

As for Vera, she came back and visited us many times and was a continuing joy for all of us that loved her. And I'll never forget the last time I saw her that particular summer as we were sitting out on the side walk in front of our Uncle Mel's grocery store,

The Quarter Kid

eating popsicles. Along came a "Clickity, click" and before we knew it, the looming shadow of the menacing Shotgun Shorty fell over us.

"You dern worthless kids….I bet you stole those popsicles!" he growled as he shook his cane menacingly at us, his old rusty double barrel shotgun in the crook of his other arm.

Little Vera jumped to her feet and shook what was left of her half eaten popsicle at the little old man and replied, "We did NOT steal these, we bought them….and I am NOT WORTHLESS….I swaller'd a quarter and I'm worth twenty five cents…..sic'em Lady!"

And off went that old man as if his seat was on fire….which I bet it felt like, for our old German Shepard Lady Dog had been a laying down just around the corner in the shade, or at least "WAS" laying around the corner, right up until she became attached to Shotgun Shorty's backside.

Archie Matthews

THE END